OXFORD STUDIES IN
SOCIAL AND LEGAL HISTORY

OXFORD STUDIES
IN SOCIAL AND LEGAL
HISTORY

EDITED BY

PAUL VINOGRADOFF

M.A., D.C.L., LL.D., DR. HIST., DR. JUR., F.B.A.

CORPUS PROFESSOR OF JURISPRUDENCE IN THE UNIVERSITY OF OXFORD

VOL. IV

THE HISTORY OF CONTRACT IN EARLY ENGLISH EQUITY

BY W. T. BARBOUR

THE ABBEY OF SAINT-BERTIN AND ITS NEIGHBOUR-HOOD, 900–1350

BY G. W. COOPLAND

OCTAGON BOOKS

A DIVISION OF FARRAR, STRAUS AND GIROUX

New York   1974

Originally published in 1914 by the Clarendon Press

Reprinted 1974
by special arrangement with Oxford University Press, Inc.

OCTAGON BOOKS

A DIVISION OF FARRAR, STRAUS & GIROUX, INC.

19 Union Square West

New York, N. Y. 10003

Library of Congress Cataloging in Publication Data

Barbour, Willard Titus.
    The history of contract in early English equity.

    Reprint of the 1914 editions published by Clarendon Press, Oxford, which were issued as v. 4, no. 7-8, of Oxford studies in social and legal history.

    Includes bibliographical references.
    1. Contracts—Great Britain. 2. Equity—Great Britain. 3. Saint-Omer, France. Saint-Bertin (Benedictine abbey) 4. Land tenure—France—History. 5. Peasantry—France. I. Coopland, George William, 1896-   The abbey of St. Bertin and its neighbourhood, 900-1350. 1974. II. Title. III. Title: The abbey of Saint-Bertin and its neighbourhood, 900-1350. IV. Series: Oxford studies in social and legal history, v. 4, no. 7-8.
KD1554.Z9B37   1974   346'.42'02   73-22303
ISBN 0-374-96163-8

Printed in USA by
Thomson-Shore, Inc.
Dexter, Michigan

PREFACE

Mr. Barbour's contribution to the Studies is an attempt to characterize with some precision and detail the functions of the Chancery in the fifteenth century. The court was gradually differentiated from the King's Council, and the writs of Edward III's time calling on persons to appear under penalty of a fine or of imprisonment (subpoena), and other special injunctions, are generally framed in terms which leave it undecided whether proceedings were to be taken by the King's Council, or by the Council under the chairmanship of the Chancellor himself with or without the aid of assessors. By the time of Richard II, however, the personal jurisdiction of the Chancellor had acquired a fairly definite range, and was assuming the aspect of a standing institution. Chancery was not a court of record, but it would be idle to deny that it was none the less a court, in the sense of a tribunal taking cognizance of certain juridical disputes and deciding them by peculiar methods of investigation and procedure. The growth of trusts is the most famous expression of this interesting ' ius honorarium ', but Chancery also exercised a powerful influence in the sphere of contract, and it is from that particular point of view that its action during the fifteenth century has been studied by Mr. Barbour. A vast quantity of material was available for that study. Some documents bearing on the subject had seen the light in the specimens of petitions and disclaimers published by the editors of the Chancery Calendars and by Mr. Baildon. But most of the innumerable membranes and papers concerned with these disputes are still lying unstudied and unsifted at the Public Record Office. The early Chancery proceedings for the reigns of Richard II, Henry IV, Henry V, Henry VI, Edward IV, and Richard III number considerably more than 100,000 pieces. It is to be hoped that steps may be taken to classify and to calendar this mass of information, but students can hardly be expected to wait until the necessary funds are forthcoming, and the calendaring has been carried out in a scholarly way by the overworked staff of the Record Office or by competent volunteers. Mr. Barbour has had the courage to plunge boldly into the midst of this enormous heap of documents, and to collect observations from a sufficient number of instances to frame conclusions as to the average methods of Chancery in trying contract cases. The results seem to me to have amply justified his undertaking. The subject may be approached from two distinct points of view. It may be examined as a matter-of-fact treatment of the rights and duties of parties to contractual transactions, and there can be no doubt that it is important to ascertain exactly in what particular cases the Chancellor was expected to grant, and did actually grant, remedies to parties seeking justice before him. When this side of the problem has been examined and solved in one way or another, a second question arises— namely, What was the influence of Chancery practice on the general development of the law of contract in England and, in particular, on the treatment of contracts at Common Law? Thirdly, we may inquire into the connexion between the views held by the Chancellor and their assessors and the doctrines of Canonists and Civilians. Mr. Barbour's monograph is especially concerned with the first of these questions from which any investigation naturally has to start, and which is the condition precedent of all further study of the subject. He has also described, as far as possible, the contrasting methods of treating contractual relations at Common Law and in Chancery. As for the third part of the investigation, it could not be carried out within the limited time at the author's disposal, and he had to content himself with some observations of a general nature. It is to be hoped that the writer may be able to proceed with his analysis in this department also, and thus complete an investigation to which he has already given so much time and thought.

Mr. Coopland's monograph represents the social aspect of our studies. He had opportunities of making himself acquainted with the economic history of a

district of Northern France reclaimed from the sea and
from a state of decay by the action of a great ecclesiastical institution and by the advent of peasant
colonists, who had to pay various dues and to render
many services, but who gradually acquired a secure
tenant-right almost equivalent to ownership. An intimate knowledge of topography and natural conditions,
and laborious researches into the archives of Northern
France, have enabled the writer to trace the stages
of this process with exact details, which are necessary
in order to unravel the true factors of social development. It is not in the direction of obscure origins
that this study has proceeded : questions as to the
initial forms of agrarian occupations, the status of the
first settlers, the cross-influences of Roman and Teu-
tonic institutions, had to be left for discussion on the
broader lines of a comparative study of mediaeval
antiquities. But the late Carolingian survey of the
possessions of Saint Bertin presents a convenient
starting-point for another sequence of facts, namely for
the development of Northern France from the manorial
system of the *seigneurie* to the work of small peasant
farmers which de Tocqueville has described so effectively in his *Ancien Régime.* I should like to call
special attention to the curious way in which *morcelle-
ment* and *vaine pâture* held their own after the dis-
ruption of the regular holdings. It would have been
out of the question to encumber the account given
of this complicated process by direct comparisons with

the rural history of England: those who take up such a study may be presumed to be acquainted with the main features of this history.   It is not by pointing out obvious analogies or contrasts that Mr. Coopland's monograph is helpful to students of social history, but by concrete data in regard to the nature of the French open-field system, of the holdings and their disruptions, of the distribution of capital, of the forms and incidence of revenue assessment, of the peculiarities of land measures, and so forth.   Many of these details may be dry and not very easy to follow, but it is only by the help of conscientious studies of this kind that we may hope to substitute precise knowledge and well-founded generalizations for the hazy outlines with which the historians of the peasant class and of rural economy have too often had to content themselves.

PAUL VINOGRADOFF.

VII

THE HISTORY OF CONTRACT IN EARLY ENGLISH EQUITY

BY

W. T. BARBOUR, A.M., LL.B., B.Litt.

ASSISTANT-PROFESSOR OF LAW IN THE UNIVERSITY OF
MICHIGAN, U.S.A.

NOTE

THIS essay has been materially abridged in order to bring it within a reasonable length. Had I followed out the plan originally projected, it would have contained an additional hundred pages. Part I stands as originally written ; Part II has been somewhat condensed. I should have liked to include more extracts from the petitions and to submit a greater number of cases, but it seemed desirable to make this study as brief as possible. As it is, I have burdened the text with numerous quotations, but, as the chancery material is not available in published form, a mere reference to a petition by number without indicating its content would not be convincing. I hope, however, that I have not obscured the argument by too frequent quotation.

The chancery petitions are cited by indicating the bundle number in Roman numerals and the number of the petition in Arabic numerals. Thus, XII. 10 means Bundle twelve, Petition number ten.

In the Appendix I have given a few select petitions. They were chosen from among some 500 transcripts which I made at the Public Record Office.

ANALYSIS

INTRODUCTION

THERE is scarcely a subject in legal history which has occasioned more discussion than the history of contract. Particularly in English law it has excited the attention of many able investigators;[1] and as so much has been written, it may seem presumptuous to undertake to say anything more. The only excuse for such an essay as this is that the material upon which it is based is new and, so far as I am aware, has never been published.

I propose to discuss the history of contract in chancery in the fifteenth century, and I shall base my argument largely upon the petitions which were brought before the chancellor during that period. It is my purpose not alone to show what was actually done in equity, but also to determine so far as possible the principles upon which the chancellor acted. Our chief interest lies in the development of parol contract, but it seemed to me desirable to give some consideration to the contract under seal as well. My reasons for so doing will appear later.

[1] e. g. Holmes, The Common Law, Lecture VII; Pollock and Maitland, History of English Law, vol. ii, chap. v; Ames, History of Assumpsit, *Harvard Law Review*, vol. ii, pp. 1–19, 53–69; Ames, Parol Contracts, *idem*, vol. viii, pp. 252–64; Salmond, History of Contract, *Law Quarterly Review*, vol. iii, pp. 166–79; Salmond, Essays in Jurisprudence and Legal History, Essay IV; Jenks, The Doctrine of Consideration (Yorke Prize Essay, 1891); Holdsworth, History of English Law, vol. iii, chap. iii. See also Holmes, Early English Equity, *Law Quarterly Review*, vol. i, pp. 162–74; Vinogradoff, Reason and Conscience in Sixteenth-Century Jurisprudence, *idem*, vol. xxiv, pp. 373–83.

This essay then deals chiefly with the development of contract in equity. But it is impossible to consider equitable doctrines alone and by themselves. Their significance is apparent only when they are placed side by side, and contrasted with the doctrines of the common law. Accordingly I have divided this essay into two parts. Part I, which is introductory, gives a brief review of the history of contract in the common law. Part II is an attempt to set forth the equitable doctrines with regard to contract.

PART I

CONTRACT IN THE COMMON LAW

CHAPTER I

INTRODUCTORY

THE theory of contract as it existed in the common law must be found in the history of the common law actions. 'So great is the ascendancy of the Law of Actions in the Courts of Justice', remarked Sir Henry Maine,[1] 'that substantive law has at first the look of being gradually secreted in the interstices of procedure.' And so we find it in the common law in the fourteenth and fifteenth centuries. Accordingly I have based the discussion of contract on the actions of Account, Covenant, Debt, Detinue, and Assumpsit. These are practically the only common law actions which had any effect upon the development of the substantive law so far as contract is concerned.

As one looks at the common law as a whole, one must continually notice the insistent testimony which it bears to its feudal origin. This appears in the division of society into classes of men, upon whom certain liabilities are imposed. It will become very evident in our discussion of assumpsit. Again, it is seen in the dominating position given to the land law. For example, in 1285 a new rule was introduced by statute, that an Assize of Novel Disseisin would lie for a corody. A corody is really a benefit derived from contract; yet the right to receive it is treated as if it were a right in land.[2] This situation must have had its effect in the development of contract. I merely wish to call attention to it here.

---

[1] Early Law and Custom, 389 (quoted, Maitland, Equity, 295).
[2] See P. and M., ii. 135.

In reviewing the common law I am considering a subject which has been very fully discussed elsewhere. Hence I shall be as brief as possible. I have treated at some length cases which do not seem to have been considered heretofore ; and in one or two places I have sought to put a different interpretation upon cases that are well known. In general, however, what is said here is merely a summary of the work of previous writers.

At the same time I have adopted a different point of view. I have sought to show not so much the efficiency of the common law as its inefficiency ; I have stressed the defects of the actions, and have attempted to set forth the important types of contract for which there was no remedy. In the second place, the study of the common law is not carried beyond the year 1504, when assumpsit first obtained general recognition as an action on contract. In that respect it is fragmentary, but it suffices for the present purpose. In equity I have considered only the fifteenth century, and in consequence the contrast is with the common law of the same period. By the action of assumpsit the common law was able in the sixteenth century to retrieve its lost jurisdiction over contract, but we are here dealing with an earlier period. In brief, I have treated the common law as a means of approaching chancery, and in this light I have attempted to sketch the history of the different actions.

CHAPTER II

THE COMMON LAW ACTIONS

SECTION I. ACCOUNT

THE precise moment when the action of Account made its first appearance cannot be fixed with certainty, but one of the earliest known cases in which it was used was in 1232.[1] From that time onward it appears with greater frequency, until at length it succumbed to the competition with chancery ; but in the Year Books it is a common form of action. The form of the writ[2] shows that it was modelled upon the proprietary writs; the 'command' was that the defendant should render the plaintiff an account, while the plaintiff in stating his case must show how the liability to account arose, and how and where the money claimed was received.[3]

According to the theory of the common law the action existed for one purpose only:[4] to enforce the obligation to account. It becomes important, therefore, to inquire into the precise nature of this obligation. It was not founded upon contract ; rather was it an independent creation of the law itself, and though a bond were conditioned to render an account, it would not support the action unless the necessary conditions which created the obligation to account did exist.[5]

---

[1] P. and M., ii. 221 ; Note Book, pl. 859.

[2] 'Precipe A quod iusta et sine dilatione reddat B rationabile compotum suum de tempore quo fuit ballivus suus in C receptorum denariorum ipsius B ut dicit . . .' Pollock, H. L. R., vi. 401. See Maitland, Equity, 382.

[3] e. g. 'Un homme porta un bref d'acompte vers un autre et assigna les resseites par my la mayn un tiel.' Y. B. 11 & 12 Ed. III [R. S.] 315.

[4] For this statement of the obligation to account I am indebted to Langdell, H. L. R., ii. 242-57.

[5] H. L. R., ii. 243, and cases cited.

We may enumerate four essentials, without the concurrence of which the action did not lie : [1]

(1) The person on whom the obligation is to be imposed must have received property not his own, of which the person imposing the obligation is owner.

(2) The receipt of the property must not amount to a bailment.

(3) The receiver must have possession, as distinguished from custody.

(4) There must be privity between the parties.

It will be obvious, then, that account was confined to a narrow orbit. Indeed, the common law recognized as accountable only three classes of persons: guardians, bailiffs, and receivers, and the extension by statute [2] to the guardian in socage was not a material enlargement. In none of these cases does contract, as such, have any function.

It should be noted, however, that the law was making an attempt, confessedly awkward, to meet the widening demands of commerce. There is some indication in the early cases that primitive arrangements, which to the modern eye suggest partnership [3] or agency, were attempting to take shelter beneath the mantle of account. Thus, where two embarked on a commercial venture, one sought to hold the other to an account for the time when he 'fuit receptor denariorum ipsius A ex quacumque causa et contractu ad communem utilitatem A et B proveniencium'. [4] In 1340 [5] a plaintiff seeks to compel a defendant to account for money received to trade with. But such instances are comparatively rare. The action never acquired sufficient flexibility to serve any useful purpose for

---

[1] See more fully H. L. R., ii. 243-8.

[2] Prov. Westm. (1259), c. 12 ; Stat. Marlb. (1267), c. 17, and see Y. B. B. 12 & 13 Ed. III [R. S.] 321 ; 18 & 19 Ed. III [R. S.] 325 (action does not lie till heir is of full age) ; 19 Ed. III [R. S.] 449.

[3] In later common law co-partners as such were not accountable to each other (see Langdell, H. L. R., ii. 265, citing Lindley, Partn. [4th ed.] 1022 n. R.), but I am referring to the early cases.

[4] Y. B. 33-5 Ed. I [R. S.] 295.

[5] Y. B. 14 Ed. III [R. S.] 283 ; and note a curious case in 16 Ed. III (pt. i) 191, where an action was brought against the keeper of a marsh who dug turves and sold them, keeping the profits himself.

merchants or traders, and we note the above cases as exemplifying a tendency, and nothing more.

It is sometimes asserted that Debt, and later Indebitatus Assumpsit, superseded Account. Such an assertion rests upon a confusion of ideas ; for a *debt* was necessary to support either of those actions, and obviously an obligation to account could not constitute a debt.[1]

Circumstances might of course arise in which the receiver had so dealt with the property [2] that the obligation to account could be treated as having been converted into a debt ; in such case the plaintiff would have the option of holding the receiver to account or of waiving the account and bringing debt. Thus, where a receiver granted by deed that he had received £46 of the plaintiff, to be employed to his use, and further granted to repay the £46 to the plaintiff; there account might be brought, or if the account were waived, debt would lie on the grant to repay.[3] This became important if there were a death on one side ; for account would not lie against the executor or heir of the receiver, whereas debt would, provided there were a deed.[4]

The suspension of the action in case of death was a vital defect. Though by statute [5] it was extended in favour of the executor of the obligee, the common law never regarded the executor or administrator of the obligor as answerable in account.[6] Furthermore, damages were not recoverable,[7] nor could a receiver be held accountable for profits,[8] and if the plaintiff counted of a receipt by his own hand, the defendant might wage his law and acquit himself by oath.[9] But, in

---

[1] The point is fully discussed in Core's Case, 28 H. VIII, Dyer, 20 (*a*).

[2] e. g. by converting it to his own use.

[3] See Y. B. 16 Ed. III (pt. ii) [R. S.] 383.

[4] ' Tut fut ceo a derener par voie d'acompte en sa vie ceo q'il devoit, apres sa mort il ne poet aver accion forsqe par voie de dette.' Kershuile J. in Y. B. 16 Ed. III (pt. ii) [R. S.] 383.

[5] 13 Ed. I (Westm. ii), chap. xxiii : and see Coke, 2nd Inst., 404.

[6] Y. B. 16 Ed. III (pt. ii) [R. S.] 383. This was remedied by statute, but not till 1705 : 4 Anne, c. 16, s. 27.

[7] Y. B. 14 Ed. III [R. S.] 287 (per Schard J.).

[8] Langdell, H. L. R., ii. 247 ; Rol. Abr. *Accompt* (o) pl. 14, 15.

[9] Y. B. 13 & 14 Ed. III [R. S.] 289; otherwise where receipt could be proven by deed, Y. B. 16 Ed. III (pt. i) [R. S.] 5.

addition to these technical defects, there was one still more grave. The only adequate remedy was specific performance; that is, the defendant must be compelled to account; to the accomplishment of such a purpose the machinery of the common law was ill adapted.[1] Doubtless this occasioned the early intervention of equity; for in the Bill for account the chancellor had a more efficient remedy.[2]

An application to equity was made as early as 1385.[3] No reason is mentioned for applying to the chancellor, but the explanation may lie in the fact that the complainant was a 'clerc de la Chauncellerie'. Thenceforth appeals to equity become more frequent. In the early cases the complainant usually assigns his poverty,[4] or inability to get hold of the defendant by common law process,[5] as the occasion for coming to chancery; but at length the subject-matter of an account itself was treated as a sufficient cause.[6]

From this brief consideration of the action, it is apparent that account could do little for the law of contract. Founded upon an obligation which was essentially a creation of the

---

[1] Sometimes the common law endeavoured to coerce an obstinate defendant by putting him in irons. By statute (St. Westm. ii, c. 10) auditors had power to award a defendant to prison if he were found in arrearages and refused to account. See Termes de la Ley, fol. 4; in Y. B. 18 & 19 Ed. III [R. S.] 413 it was held that a defendant should be put in irons.

[2] A defect in the action arising from its being purely legal is well stated in the words of Mr. Hening: 'The plaintiff in account was compelled to undergo the delay of two distinct trials, the first before a jury to determine his right to an accounting, the judgment for the plaintiff being that the defendant do account (*quod computet*), and the second trial being the accounting itself before the court-appointed auditors.' Anglo-Am. iii. 350.

[3] III. i (10 S. S. 1).

[4] XI. 358 (where a complainant says that because of his poverty and the defendant's wealth he has no power to sue the common law).

[5] Thus in VI. 168 it is alleged that the defendant 'luy purpose de passer hors de jurisdiccon dicest Royalme', and by no process of law can he be restrained. The prayer asks for a writ of subpoena in a penalty of £1000.

[6] It is not always easy to distinguish Bills for accounting from other applications; for commonly the relief sought is 'general', i.e. the complainant trusts to the chancellor's discretion. See VII. 186; IX. 382. If the true intent of XVII. 335 (10 S. S. 107) is to have an account, it would seem that the common law requirement of privity was not strictly enforced in equity. However, the jurisdiction of equity in account is scarcely within the range of this essay.

law, and restricted even within its narrow sphere by procedural disadvantages, it could not be the source of any important substantive doctrine.   For the common law theory of contract we must look elsewhere.

SECTION II.   COVENANT AND THE CONTRACT UNDER SEAL

The Action of Covenant.

Nothing shows more forcibly the insistent conservatism of the common law than the development of the action of Covenant.   Here was an action which drew its name and being from agreement (*conventio*), and remained throughout the early period the most purely contractual action of English law,[1] indeed for two centuries and more the only vehicle for enforcing executory contracts which gave unliquidated damages[2]; and yet when its claims are evaluated it will be found that it contributed very little to the substantive law of contract.   Even its position as a contractual remedy was attained only by a struggle.

In England of the early twelfth century the dominating force, juristically considered, was the land law ; it is not surprising, therefore, that Covenant first manifests itself in connexion with agreements relating to land.   We find it in the earliest extant plea roll,[3] which comes from the reign of John, and by the time of Henry III[4] it was a common form of action and might be had ' as of course '.[5]   ' En auncien temps ', remarks one of counsel of a later period, ' homme soleit lever fynes par bref de covenant,'[6] a practice which may account for its popularity, but the occasion of its invention was not a desire to simplify conveyance, but to protect the termor.   For while the termor had at this time no real right, he was allowed the benefit of a covenant ;[7]   the need for

---

[1] Holdsworth, iii. 326.   [2] Holdsworth, ii. 310.
[3] Select Civil Pleas (3 S. S., pl. 89) ; P. & M., ii. 216.
[4] See Maitland, Register of Writs, H. L. R., iii. 113-15 (especially p. 115, No. 6).
[5] P. & M., ii. 216.   [6] Y. B. 16 Ed. III (pt. ii) 523.
[7] P. & M., ii. 106.

protection of leases brought the writ into existence. Bracton[1] says that it had become the ordinary remedy of the lessee, who might thereby obtain a judgement for specific performance: that he recover possession of the land.

Gradually the action was extended to covenants not relating to land, though in the time of Glanville[2] the king's court showed great reluctance to concern itself with mere private agreements (*privatae conventiones*). By the time of Bracton,[3] however, Covenant was regarded as a general remedy, and any doubt which might have remained was set at rest by the Statute of Wales[4] (1284), where the action is treated as co-extensive with agreements. This looks as if a flexible and elastic contractual remedy had been evolved in the thirteenth century;[5] indeed it had possibilities, which were, however, negatived by two limitations, and its sphere of action was materially restricted.

These limitations are curious, but at the same time characteristic of the common law. The first appears from the rules of evidence, when we inquire as to what was necessary to support the action. Could the plaintiff sustain his case by the production of suit? There is a time (e. g. in the middle period of Edward I's reign)[6] when the judges show some uncertainty, but it was ultimately settled that Covenant could not be maintained without a deed.[7] This decision was fraught

---

[1] 'Solent aliquando tales cum eiecti essent infra terminum suum perquirere sibi per breve de conventione.' Bracton (R. S. ed. Twiss), iii. 468 (bk. iv, chap. xxxvi, fol. 220); and see Digby, Hist. R. P. (5th ed.), 176, 178. See also Y. B. B. 20 & 21 Ed. I [R. S.] 279; 2 & 3 Ed. II [S. S.] 84; 18 & 19 Ed. III [R. S.] 409; 19 Ed. III [R. S.] 17; 20 Ed. III (pt. i) [R. S.] 107; and cf. Y. B. 18 & 19 Ed. III [R. S.] 523.

[2] Glanville, x, cap. 8; 'privatas conventiones non solet curia domini Regis tueri . . .' (*idem*, x, cap. 18).

[3] P. & M., ii. 218, n. 3.   [4] Holdsworth, iii. 325.

[5] Maitland, Equity, 358.

[6] Y. B. 20 & 21 Ed. I [R. S.] 223. Mr. Salmond (Essays in Jurisprudence, 184) cites this case as deciding 'that a writing was the only admissible proof of an agreement'. It is submitted that the case makes no such decision. Witness the dialogue: '*Lowiere*: Quey avez del covenant? *Spigurnel*: Sute bone. *Lowiere*: Avez autre chosse? *Spigurnel*: dit ke non. *Lowiere*: Jugement, si nus devum respundre a sa sute sans escrit, &c.' Here the case ends. The reporters leave us uncertain as to the decision, but it was evidently still doubtful whether or no suit would support an action of Covenant.

[7] Y. B. 32 & 33 Ed. I [R. S.] 201; see P. & M., ii. 220, n. 1.

with tremendous consequences. It swept to one side and gave a peculiar character to obligations under seal; it left executory parol contracts helpless until the rise of Assumpsit restored them to their rightful position.

These remarks apply only to the king's court. Though the authority is very meagre, it seems to be pretty clearly established that a different rule prevailed by special custom. In London[1] and probably in Bristol,[2] Covenant lay without a sealed instrument. The origin of this peculiar custom has occasioned much speculation, with which we are not here concerned. We may note in passing, however, that there is some significance in the fact that the custom subsisted in communities which were essentially mercantile and affected by commerce. Perhaps it is more than a coincidence that Covenant without specialty abode in the same county with gavelkind. At all events the special custom had small effect on the substantive law; it never received recognition in the royal courts, and from the frequency with which citizens of London appeal to the chancellor when they wish to bring Covenant but have no deed, one may well doubt whether it ever obtained general recognition.

The second limitation upon the action is so curious as to excite some surprise. Covenant did not lie for a sum certain, but only for the recovery of damages for the breach of a promise in writing. The remedy to enforce a covenant to pay a definite amount of money or chattels was Debt, and not Covenant.[3] Hence though a debt be proved by a writing under seal, Covenant would not lie upon it. This rule persisted till the late sixteenth century, and even in 1613 the

---

[1] 'And note well that no writ of covenant shal be mayntenable wythout especialty, but in the Cytie of London or in other suche place privileged, by the custome and use.' Termes de la Ley, *sub tit.* Covenant ; and see F. N. B., 146 A ; Liber Albus (ed. Riley), 181, 189. It would seem that the whole transaction must have taken place within the City of London. See XIX. 354 *b*, XIX. 354 *c*, *Appendix of Cases*, p. 205, XIX. 493, *ibid.*, p. 209. In Y. B. 48 Ed. III. 6. 11 Candish J. called trespass on the case an 'action de covenant', and said it was maintainable without specialty. There appears to have been some confusion in the learned judge's mind.

[2] *Wade and Bemboe' Case* (H. 25 Eliz.), 1 Leon. 2.

[3] Ames, H. L. R., ii. 56.

judges of the Common Bench remarked [1] : 'If a man covenant to pay £10 at a day certain, an action of Debt lieth for the money and not an action of Covenant.' The common law was ever chary of allowing concurrent remedies. There was already in existence an action the function of which was the recovery of specific sums, and the judges consequently restricted Covenant to claims for unliquidated damages.[2]

The advantages and disadvantages of Covenant may be briefly summarized. The proof required was simply the production of the deed itself [3] ; and as the action was supported by specialty it lay against the executors or administrators of the original covenantor, and even against his heir if he were named in the covenant.[4] On the other hand, a plaintiff could never recover a greater sum than he claimed [5] ; the exact point in which each covenant was broken, and how and wherein damage was sustained, must be stated with great particularity ; and the necessity for the assessment of damages required the presence of a jury.

The Contract under Seal.[6]

Our discussion would be incomplete without some detailed consideration of the obligation which was the basis of the action of Covenant—the contract under seal.[7] It is true that the sealed instrument was broader than Covenant, and, as we have already seen, in certain cases would support Debt, but it is proposed for the time being to drop the procedural point of view, and to look at the substantive law.

[1] *Chawner* v. *Bowes*, Godb. 217 (cited Ames, H. L. R., ii. 56).

[2] '... cety bref de Covenant, ke est naturelement done a recoverir damages ...' (Aseby, in Y. B. 21 & 22 Ed. I [R. S.] 183).

[3] e.g. ' *Tiltone* : Quey avez de covenant. *Rauf* : Bone escrit.' Y. B. 20 & 21 Ed. I [R. S.] 181 (sp. ref. 183).

[4] Britton, i. 29. 15 ; Jenks, 162.

[5] Y. B. 16 Ed. III (pt. i) [R. S.] 183.

[6] The discussion of the contract under seal is put here for the sake of convenience. Of course in a great many cases a deed was the basis of the action of Debt. These remarks apply to Debt as well as Covenant, in all cases in which the former was brought on a sealed instrument.

[7] There is a curious remark in the Kentish Eyre (6 Ed. II), wherein a deed (*fet*) is distinguished from a specialty (*especialte*). The plaintiff in support of his claim had introduced a tally. Counsel for the defendant calls the tally a ' deed ' and remarks : ' Jugement si par tiel fet qe nest especialte deit estre response.' *Anon.* v. *Anon*, Y. B. 6 & 7 Ed. II [S. S.] 35.

A distinguished writer has objected to the term 'formal contract' when applied to the sealed writing. 'Consideration', he remarks,[1] 'is as much a form as a seal.' Doubtless this is true to-day, when modern law, especially in the United States, has practically abolished all distinctions between sealed and unsealed writings, but any such proposition would have received scant appreciation from a mediaeval lawyer. His eye never penetrated beyond the seal into the genesis of the contract ; to him a deed was more than evidence, it was *the contract itself*.[2]

We are not concerned here with the origin of the doctrine which gave a sacramental importance to the presence of a seal. To be able to write was in the twelfth century a tremendous accomplishment, and any written document was bound to be impressive to the ordinary person. Moreover, the belief certainly existed at this time that the Romans did stipulate by writing, and this belief was fostered by the confused account of 'stipulatio' in the Institutes,[3] wherein substance and proof are hopelessly confounded. Doubtless these elements combined to give peculiar significance to any written document; and apparently such writings were always sealed, for when an attorney or judge speaks of a writing he means a sealed instrument.[4] At all events, the contract under seal attained a peculiar position, of which we must note two consequences.

1. The mere attaching of the seal to a writing bound the party to whom the seal belonged. Even if one carelessly lost his seal,[5] and another made improper use of it, there was no defence. It follows that the use of the seal bound the owner, whether he were actually a party to the contract or not. This

---

[1] Holmes, 273.

[2] 'En dette sur contract le plaintiff monstra in son count pur quel cause le defendant devient son dettour ; autrement in dette sur obligation, *car l'obligation est contract in luy mesme*.' Bellewe, 8 Rich. II, 111 (ed. 1869) ; see Salmond, Anglo-Am., iii. 323, n. 2.

[3] Institutes, iii. 21 ; see Girard, Manuel élémentaire de Droit romain (4th ed.) 500. Of course in Roman law the written instrument does not bind ; it is merely evidence, and the binding force comes from the stipulation which it attests. Thus Paulus, Dig. xliv. 7. 38 'non figura litterarum, sed oratione, quam exprimunt litterae, obligamur.'

[4] See Williams, R. P. (20th ed.), 149–50, and authority there cited.

[5] Glanville, x. 12. But cf. Britton, i. 29. 21.

situation is well illustrated by a case in 6 Ed. II, *Bokelande v. Leanore*.[1] An agreement was made between one Peter the Mason and John Bokelande (the plaintiff) that the said Peter should build two mills for the plaintiff. When the deed which recited the transaction was read, it appeared that the original agreement was made between Bokelande and Peter the Mason only, but that for greater security the names of Roger Leanore and others were added, and that they affixed their seals. Obviously this was a clumsy attempt to produce a relation of suretyship. The mills were not built according to the covenant, whereupon the plaintiff sued a writ of Covenant against Roger Leanore, who objected that he was not a party to the contract, and that he attached his seal only 'for further security'. Spigurnel J. disposed of this defence summarily and said : ' Si un home se oblige a vous en dette par escrit et die en l'escrit, " et a greignour surte ieo troef un tiel qe se oblige " et il met le seal al escrit, *coment q'il ne parlent pas ceo* que l'autre parle, il afferme par le mettre du seal, par quei responez au fet.' The judge, arguing from the analogy of a covenant to pay money, compelled the defendant to answer to the deed. He could not contradict by extrinsic evidence what he 'affirmed' by his seal. There could scarcely be a better example of the strict and relentless logic of the common law.

2. The second consequence is really only another phase of the first. The written instrument was interpreted very strictly ; the obligor was taken to mean exactly what he said. As he could not show that he was not a party to the contract, if he had attached his seal, so he could not deny nor explain anything he had written. ' By a writing,' says Fleta,[2] ' . . . any one will be bound, so that if he has written that he owes it, *whether money was paid or not*, he is bound by the writing, and he will not have an *exceptio pecuniae non numeratae* against the writing, because *he said he owed the money*.'[3] Fleta is not a compelling authority, but his statement finds support in the

[1] Y. B. 6 & 7 Ed. II [S. S.] 9.
[2] Fleta (Selden), ii. 56, § 20.
[3] Bracton makes practically the same statement ; see f. 100 b.

Year Books. A promise to pay money was enforceable though conditional upon the happening of an impossible event, as some defendants, who wrote not wisely but too well, must have learned to their cost. Indeed such a situation was explained by the use of a delictual maxim, when a reporter [1] remarks: ' Note that the Law will suffer a man of his own folly to bind himself to pay on a certain day if he do not make the Tower of London come to Westminster ; whereof said Bereford C. J. : " *Volenti non fit iniuria*[2] although the written law says, *Nemo obligatur ad impossible*".' We thus see that the fundamental principle of the sealed writing is its absolute conclusiveness against the obligor.

A graphic illustration of this principle is afforded by a consideration of the defences which might be brought forward. We might better say defence ; for there was scarcely more than one real defence. However grievous might have been the misconduct of the obligee in procuring the obligation, it was of no avail to the obligor, save in one case ; [3] for the common law made an exception in favour of duress.[4] But fraud,[5] failure of consideration [5] and accord and satisfaction [6] were not pleadable against a specialty. It was, of course, open to the defendant to deny the authenticity of the writing and tender an averment to the country that it was not his deed, a plea technically described as ' nient son fait '.[7] Otherwise he must show a sealed release or acquittance ; for what was

---

[1] Y. B. 3 & 4 Ed. II [S. S.] 199.

[2] To-day the maxim is interpreted to mean that damage suffered by consent is not a cause of action. Broom, Legal Maxims, 217 ff.

[3] Ames, H. L. R., ix. 57.

[4] Britton, i. 29. 20. The mere fact that the obligor made a bond in prison in order to obtain his freedom was not evidence of duress. *Anon.* v. *Anon.*, Y. B. 6 & 7 Ed. II [S. S.] 36.

[5] Ames, H. L. R., ix. 51. Fraud was not an admissible defence at common law until the Common Law Procedure Act (1854).

[6] Y. B. 3 & 4 Ed. II [S. S.] 145. And though the obligee has already brought suit and recovered, the obligor has no defence, unless he can show acquittance. *Anon.* v. *Anon.*, Y. B. 6 & 7 Ed. II [27 S.S. 37]. In such a case Shardelow J. said : ' He charges you by an obligation ; why then was it not cancelled ? (i. e. in the previous action). And you do not produce any acquittance of the debt.' Y. B. 17 Ed. III [R. S.] 297.

[7] Y. B. 3 H. IV. 2. 8. Where a seal was ' glue al fait ', the court held it to be suspicious and declared the deed void. Y. B. 7 H. VI. 18. 27.

done by deed could only be undone by deed.[1] 'Quand un homme conust un fait et ne monstra especial matier de voider ceo, le plaintif ad cause de recouvrer meintenant sans plus.'[2]

Perhaps it was not always so. Some judges, particularly in the early cases, show an inclination to go behind the seal, and allow parol evidence to be introduced. Thus where Debt was brought on a deed to recover £10 for a lease, the defendant was permitted to show that as a matter of fact he had been ousted.[3] This looks like an attempt to apply the doctrine of *quid pro quo* to sealed instruments. In 1292 a plaintiff was allowed to bring Debt for chattels which were given by deed unconditionally, and to aver that the gift was conditional upon the defendant's marrying her.[4] 'Fut ceo la cause du don ke vous la dussez esposer ou non?' was the incisive question put by Metingham J., and issue was joined on the condition. These are early and isolated cases and cannot be said to affect the trend of judicial opinion. If they indicate anything, it is that the rigid enforcement of the general rule produced so much hardship that occasional attempts were made to consider a particular case upon its merits. But there was never any general admission of parol evidence to engraft a condition upon a deed. To do so the defendant must show 'lettre del plaintiff ou enroullement de court qe porte record[5].' Parol evidence was of no avail. In *Esthalle et Herlison* v. *Esthalle*[6] the defendant bound himself in a simple obligation, but there was a separate defeasance bond, bearing a condition. Both these obligations were delivered to one G. for safe-keeping. The condition was performed, and after G.'s death the obligations

---

[1] Y. B. 3 & 4 Ed. II [S. S.] 145. 'Rien luy doit' cannot be pleaded against a deed. Y. B. 9 Ed. IV. 48. 3 (continued, 53. 17).

[2] Paston J. in Y. B. 9 H. VI. 37. 12.

[3] Bereford J. said: 'When the Parson ought to have had an estate by the grant of the Prior, he had nothing. (And he drove them to answer over.)' Y. B. 1 & 2 Ed. II [S. S.] 160. See Holdsworth, iii. 327, n. 3.

[4] Y. B. 20 & 21 Ed. I [R. S.] 367. But see Fitz. Abr. *Debt*, 169 (T. 4 Ed. II), where it was held that no evidence of a condition could be introduced 'sans monstre fait del condicion'. If a condition were endorsed on the deed, parol evidence was admissible to prove performance of the condition. Y. B. 20 H. VI. 23.

[5] Britton, i. 29. 22.

[6] Y. B. 6 & 7 Ed. II [S. S.] 19 [22].

came into the hands of his executors, one of whom was an obligee in the simple obligation. The executor brought suit against the defendant, who endeavoured to set up the condition. Then ensued the following dialogue :

Spigurnel J.: Ou est le fet devenuz qe tesmoigne la condicion ?

Malmerthorpe: Geoffrei l'avoit en garde et nous avoms bille pendaunt vers ses executours, cesti Reynaud (*the plaintiff*) et altres, de cel escrit et des autres.

Spigurnel J.: Ceo fut folie a lesser vostre bastoun hors de vostre main.

The court refused to stay judgement till the defendant could recover his defeasance bond and put it in evidence, deciding rigidly on principle : ' pur ceo qe J. et R. mettent avaunt le fet Richard de E., q'est simple, et il allege une condicioun destourtre de la dette et de ceo ne moustre rien &c. ne nul autre chose qe luy peuse valer encountre l'obligacion q'est son fait, si agard la curt qe J. et R. recovere les C li vers Richard de E. et lour damages de C s. et Richard en la merci.' If one had an acquittance and lost it, he would be in the same unenviable position. It was his folly; the court turned a deaf ear to his plaint.

In the end, we come back to the remark of Lord Bacon : ' The law will not couple and mingle matter of specialty, which is of higher account, with matter of averment, which is of inferior account in law.' [1]

SECTION III.   DEBT AND DETINUE

Debt and Detinue were intimately related, and may profitably be considered together. While it would be venturesome to say that the latter action descended from the former,[2] there was a close connexion between them which was recognized after they had become distinct forms of action; for Detinue was held to be within the purview of a statute [3] which referred

---

[1] Bacon, Maxims of the Law, Reg. 25 [cited, Salmond, Essays in Jurisprudence, 57].
[2] See P. & M., ii. 177.   [3] 9 Ed. III, st. 1, c. 3.

in express words to Debt alone. In so deciding, Hillary J. remarked: ' The process is quite the same in Debt and Detinue ; and in a plea of Detinue the essoin and warranty of attorney shall be in the words " de placito debiti ".'[1] Before we attempt to point out the line of cleavage between the two actions, it will be well to examine the origin and form of the writ of Debt.

Debt represents an archaic conception.[2] The active party appears at first as a demandant rather than a plaintiff, and the action is itself ' petitory '.[3] One claims what is *his own*.

This comes out forcibly in Glanville's statement of the writ of Debt (which was modelled on the Praecipe in capite), where the defendant is ordered to ' render A one hundred marks which he owes him and of which he (i. e. A) claims that he (defendant) *deforces*[4] him '. This suggests that the action is proprietary, and that all distinction between obligation and property is obliterated. It would be dangerous, however, to assert this as a general proposition.[5]

Gradually the word ' deforces ' disappears, and the plaintiff asks that the defendant render him so many pounds, &c., which ' he owes and unjustly detains '.[6] We have here Debt in the ' debet et detinet '; it seems better able to express the relation between debtor and creditor.

At the same time a notion is coming to the fore that there are certain cases in which the word ' debet ' ought to be used, and certain other cases in which one should say ' detinet ' only. ' Debet et detinet ' is proper enough so long as the original creditor sues the original debtor, but if there has been a death on either side the word ' debet ' is out of place. The representative of the debtor ' detains ' money ; he does not ' owe ' it.[7] If the situation be reversed, and the representative of the

---

[1] Y. B. 17 Ed. III'[R. S.] 141.
[2] Maitland, Equity, 332.
[3] P. & M., ii. 207, n. 1 (citing Note Book, pl. 645, 732, 830).
[4] Glanville, x. 3 ; see Maitland, Equity, 332.
[5] Cf. P. & M., ii. 204.
[6] P. & M., ii. 173.   And see Britton, i. 29. 12.
[7] ' Nota ke en bref de dette porte vers un homme de autri fet cum ver le heyr de le fet et de le dette le pere ou ver executour de le fet le testatour, ne deyt pas mis le debet mes tout solement le injuste detinet.' Y. B.

creditor sue the original debtor, he must use the 'detinet' alone. The property in the debt was supposed to be in the testator ; it was merely 'detained' from his representative.[1] Curiously enough, the position of the heir was distinguished in some decisions. One of counsel in 1339 remarks that the heir demands a profit which is due to himself and shall say ' debet' ; at the same time care is taken to distinguish the case of the executor.[2] This distinction between ' debet' and ' detinet' is far remote from any idea of obligation.

At the same time an attempt is being made to base the distinction on another ground. Slowly men awake to a nascent perception of obligation ; they begin to discriminate between a *mutuum* and a *commodatum*. The use of ' debet' or ' detinet' is to be determined by the nature of the claim which is sought to be imposed. A reporter[3] in the time of Edward II distinguishes a claim for money (i. e. current coins) from a claim for movable goods ; in the first case one should say ' debet', in the second ' detinet'. It is evident, however, that in the early Year Books this distinction has not obtained a firm footing. Debt in the ' detinet' was brought for £4 due on a sale of goods,[4] money due on a lease,[5] against an abbot for the price of goods bought by his monk,[6] and for twenty shillings in silver.[7] On the other hand, Debt in the ' debet et detinet' was brought to recover sixty marks, where it appears that the

21 & 22 Ed. I [R. S.] 615. See also Y. B. 21 & 22 Ed. I [R. S.] 255. It is not clear that a ' debet' would not lie against the heir. Thus note this dialogue in 1340 :
'*Pole*: Judgement of the writ ; for the writ is in the words " quas debet ", whereas against heirs and executors it should be only " detinet ".
Pult: It is not so; against executors it is " detinet " only and against heirs it is " debet et detinet ".'
(*Semble*) The writ in the ' debet' against the heir was upheld. Y. B. 16 Ed. III (pt. ii) [R. S.] 383. And note that where one granted for himself and his heirs, a writ in the ' debet' against the heir was upheld. Y. B. 3 & 4 Ed. II [S. S.] 198.
  [1] Per Shardelow J., Y. B. 17 & 18 Ed. III [R. S.] 355.
  [2] Y. B. 12 & 13 Ed. III [R. S.] 171 (per Trewith).
  [3] Y. B. 3 Ed. II [S. S] 26.
  [4] Y. B. 21 & 22 Ed. I [R. S.] 293.
  [5] *Anon.* v. *Anon.*, Y. B. 6 & 7 Ed. II [S. S.] 33.
  [6] *Raudolf* v. *L'Abbé de Hughes*, Y. B. 6 & 7 Ed. II [S. S.] 32.
  [7] *Walewayn* v. *Rem*, Y. B. 6 & 7 Ed. II [S. S.] 38. (In this case there is no evidence that the plaintiff was seeking to recover the specific coins which were lent.)

plaintiff was demanding certain specific coins as bailor.[1]   But
at length Debt in the ' debet ' drew apart, and the form of
action in the ' detinet ' became indistinguishable from Detinue.
Detinue was recognized as a separate action as early as 1292,[2]
and as its province became more clearly defined,[3] it became
important to distinguish it from Debt.   Both lay to recover
chattels or money; for one might *owe* the one as well as the
other.   Roughly speaking, the distinction was between obligation and property.   Where the plaintiff's right was *in
personam*, that is, where he was enforcing an obligation to
pay money or chattels, the proper remedy was Debt.   But if
he sought to recover certain *specific* property of which he
claimed ownership, Detinue was the proper form.[4]

Detinue.

The importance of Detinue in the law of contract lies in the
fact that all bailments were left to its protection, and as the
action developed but little, the law of bailment remained practically stationary until Assumpsit superseded Detinue.   We are
concerned here with two questions relating to the action : its
nature, and the limitations imposed upon it.

I. *The nature of Detinue.*

We have said that in bringing Detinue the plaintiff was
asserting ownership of the chattel claimed.   This, however, is
a statement which many writers would not permit to pass un-
challenged.   We cannot consider very fully the perplexing
question of the fundamental nature of the action; for the
whole theory of the law of movable goods is involved.   But
on the other hand we cannot ignore it ; the mediaeval lawyer's
attitude toward bailment is best seen in connexion with the

---

[1] Y. B. 33–5 Ed. I [R.S.] 455 (The fact that the writ was not
challenged excited the attention of the reporter).

[2] Y. B. 20 & 21 Ed. I [R. S.] 189.

[3] Even in the time of Edward III there was still confusion.   See Y. B.
17 Ed. III [R.S.] 517.

[4] See Salmond, Essays, 176 ; Salmond, Anglo-Am., iii. 321, and cases
cited, Ames, H. L. R., viii. 260, n. 1.   And note Y. B. 12 & 13 Ed. III
[R. S.] 245 (Detinue for a sealed bag containing £20.   The defendant
asserted that as the demand was for money, Debt was the proper action.
Shardelowe J. supported Detinue, on the ground that the defendant had
no power to take the money out of the bag).

action. Was it founded on contract, or was it in a sense
proprietary? Was the gist of the action a breach of contract,
or a tort? There does not seem to be any categorical answer
to these questions.

A very keen student of the common law has asserted that
Detinue was, in its origin, founded on contract, and that the
gist of the action was a breach of contract, namely, the refusal
to deliver up the chattel on request, which refusal or unjust
detainer was a tort, only in so far as every breach of contract
is tortious.[1] This explanation is very simple, and if it is
sound it has far-reaching consequences. Much as I hesitate
to differ with Professor Ames, I venture to question his conclusion. Before stating reasons for so doing, it is well to
examine certain cases.

Y. B. 20 & 21 Ed. I [R. S.] 189. A charter was bailed to
one Maud de Mortymer, while she was married; her husband
died, and after his death the bailor attempted to bring Detinue
against the widow. Now it is admitted that a married woman
cannot bind herself by contract. The plaintiff, however, contends that she must answer for her tort; 'In this case,' he says,
'the action arises from the tortious detainer, and not from the
bailment.' It is unlike Debt. The question is debated at some
length, but just at the point where one's curiosity is thoroughly
aroused, the report ends, and we are at loss to know what was
decided.[2]

Y. B. 21 & 22 Ed. I [R. S.] 466. A reporter in a note says
that one may count in Detinue by alleging that the defendant
found the chattel which is claimed (. . . 'la ou meme cele
chosse ly fut endire . . . la vynt yl (the defendant) . . . e le
trova ').[3] It is difficult to see what notion of contract is present
here.

---

[1] Ames, History of Trover, Anglo-Am., iii. 432–4.

[2] It is believed that Mr. Ames (Anglo-Am., iii. 433) has misunderstood
this case. He quotes it as *deciding* that Detinue will not lie against
a widow for a charter bailed during coverture. The question is discussed
—but no definite inference can be drawn. The decision can only be
settled by looking up the case in the Rolls, which I regret to say I have not
had time to do.

[3] This looks as if Detinue by a loser against a finder might have been
used at an early date. Ames (Anglo-Am., iii. 439) says that no instance
has been found prior to 1371. A reporter's note has not the force of
a decision, but it should be noted. Littleton, however, in 33 H. VI.
26. 12 describes the declaration *per inventionem* as a 'new-found
Halliday'.

Y. B. 1 & 2 Ed. II [S. S.] 39. A son brings Detinue against his father's executors for a bairn's part of his father's goods. The count relies, not upon any bailment, but upon a *usage of the country* (*par usage du pays*). The defendant objected that the writ could not be maintained, because the plaintiff did not show that he bought the goods or bailed them, nor was there any contract, to which Staunton J. replied, 'You must answer to the writ.' The son would seem to have claimed his portion of the goods as his *right*; and he did this through the action of Detinue.[1]

Y. B. 6 & 7 Ed. II [S. S.] 18. In Detinue for charters, Stanton J. remarked: 'They have counted that the charters came into your possession as their mother's executor after her death. By what law can you detain these charters, seeing that you do not hold them by the delivery of one who had a right to them . . . ?'

Y. B. 17 Ed. III [R. S.] 141. Detinue, for a wife's reasonable portion of her husband's chattels. *Semble*, the action is maintainable. Later a writ 'de rationabile parte' was brought, and it was referred to as ' in the nature of a writ of Detinue' (17 Ed. III, 145).

6 Hen. VIII (Comyn's Digest, sub tit. Detinue) per Brian J. The plaintiff must have the general or special property at the time of the action to maintain Detinue.

In most of these cases there was no bailment; but even where the action was ostensibly founded on a bailment, it is not clear that the idea of contract was predominant. A denial of the bailment was not a sufficient answer; the defendant must also deny the detainer.[2] Again, though the plaintiff alleged a bailment, he based his right to recover on his ownership in the thing bailed. This comes out clearly in a case in 1344. Detinue was brought for a horse, bailed by the plaintiff to the defendants' testator. The defendants contended that, as executors, they need not answer without specialty. It was admitted that Debt did not lie against executors without a specialty, and the contention was that the situation in Detinue was the same. In answer, Mowbray said, ' Sir, in

---

[1] It is admitted that actions of this kind were comparatively rare. More often the plaintiff went to chancery, e. g. IV. 158, *Cases*, p. 174.

[2] Y. B. 20 & 21 Ed. I [R. S.] 193. And see Y. B. 16 Ed. III [R. S.] 167, holding that issue must be taken on the *Detinue* and not on the manner of bailment. See also Y. B. 20 & 21 Ed. I [R. S.] 213.

a writ of Debt, if the debt be recovered against executors, the execution shall always be made of the testator's goods found in the possession of the executors, in which case it is not right that he should recover without a specialty ; but now on this writ we are seeking to recover a horse ; that is *our own chattel* and not that of the deceased; wherefore . . .'   And Sharshulle J. ruled that the plaintiff should be answered without specialty, because ' *this action does not arise on obligation*'.[1]

We may now summarize our objections :

(1) Even in the early Year Books, as the cases cited show, Detinue lay where there was no bailment.   The son's action for a bairn's share of his father's goods, the wife's claim for a share of her husband's chattels, the action by the loser against the finder, none of these sound in contract.   Each is an assertion of the right of ownership as distinct from a right by obligation.   Now it is possible that Detinue began as a contractual action, and was later extended to cases where there was no contract.   But so far as our evidence goes, this remains unproven.   We do know that there are very early cases in which Detinue was brought, where there was no contract.   It is incumbent upon supporters of the contractual theory to give some explanation of these actions.

(2) If Detinue 'sur bailment' were founded on contract, it would follow that the bailor's right was only *in personam*. The fact that Detinue did not lie against a third hand seems to support this.   But we know that gradually the bailor did acquire a general property in the thing bailed without the assistance of any statute.[2]   In other words, a purely contractual right somehow developed into ownership.   This extraordinary transformation of a right *in personam* into a right *in rem* by a process of development is not impossible ; but we decline to accept a theory which thrusts so heavy a burden on the common law, unless it be shown that no other is tenable.[3]

---

[1] Y. B. 17 Ed. III [R. S.] 517 ff.   This is not the same thing as saying the 'action does not arise on contract', but such seems to be the implication.

[2] P. & M., ii. 177.

[3] 'The transformation . . . of the bailor's restricted right against the bailee alone, to an unrestricted right against any possessor of the chattel

(3) In later days Detinue lay against a seller on a bargain and sale. The payment of the purchase money, or the delivery of the buyer's sealed obligation, constituted the *quid pro quo* which supported the action.[1] But the principle was extended farther, so that Detinue lay upon a mere parol bargain of sale, where nothing was delivered to the seller. This might appear to indicate that the buyer was enforcing a personal right against the seller, but the remark [2] of Fortescue C. J. destroys any such notion. Detinue was allowed because the property in the thing sold passed to the buyer; he claimed it as his own.[3]

We have presented only one side of the argument. It cannot be said that Detinue was proprietary, for in the early cases there is convincing evidence that it was not. But the point to be made is this. It is not believed that the mediaeval lawyer had any theory of the nature of Detinue at all. When he wrote text-books, he talked in Roman terms, but when he came into court, he dismissed any theories of substantive law and looked only at procedure. It did not matter whether Detinue sounded in contract or in tort; the primary question was whether it would lie upon a given state of facts. Limitations were imposed on the action, or its sphere was slightly extended, without any thought of the effect upon the substantive law of contract. Indeed, nothing more impresses the student of the Year Books than the absence of general doctrines and the disinclination to make generalizations. In the interest of analytical jurisprudence it may be desirable to frame a theory of the nature of Detinue; but one imposes

---

bailed, virtually converted his right *ex contractu* into a right *in rem*.' (Ames, History of Trover, Anglo-Am., iii. 435.) Mr. Ames seems to assume that because the bailor's right was originally restricted to an action against the bailee alone, that the right must have been *ex contractu*. This does not follow. Nor has the learned writer shown conclusively that Detinue was founded on contract.

[1] Y. B. 21 Ed. III. 12. 2 ; and see Ames, H.L.R., viii. 259 and cases cited.

[2] 'If I buy a horse of you, *the property is straightway in me*, and for this you shall have a writ of Debt for the money, and I shall have Detinue for the horse on this bargain.' Y. B. 20 H. VI. 35. 4, quoted Ames, H. L. R., viii. 259.

[3] Thus a buyer appeals to equity, alleging that he has no remedy at law because the property in the goods sold never vested in him. The reason was that the vendor had no title. LIX. 185, *Cases*, p. 230.

such a theory on the early decisions at his peril. Down to the nineteenth century Detinue pursued its mysterious way, continuing to confound judges and lawyers in their speculations as to its origin.[1]

II. *Limitations in the use of the action.*

(1) If the defendant persisted in retaining the chattel, the common law afforded no means by which its delivery could be compelled. The plaintiff in Detinue had to be content with damages, if worst came to worst; because in the rough generalization of early common law, 'all things may be resolved into damages as an equivalent'.[2] So the law remained till modern times.[3]

(2) In case of bailment the bailor could bring Detinue only against the bailee, or his representative.[4] That is, the defendant's possession must be connected with that of the bailee, 'as by showing that the possessor was the widow, heir, or executor of the bailee, or otherwise in a certain privity with him'.[5] If the chattel passed with or without the bailee's consent into the hands of a third party, the bailor was helpless.[6]

(3) While inability to re-deliver, as through the destruction of the thing, was no defence,[7] still if the bailee wasted or misused the thing bailed, Detinue afforded no remedy.[8]

---

[1] See Note A, p. 169.

[2] 'Nota. Detinue de chateux. Le pleintif recoveri damages et noun pas le principal, pur ce qe tout court en damages al contra.' 14 & 15 Ed. III. 31.

[3] Ord. XLVIII. v. 1 (R.S.C. 1883) empowers the court or judge to order execution to issue for the delivery of a specific chattel, without giving the defendant the option of retaining the same upon payment of its assessed value.

[4] P. & M., ii. 175. It is a question whether the executor of the bailor could bring Detinue. In VI. 177, appeal is made to equity, and petitioners allege that as they are executors they cannot bring Detinue.

[5] Ames, H. L. R., iii. 33. In Y. B. 16 Ed. II. 490 a plaintiff counted that he had bailed a writing to D. to rebail, &c., 'issint qe apres la mort l'avant-dit D. l'escript devynt en la mayn celui B. . . .' The writ was brought against B., and Mutford J. remarked: 'Pur ceo qe vous n'avez mye dit coment il avynt a l'escript, ne vous luy fait mye prive a D. come heir, ne come executour, ne en autre manere, si agarde la court qe vous ne preignez rien par vostre breve.' Cf. VI. 245 (10 S. S. 113).

[6] Ames, H. L. R., iii. 33; Y. B. B. 24 Ed. III. 41a. 22; 43 Ed. III. 29. 11.

[7] Y. B. B. 14 Ed. III [R. S.] 35; 20 H. VI. 16. 2.

[8] Ames, Anglo-Am., iii. 441.

D

(4) In certain cases the defendant might wage his law, e. g.
if the plaintiff delivered the article by his own hand.[1]

Debt.

We turn now to a more particular examination of Debt.[2]

I. *Characteristics of the action.*

1. The writ of Debt was general. It merely specified that
something was due ; the form was the same whatever the
nature of the claim. The count particularized and made
mention of the specific nature of the demand.[3]

2. According to Langdell[4] a debt itself was regarded as
a grant ; this theory seems to be confirmed by the fact that
Debt was the exclusive remedy upon a covenant to pay
money, till a late period.[5] Covenant would seem to have
been the more natural remedy, but it was restricted to claims
for unliquidated damages. A parol grant,[6] however, would
not support Debt, except by special custom.[7]

The idea that a debt was a grant throws some light on the
conception of Debt itself. The claim in the action was that
the defendant owed a certain sum ;[8] he was conceived to
withhold something from the plaintiff, which it was his duty
to surrender.[9] Hence, it followed logically that :

3. The claim must always be for a sum certain.[10] The

---

[1] Y. B. 16 Ed. III [R. S.] 329. On this ground appeal was made to
equity : XI. 427*a*, *Cases*, p. 187.

[2] In the thirteenth century many actions of Debt were brought, not to
enforce a loan, or claim money, but that judgement might be had by
default ; creditors were using the action as a means of obtaining security
before making a loan. This primitive form of security passed out of use
with the development of the recognizance and statute merchant. See
P. & M., ii. 203-4.

[3] ' Each writ of Debt is general and of one form and the count special
and makes mention of the contract, obligation, record, &c.' Colepepper J.
in Y. B. 11 H. IV. 73.

[4] Langdell, Contracts, § 100.

[5] Ames, Anglo-Am., iii. 279, n. 4, and cases cited.

[6] Y. B. 3 Ed. II [S. S.] 191.

[7] e. g. by custom of London and Bristol. Ames, H. L. R. viii. 254, n. 2,
and cases cited.

[8] ' Le demand est un dutie et le ground de la action est un dutie.'
Y. B. 7 H. VI. 5. 9.

[9] Ames, H. L. R., viii. 260.

[10] Fitz., Abr., *Debt*, 158. See Martin J. in Y. B. 4 H. VI. 19. 5 (cited
Jenks, 165), and note remarks of counsel in Y. B. 4 H. VI. 17. 3.

defendant could not owe a duty to pay an uncertain sum ; it must be reduced to certainty. Thus, in case of a sale of goods, the vendee's promise to pay what the goods were worth would not support Debt. 'If I bring cloth to a tailor to have a cloak made', remarked Brian C. J. in 1473,[1] 'if the price be not determined beforehand that I shall pay for the making, he shall not have an action of Debt against me.' Even when Indebitatus Assumpsit first supplanted Debt, it assumed this limitation, which was afterwards removed. This statement is not contradicted by the fact that damages were recoverable, that is, not damages as a sole claim, but damages for the detention of the debt.[2]   In many cases the judgement is that the plaintiff do recover his debt and damages,[3] the damages being usually taxed by the court,[4] though if the defendant waged his law and afterwards made default, the plaintiff might recover such damages as he himself alleged in the count.[5]

4. It may be inferred from what has already been said that the action of Debt was wider than contract. It was based upon the duty to pay money or goods, a duty which arose from some source recognized by law.[6] No one thought of a promise as the basis of the action. If money were promised one for making a release, and the release were made, Debt would lie for the money promised ; but it was the act of making the release, the something done, which supported Debt, not the promise to pay.[7] A does not bring an action against B and allege that B promised to pay him ; he says simply that B *owes* him a certain sum, and sets up a *insta causa debendi*, that is, some 'cause' recognized by law by which money is due.

---

[1] Y. B. 12 Ed. IV. 9. 22 ; Ames, H. L. R., viii. 260.

[2] Of course the plaintiff might bring Debt for damages due as the result of some other action, e. g. damages recovered in a writ of waste (43 Ed. III. 2. 5).   But in such cases the amount due was definitely determined, and the defendant's duty to pay arose from the judgement against him.

[3] e. g. Fitz., Abr., *Debt, passim* ; *idem* 164 (34 Ed. I).

[4] Where debt was proved by a deed which the defendant could not deny, damages were taxed by the court. Y. B. 1 & 2 Ed. II [S. S.] 91.

[5] Y. B. 12 & 13 Ed. III [R. S.] 119; but cf. Y. B. 17 & 18 Ed. III [R. S.] 623. The point may be doubtful.

[6] See The Exposition of the Terms of the Lawes of England, fo. 32-3, (*sub tit.* Debt).   [7] See remarks (*ad fin.*) Y. B. 12 H. VI. 17. 13.

Among such causes were the following: Debt would lie
to recover statutory penalties, amercements, forfeitures;[1]
arrears of an annuity;[2] a claim against a sheriff for allowing
a recognizor by a statute merchant to go at large;[3] arrears
of rent service;[4] arrears of a parker's wages;[5] damages recovered in a writ of waste;[6] a debt confessed by a sealed
instrument;[7] money lent;[8] price of goods sold;[9] money due
from a surety.[10] Instances might be multiplied, but those
already given are characteristic.

If we except the cases of Debt on a sealed instrument or
some kindred security, it will be found that the action is
never brought unless the defendant has received something
from the plaintiff. It therefore became possible to deduce
a general principle from these typical 'causes' which supported Debt, and this deduction resulted in the well-known
doctrine of *quid pro quo*. There was no such requirement
where Debt was brought on a judgement or a sealed instrument; but in other cases the action was not maintainable
unless a *quid pro quo* were present.

II. *The doctrine of* quid pro quo.

1. When this generalization was first made cannot be settled
with certainty. In 1293[11] there is what appears to be such
a generalization, though the technical name is absent; and
indeed, under Edward II, Bereford[12] endeavoured to apply the
same reasoning to sealed instruments; for we find him peering

---

[1] P. & M., ii. 210.
[2] Y. B. B. 12 & 13 Ed. III [R. S.] 109; H. 3 H. VI (Fitz., Abr., *Debt*, 16).
[3] Y. B. B. 12 & 13 Ed. III [R. S.] 131; *id.* 355; 18 & 19 Ed. III [R. S.]
65.   [4] Y. B. 17 & 18 Ed. III [R. S.] 63.
[5] Y. B. 17 & 18 Ed. III [R. S.] 623.   [6] Y. B. 43 Ed. III. 2. 5.
[7] *Supra*, under Covenant.   [8] P. & M., ii. 211.
[9] Y. B. 21 & 22 Ed. I [R. S.] 293.
[10] But by the reign of Edward III it was settled that a surety could not
be held unless he bound himself by deed. Holmes, 264.
[11] Y. B. 21 & 22 Ed. I [R. S.] 293. The plaintiff delivered chattels to
the defendant, for which the latter did not pay £4. It was held that the
defendant's admission of the receipt of the chattels raised the duty to pay
the £4. Thus:
Metingham J. 'Pur ceo ke Thomas ad reconu ke yl ressut les chateux
de Ricard e yl ne pout dedire le contract entre ly e Ricard, sy agardom ke
Ricard recovere le iiij livres ver Thomas,' &c.
[12] Y. B. 1 & 2 Ed. II [S. S.] 160.

behind the seal, and inquiring into the question, Did the defendant get what he bargained for?

In 1338 it is clearly recognized.   By covenant between the plaintiff and defendant, the plaintiff was made the defendant's attorney for ten years at 20s. per year.   The payment was in arrear, but the plaintiff had no specialty to show for his covenant.   Sharshulle J. remarked : 'If one were to count simply of a grant of a debt, he would not be received without a specialty ; but here you have his service for his allowance, of which knowledge may be had and you have "quid pro quo".'[1] The appearance of the phrase in other actions without technical significance[2] indicates that it was some time before it became a settled term of art.[3]

2.   At all events, whatever the date of the enunciation of the doctrine in technical form, it is very doubtful if an action of Debt could ever be maintained in the king's court, unless the plaintiff could show either a specialty, or a *quid pro quo* received by the defendant.[4]   By *quid pro quo* is meant some substantial benefit received, and whatever the law could regard as such would support Debt.   This is clearly a benefit to the promisor.

3.   Suppose, however, the benefit were conferred upon a third party at the request of the defendant.   Would Debt lie?   At first this was doubted, but at length the reasoning of Moyle J.[5] in its favour made its way, and it became settled

---

[1] Y. B. 11 & 12 Ed. III [R. S.] 587.

[2] e. g. Y. B. 16 Ed. III [R. S.] 527 : in an action of Covenant, there is the remark of Mowbray : ' Quant le Priour se retreit, et puis accorde se prist, cele retrere ne put estre entendu forque pur le covenant ensuant, issint *quid pro quo*.'

Mr. Pike's translation of ' forque pur ' as ' in consideration of ' is unfortunate, in that it seems to suggest a technical meaning.   What is implied is plain enough, namely, that in the process of levying land by fine, the fact that one party retires and permits judgement to go against him, does not mean that he abandons his rights.   The prior's retreating is to be interpreted *in the light of* the ensuing covenant.   He withdrew in order that he might receive something else in return.   This is quite a different thing from the technical generalization in *quid pro quo*.

[3] Salmond says the phrase was first used in 39 Ed. III (in a case unconnected with contract).   But this is disproved by the cases cited, which are earlier.

[4] Ames, H. L. R., viii. 254.

[5] In Y. B. 37 H. VI. 8. 18.

law.[1] But it was an essential condition that the defendant, at whose instance the benefit was conferred, should alone be liable ; for :

4. One *quid pro quo* would not support two distinct debts.[2] If A requested B to furnish goods to C, and B did so, relying on A's request, B might maintain Debt against A ; but it was otherwise if C became personally liable.

III. *Debt might be maintained against a principal on the contract made by his agent*, provided the principal received the benefit ; there must be *quid pro quo*, and the *quid* must pass through the agent to the principal.

Thus goods are sold to an abbot by the hand of T, his monk. The monk may be charged in Debt, if the goods went to the profit of the house.[3] It is this which makes the ' simple contract to bind the house ' ;[4] the monk is a mere conduit. In fact, the law of agency is extremely rudimentary ; for the only means of bringing suit against a principal was Debt, and in that action the requirement of *quid pro quo* reduced the agent to a nonentity.

IV. *Proof.*

1. Suit or secta. The plaintiff might produce secta, or transaction witnesses. This practice has been so thoroughly examined elsewhere[5] that it is needless to review it here. It soon became obsolete.[6]

2. Deed. A specialty was proof conclusive, and could only be met by a specialty.[7]

---

[1] Ames, H. L. R., viii. 263. However, it did not become settled law during the fifteenth century (the period considered in this essay), and so far as appeals to equity are concerned may be ignored. In the meantime the rise of Assumpsit had lessened the importance of this principle in Debt. See Holdsworth, iii. 328.   [2] Ames, H. L. R., viii. 263.

[3] Y. B. 33–5 Ed. I [R. S.] 537 ; Y. B. 6 & 7 Ed. II [S. S.] 32. It was objected that the abbot was not a party to the contract. Bereford C. J. replied : ' Jeo maundrai moun homme al marche, il achatera a mon oeps divers marchandises et il les fra venir a moun hostiel et ieo les dependrai, ne quidez vous qe ieo responde : quod diceret sic.'

[4] ' . . . la conversion de la summe a la oeps de la Measson fait le simple contract de lier la Meason.' Y. B. 20 H. VI. 21. 19.

[5] Holmes, 255 ff. ; Jenks, 174–86.

[6] The last case alluding to the practice appears to be Y. B. 13 Ed. III [R. S.] 44, in which it was said that the mention of suit was a mere form.

[7] Y. B. B. 30 & 31 Ed. I [R. S.] 159 ; 33–5 Ed. I [R. S.] 331 ; *supra* under Covenant.

3. Tally.

(*a*) Doubtless the difficulty of securing sealed writings opened the way for some simpler mode of proof. This was found in the tally. A tally, however, was not considered a very valuable means of proof, as it was too easy to alter it ; indeed Herle in disparagement referred to it as a mere 'fusselet'.[1]

(*b*) Except by the law merchant,[2] the defendant might wage his law against a tally.[3] An early case shows an inclination to extend the custom of the law merchant to the royal courts, at least in such cases as concerned merchants,[4] but subsequent decisions do not indicate that the tally was thus favoured.

(4) If the plaintiff could produce neither specialty nor tally, he must show that the defendant had received a *quid pro quo*.

V. *Disadvantages of Debt.*

(1) The claim must always be for a sum certain. Thus damages for the breach of an executory parol contract could never be obtained in Debt.

(2) The plaintiff must prove the precise amount of his claim.[5]

(3) Great particularity was required in the count.[6]

(4) If the plaintiff could not produce a specialty the defendant might wage his law. Wager of law remained a glaring defect of the action.

(5) Wherever wager of law was possible, the action would

---

[1] '. . . mais ceo qe vous mettez avant pur especialte n'est qe un fusselet en le quel n'est pas la demand note . . .', per Herle in *Anon.* v. *Anon.*, Y. B. 6 & 7 Ed. II [S. S.] 35. Herle went on to say that the amount due was indicated only by notches, which might be increased or whittled away at pleasure.

[2] Y. B. 20 & 21 Ed. I [R. S.] 69.

[3] There may have been an exception in favour of a sealed tally. See Y. B. 3 Ed. II [S. S.] 46. As examples of wager of law against a tally, see Y. B. B. 20 & 21 Ed. I [R. S.] 331 ; 20 Ed. III (pt. ii) [R. S.] 449.

[4] Y. B. 21 & 22 Ed. I [R. S.] 457. (Note the remark of Metingham.)

[5] 'If he (i. e. the plaintiff) demanded a debt of £20, and proved a debt of £19, he failed as effectually as if he had declared in Detinue for the recovery of a horse and could only prove the detention of a cow.' Ames, H. L. R., viii. 261.

[6] Ames, H. L. R., ii. 57.

not lie against executors. The deceased might have waged his law, but the executors could not do this for him ;¹ hence the action failed.

SECTION IV. ASSUMPSIT

From the foregoing discussion the rigid limitations of the old contract remedies are quite obvious. Agreement, or 'accord', as such played no part in the theory of the common law ; and yet it is inconceivable that the transactions of a busy commercial life could have been satisfied by such meagre recognition. Pressure was being exerted from without ; suitors weary of the ineffectuality of the existing remedies were turning to the chancellor for aid. If the common law were to retain its commercial jurisdiction, the idea of 'contract' must be widened. This is what was done, in effect. But the method was characteristic. No new remedy was invented ; an old one was taken and perverted from its original purpose. The vitalizing force for agreement came from an unexpected source, from an action which sounded originally purely in tort, trespass on the case.² The perversion which so vitally

---

¹ Y. B. 17 & 18 Ed. III [R. S.] 513. Shardelowe J. remarked : ' Quele est la cause en Dette pur quei executours ne respoundrount pas saunz especialte de dette due par lour testatour ? Pur ceo qe lour testatour poait aver fait sa ley, et cel respons faut a eux.' And see Holdsworth, iii. 455.

² In H. L. R., xxv. 428 (March, 1912), Mr. Deiser puts forward an ingenious theory. He contends that by means of the Statute of Westminster II a remedy was found 'not merely for trespasses, but for all those miscellaneous instances of litigation that did not fall into any well-defined category'. He believes, therefore, that at this early period a remedy was found 'for breaches of covenant or contract in the action on the case'. But there appear to be insuperable objections in the way of this theory.

1. All actions in which an Assumpsit was laid would sound in contract and not in tort. In consequence, Mr. Ames's explanation of the presence of an Assumpsit in Trespass on the case is gratuitous. Mr. Deiser fails to explain why this Assumpsit appears in the early cases, and *disappears* after the idea of tort became widened.

2. All the cases he cites (and he has produced none that are new) are examples of misfeasance. In other words, the breach of contract never takes the form of a mere failure to perform the promise. This is certainly peculiar. If the action were based on the promise, we should certainly expect to find examples of breach by non-feasance.

3. Upon Mr. Deiser's own showing, there are only 52 reported cases of trespass on the case from 1275 to 1471. Bearing in mind the fact that litigants began to appeal to the chancellor in the latter part of the fourteenth century, it seems remarkable that more use was not made of this convenient action (case) if in fact it was available for breach of contract.

affected the law of contract was a branch of this action, and
came to be known as Assumpsit; but to the end it retained
certain indelible marks of its delictual origin.

That the chief contract remedy of the common law should
be a delictual action perverted to another use has excited the
curiosity and indeed astonishment of many students. But
is it, after all, so very extraordinary? Doubtless from our
notions to-day it may seem so; but if we inquire into the
workings of the mediaeval lawyer's mind, the matter may
appear simpler. What was meant by the form 'contract'?
Was agreement a different thing? Was there a sharp line
drawn between contract (as we think of it to-day) and tort?
It is worth while to look for a moment at these questions
before tracing summarily the development of Assumpsit.

Perhaps no case more clearly emphasizes the distinction
between Debt and Assumpsit, or the contemporary notion
of contract itself, than an action of trespass on the case which
was brought in 1536.[1] This falls without the period considered
in this essay, but it may serve as a useful introduction to the
earlier cases. The plaintiff had imprisoned one Tatam in the
Counter for debt; the defendant came to the plaintiff's wife,
the plaintiff himself being away, and 'assumpsit super se
al' feme' that if the plaintiff would discharge Tatam from
execution, he (i.e. defendant) would pay the debt 'a tiel jour
al' baron, si Tatam ne paia devant'. When the plaintiff
returned, his wife told him of the defendant's undertaking,
whereupon he 'agrea a l'assumption', and discharged Tatam.
Tatam, however, though he rejoiced in his liberty, showed no
eagerness to discharge the debt; and then the plaintiff brought
his action on the case against the defendant, seeking to charge
him on the undertaking. The action was held to be properly
brought.

In the count the plaintiff had alleged that defendant
'assumpsit super se al plaintiff...'; defendant traversed
the assumpsit, and upon the introduction of evidence, it
appeared that the undertaking, as already stated, was made
to the wife, in her husband's absence. The defendant seized

---

[1] Y. B. 27 H. VIII. 24. 3.

upon this 'variance', and made his exception, contending
that the wife 'ne poet estre party a tiel assumption sans
commandement de son baron devant . . .' This question
afforded some difficulty to the judges, but they finally overruled the exception, and then the defendant moved in arrest
of judgement, alleging as his chief reason that the action
should have been one of Debt. This was the crux of the
case. Was there here any 'contract'? What was the basis of
this action? Brook thought Debt would not lie in such case
as this; for 'on n'aura bref de Dette mes ou un contract est,
car le defendant n'ad *quid pro quo*, mes l'action [i.e. in this
case] est solement fonde sur l'assumption, que sonne merement
en covenant . . .' Spelman J. was inclined to think both Debt
and Case would lie; but his reasoning, based on the analogy
of the concurrence of Detinue and Case under certain circumstances, is not very convincing. He could not show how the
defendant here had *quid pro quo*. FitzJames C. J. adopted
Brook's view. His comment is worthy of being quoted at
length: 'Donque, s'il aura accion [1] de Dette ou cest accion
(i.e. case); et come me semble, il n'aura accion de Det: car
icy n'est ascun contract ni le defendant n'ad *quid pro quo*;
purque il n'ad autre remedy sinon Accion sur son cas. Comme
si un estranger in London eme un piece de drap, et jeo die
a le merchant, s'il ne paie vous a tiel jour, jeo paiera; icy
n'est ascun contract parentre le merchant et moy, et il n'aura
accion de Dette vers moy . . . issint in le cas icy, pur ceo que
n'est ascun contract parentre le plaintif et le defendant, le
plaintif ne poit avoir accion de Dette, mes solement cest
accion.' The action was allowed: the motive which led to
this result was the thought (of which there is frequent expression in the course of the discussion) that the plaintiff had
no remedy 'sinon accion sur son cas'.

What, then, is the significance of the use of the word
'contract'? Why is the 'assumption' so carefully distinguished? We may examine first the use of the word
'contract' in the Year Books.

[1] The Year Book reads 'acre', which is an obvious mistake for
'accion'.

In Fitzherbert's Abridgement one solitary case supports this title, and that was an action of Debt,[1] in which the whole discussion revolved about *quid pro quo*. Counsel and judges take pains to distinguish 'contract' from a sealed writing, an obligation;[2] a grant is not a contract, for it must be by specialty.[3] In early days contract was swallowed up by the larger idea of property, and even in the time of Hale and Blackstone it was treated 'only as a means of acquiring ownership or possession'.[4] But it is used chiefly, one might say almost always, in connexion with the action of Debt.[5] True, we sometimes find a bailment of chattels called a contract,[6] though the use is not common. A sale,[7] and a loan,[8] were the characteristic examples.[9] The association with Debt, and the doctrine of *quid pro quo*, limited the use of the word 'contract' to transactions in which there was the transfer of some material thing. 'In every contract', remarks Coke, 'there must be *quid pro quo*, for *contractus est quasi actus contra actum*.'[10] In general it may be said that the simple contract of the Year Books approaches, though it is not the same as, the Roman 'real contract'; and so, speaking somewhat loosely, we may describe Debt as being founded usually on a real contract. A word of such limitations could scarcely include the idea of agreement; indeed, we do not find the thought of a promise, or consent, playing any part in the law of 'contract'. The 'assumption' which supported Assumpsit was a different thing; and as in the principal case, great care

---

[1] Y. B. 37 H. VI. 8. 18.
[2] Y. B. B. 17 & 18 Ed. III [R. S.] 73; Fitz., Abr., *Debt*, 83 (H. 35 Ed. III); 3 H. IV. 2. 8; 20 H. VI. 21. 19.
[3] Y. B. 3 Ed. II [S. S.] 191.   [4] P. & M., i. 57.
[5] Debt, of course, lay where there was no 'contract', in the early sense, at all. But the association of the word with Debt explains such anomalous dogmas of English law as a 'Contract of Record'. In the later attempts at generalizing, it seems to have been thought that wherever Debt would lie, there must be a contract, and the term was forced to stagger beneath a load which logic could not have forced upon it.
[6] Y. B. 19 Ed. III [R. S.] 329.
[7] e. g. Y. B. 20 H. VI. 21. 19.
[8] Y. B. 17 Ed. III [R. S.] 7 (at p. 11).
[9] See an instructive note by Ames, Angl.-Am., iii. 306, n. 1.
[10] Co. Lit. 47 *b*. It seems scarcely necessary to say that the etymology is purely fanciful.

is taken to make the distinction.[1] Too much may be made
of an argument based upon the use of one particular word ;
but it is not a matter of small importance that the idea of
contract became enlarged very slowly, and that many agreements became enforceable before they were thought of as
contracts at all. The damage which one may sustain from
relying upon a promise that is unfulfilled is not so remote
from damage resulting from a direct infringement of one's
rights by a tort. The ideas may exist side by side ; and that
they did so is revealed in the development of the action of
Assumpsit.

One of the first cases in which an Assumpsit was laid was
in 1348.[2] The defendant undertook to carry the plaintiff's ox
safely across the river Humber, but negligently overloaded
his boat, with the result that the ox was lost. The
objection that no tort was shown was overruled, the court
remarking that the trespass consisted in overloading the boat.[3]
One who undertook to cure a horse of sickness, but did his
work so negligently that the horse died, was also charged in
Case in the form of Assumpsit.[4] Case was, however, maintained against a smith for laming a horse where no specific
undertaking was laid.[5] All these are cases of active misconduct on the part of the defendant ; the damage resulted
directly from his wrongful act. To-day they would be
regarded as pure tort ; and the question arises at once why
any Assumpsit was laid in the first two cases, and why, in
the case of the smith, the writ was adjudged good, though
there was no express undertaking to shoe carefully.

The answer is to be found in the primitive conception of
liability for a wrongful act. The typical tort was an injury
caused to property by a stranger, one who had no authority

---

[1] e. g. Prisot J. in Y. B. 37 H. VI. 8. 18 asserted that an agreement (or
undertaking) to pay the plaintiff 100 marks if he married the plaintiff's
daughter was not a contract.

[2] 22 Ass., pl. 41.

[3] ' Il semble qe vous luy fistes tresp' quant vous surcharg' le bateau, par
que sa jument perist,' &c. 22 Ass., pl. 41.

[4] Y. B. 43 Ed. III. 33.

[5] Y. B. 46 Ed. III. 19. 19; Fitz., Abr., *Case*, 49 (T. 46 Ed. III. 19).

to deal with it in any way.[1] If a person saw fit to place his property in another's care, or to authorize another to do some act with regard to it, any damage which might result from improper action, or failure to act at all, did not raise any liability. The law did not, however, remain stationary in this respect; the narrow notion of liability was extended in two ways:

1. From motives of public policy the law placed certain persons or classes of persons in a peculiar position. Inn-keepers, common carriers, and smiths were required to show a certain amount of diligence in their respective work.[2] It was not necessary that the smith should undertake to shoe care-fully. The law imposed upon him the necessity of exercising a proper degree of skill; and this requirement removed the case from the old rule. Gradually this notion was pushed further, so that a smith incurred liability if he refused to shoe a horse, and damage resulted from his inaction, while an inn-keeper who declined to provide food and fodder at his inn [3] became liable in an action on the case. Taverners, vintners, and butchers must sell food of a certain quality; even without representation that it is good, they become liable in 'Deceit' if the food is inferior and damage results.[4]

2. If, however, the person sought to be held liable did not fall within one of these classes into which mediaeval society divided itself, he might still be held to account, under certain conditions.

The reason for stating an Assumpsit is clearly shown in the remarks of the judges in an action [5] brought against a horse doctor for killing a horse by 'contrary medicines', when he had undertaken to cure it. The defendant traversed the Assumpsit, and the question before the court was whether

---

[1] Ames, H. L. R., ii. 3 ff. Throughout this sketch of Assumpsit I am greatly indebted to Professor Ames's articles in the H. L. R. (vol. ii, pp. 2 and 53).

[2] Holdsworth, iii. 331. And note F. N. B., 94 D : '. . . it is the duty of each artificer to perform his art duly and truly as he ought.'

[3] 'Nota que fut agree par tout le Court : Que l'ou un Smith denie de ferrer mon cheval ou un Hosteler denie moy d'avoir herbage en son hos-terie, j'avera Action sur le case, nient obstant que nul act est fait, car ceo ne sound en covenant.' 18 H. VII, Keilw. 50. 4.

[4] Y. B. 9 H. VI. Mich., pl. 37 ; Holdsworth, iii. 331, n. 3.

[5] Y. B. 19 H. VI. 49. 5 (1440).

Case would lie, if there were no undertaking at all. It was agreed that it would not ; the traverse to the Assumpsit went to the root of the action. 'Vous n'avez monstre', remarked Paston J., 'q'il est un common mareshal a curer tiel cheval ; en quel cas, mesque il tua vostre cheval par ses medecines, uncore vous n'aurez accion vers luy sans assumption . . .' And Newton C. J. said : ' Si j'ay un malade en ma main et il appon un medecin a ma *heel*, par quel negligence ma main est mayhem', uncore jeo n'aurai action sinon que il assuma sur luy a me curer.' In these early cases the objection was continually raised that the plaintiff should have brought covenant ; ' ceo soun en covenant ' is constantly on the defendant's lips, but the objection was overruled. The defendant's undertaking, coupled with damage resulting from his *misdoing* what he had undertaken to do, together constituted the tort to the plaintiff. Or, as the mediaeval lawyer was fond of phrasing it, a covenant was converted by matter *ex post facto* into a tort. The breach of the undertaking was not itself the source of the liability. The promise or undertaking was laid merely to make an act wrongful to which otherwise the law attached no consequences ; it was the damage resulting from the act which was wrongful because contrary to the undertaking which was the gist of the action.

So long as the action on the case in the form of Assumpsit was confined to cases of active misconduct on the part of the undertaker, the action sounded purely in tort. But as one follows the decisions, he notices a constantly recurring attempt to extend the action from damage which resulted from improper action, to damage which ensued from failure to act at all. The thought of the promise is still in the background ; the judges are not troubled by questions of gratuitous promises or promises given for a consideration. Before that question can arise, it must be determined whether Assumpsit will lie for any non-feasance at all, and it is the struggle to carry over the action from misfeasance to non-feasance which stands forth so vividly in the reports. It is this which we may now trace very briefly.[1]

[1] For the sake of brevity, I have omitted the cases involving bailees,

Let us suppose that a carpenter undertakes to build a house, but for some reason fails to begin the work at all. This is pure non-feasance ; is there any remedy ? If the undertaking were under seal a writ of Covenant would lie against him. This thought seems to have been prominently in the minds of the judges. Why, therefore, allow another remedy, when the plaintiff might have protected himself by having a deed ? So when one Lawrence Watton sought to charge Thomas Brinth in Assumpsit because he had undertaken to rebuild certain houses and neglected so to do, Rickhill J. dismissed the action;[1] the plaintiff had counted on a covenant, and had nothing to show for it. In a similar case,[2] which arose nine years later, the plaintiff argued that if the defendant had built the house badly, he would have his action on the case ; why then should he not be allowed his action where he sustained damage because the defendant had refused to carry out his undertaking? The court, however, could observe no analogy. In neither of these cases is there any discussion of what the defendant was to receive for his promise.

That it was the question of allowing an action for non-feasance, irrespective of the nature of the promise, which absorbed the attention of judges and reporters is emphasized by the case against one Watkins,[3] mill-maker. The action was trespass on the case for not building a mill; and the plaintiff counted that the defendant undertook to build him a mill within a certain time, but failed to do so, to the plaintiff's damage in 10 marks. The defendant objected that there was no showing that he was to have anything for his work; the plaintiff replied that this did not matter. The contention was dismissed lightly, with the suggestion that it must be intended that the defendant would be properly rewarded for his work, and the discussion settled down to a reconsideration of the old problem. Martin J. was convinced that the action could not lie. Case would only lie where some tort was shown ; to fail to act was no tort, and the plaintiff had been

such as Y. B. B. 12 Ed. IV. 13. 9 ; 12 Ed. IV. 13. 10 ; 16 Ed. IV. 9. 7 ;
2 H. VII. 11. 9.
[1] Y. B. 2 H. IV. 3. 9.   [2] Y. B. 11 H. IV. 33. 60.
[3] Y. B. 3 H. VI. 36. 33 (1425).

able to produce nothing but a promise, which would support an action of Covenant if under seal, but nothing more. He admitted that if Watkins had begun the mill and left it incomplete or built it improperly an action would lie ; for doing the work badly converted what was covenant into a tort. ' Mes en le cas al' barr n'est mye issint,' he interjected, ' car la nul tort est suppose par le bref par le fesance d'un chose eins le non-fesance d'un chose etc., le quel sonne seulement en covenant.' Babington C. J. was not so certain. He thought that if one undertook to roof a house, and from his inaction damage resulted, as by rain ruining the timbers, a good cause of action arose. The illustrations which he gave involve non-feasance followed by subsequent damage, and it is obvious that the distinction between non-feasance and misfeasance was beginning to be felt oppressive. Cokayne J. agreed with Babington in favouring the action, but Martin J. kept resolutely to his position, asserting that if this action were maintained, one could bring trespass for the ' breach of any covenant in the world '. All this discussion passed without arriving at a decision ; for the parties did not ' demur in judgement '[1] on this question. The defendant, evidently fearing that his contention would not be sustained, proceeded to allege that he had completed the mill a long time after the ' covenant ' was made, and that the plaintiff discharged him. Issue was joined thereon, and with that the report ends, leaving us uncertain as to what was decided.

Babington's inclination to allow the action finds support in the dicta of some of the later judges of Henry VI's reign. Apparently strong pressure was being exerted from some source other than the common law. Restricting trespass on the case to misfeasance left parol executory contracts unenforceable ; and, after constant attempts to get a hearing at common

---

[1] Babington C.J. cut short the discussion by saying that it was idle to talk, since the parties had not definitely joined issue. Ames (H. L. R., ii. 11) interprets this to mean that Babington was shaken in his opinion by Martin's remark. I do not think there is any such implication. It is obvious that the defendant did not feel very secure of his position, or he would not so hastily have abandoned it, directly Babington stopped the discussion.

law, disgusted litigants were flocking to the chancellor. It was only a question of time till the distinction should break down, and in 1436[1] Paston and June JJ. agreed in holding that Case in the form of Assumpsit would lie for non-feasance, provided damage ensued from the failure to act.

This decision has been attacked by Professor Ames,[2] as being anomalous, and against all authority. He regards it as an enforcement of a gratuitous parol promise, a decision 'which was made without precedent and had no following'.[3] It is with great reluctance that one ventures to disagree with so learned a student of the common law; but as this may be considered a pivotal case, it is worthy of being examined with care.[4]

All the facts, so far as they are available, are given in the statement of the count: 'Un R suist un bref de trespas sur le cas et counta coment le plaintif avoit bargaine certein terre pur certein some del defendant et monstre tout en certein, et que le covenaunt le defendant fut que il doit faire estraunge person avoir releas a luy deinz certein terme, le quell ne relessa poynt; issint l'accion accrue a luy.' We may note the following points:

1. The use of the word 'covenaunt' does not imply a deed; the word was frequently used to describe the undertaking, upon which Assumpsit was based.

2. It is impossible to determine from the report whether or no the undertaking was gratuitous. From a somewhat blind remark of June J. at the conclusion of the case, it is apparent that this 'covenaunt' was regarded, not as 'accessory to' the main agreement, but the principal thing itself. It is submitted that the following interpretation is justifiable: the plaintiff 'bargained' land of the defendant 'pur certein some'; this sum was paid or to be paid (we do not know which) in return for the release to be made by a stranger to the plaintiff, without which he could get no title to the land. If such be

---

[1] Y. B. 14 H. VI. 18. 58. [2] H. L. R., ii. 10-11.
[3] H. L. R., ii. 11.
[4] As the Year Book report is somewhat unsatisfactory, I have given a complete transcript of the case, taken from MS. Harl. 4557. See Note B, p. 170.

true, the 'covenaunt' was not gratuitous, and if, as seems not improbable, the money was actually paid, the decision, instead of having no following, is simply an earlier declaration of the principle which was later generally accepted.[1]

3. However, this question of 'consideration' was thrust into the background. The reporters wanted to know if an action were to be allowed for non-feasance; the time-worn argument that the matter sounded in covenant was brought again to the fore. Elleker, as counsel for the defendant, introduced the carpenter and the house that was so long a-building, nor did he forget the case of the smith.[2]

The defendant had undertaken to cause a stranger to release to the plaintiff; this was covenant pure and simple: the writ must abate. Newton replied for the plaintiff, arguing from the analogy of the action for misfeasance. The plaintiff sustained damage in this case, from the defendant's failure to carry out his undertaking; this was parallel to those cases in which the damage resulted from improper action, and the action should be allowed. This argument prevailed upon Paston and June JJ. The principle upon which these two judges acted was that the breach of an undertaking (be it by misfeasance or non-feasance) was actionable, *if damage to the plaintiff ensued*. At last the absurd distinction between misfeasance and non-feasance was broken; Assumpsit was shaking off the shackles of tort and becoming a contract remedy. Not that Paston J. necessarily realized this; but the decision is significant and fraught with great consequences.

[1] It is not asserted that the conclusion reached in this case, namely that Assumpsit would lie for non-feasance, obtained immediate acceptance. The cases which Mr. Ames cites (e. g. Y. B. B. 20 H. VI. 25. 11 ; 20 H. VI. 34. 4; 21 H. VI. 55. 12; 37 H. VI. 9. 18; 2 H. VII. 11. 9, &c.), to prove that Paston and June JJ. were merely giving effect to an inclination of their own, only show how slowly the notion of an action for non-feasance made its way. But in the famous case in 1504 (Keilw. 77. 25) Frowyk C.J. said : ' If I sell my land, and covenant to enfeoff you and do not, you shall have a good action on the case, and this is adjudged.' And yet this failure to enfeoff is a mere non-feasance. The difference between the covenant in 1504 and the case at bar is too slight to make a sound distinction. Granted that the reasoning of Frowyk proceeded on different lines, still the two decisions make for the same end.

[2] Elleker's reference to the smith was not peculiarly happy. At all events, in later times the smith was made answerable if he refused to shoe a horse. 17 H. VII, Keilw. 50. 4.

But the principle of the decision was too wide. The common law after much travail had determined to allow an action for non-feasance; it now became necessary to classify non-feasances, to impose limitations. Otherwise it would become impossible to distinguish between agreements which were enforceable and those which were not; 'Pacta sunt servanda' would have been received with a vengeance. The test which was ultimately selected was reached through another line of decisions: the actions of Deceit on the Case. These we may pass in brief review.

In 1429 [1] a plaintiff sought to charge a defendant in Deceit, because there was an agreement that the plaintiff should marry the defendant's daughter, and that the defendant should enfeoff them of certain land. The daughter was married to another and the conveyance never made. The action failed, but it is noteworthy as showing an attempt to find in Deceit a remedy for the breach of an undertaking. Four years later another plaintiff was more successful. The defendant,[2] for a sum to be paid him, undertook to buy a manor of one J. B. for the plaintiff, but, 'by collusion between himself and one M. N. contriving cunningly to defraud the plaintiff,' disclosed the latter's evidence and bought the manor for M. N. The judges treated this as more than a mere non-feasance; the betrayal of the plaintiff's secrets was an act which amounted to an invasion of his rights;[3] the fraudulent act changed what was Covenant before into a tort. 'Jeo die', said Cotesmore J., 'que mater que gist tout en covenant, par mater ex post facto peut estre convert en deceit; . . . uncore quand il est devenu de Counsail d'un autre, *c'est un deceit et changer' tout cest que fuit devant forsque covenant entre les parties*, des quel deceit il aura accion sur son cas.'[4]

Suppose there were, however, no 'matter ex post facto' to achieve this miraculous conversion. This was the situation which the court was at length compelled to face, when, in 1442, a bill of Deceit was brought against one John Doight.[5]

[1] Y. B. 7 H. VI. 1. 3.   [2] Y. B. 11 H. VI. 18. 10, 24. 1, 55. 26.
[3] Ames, H. L. R., ii. 12.
[4] See Ames's quotations from same case, H. L. R., ii. 12.
[5] Y. B. 20 H. VI. 34. 4.

The plaintiff counted that he had bargained with the defendant to buy land for him for £100 in hand paid, but that the defendant enfeoffed another of the land and so deceived him. So far as the plaintiff was concerned, the defendant was guilty of nothing more than a non-feasance; this act in conveying to another could be no infringement of the plaintiff's rights, unless his undertaking gave the plaintiff some claim against him; for there was no difference, from this point of view, between merely *failing* to enfeoff the plaintiff, and enfeoffing another in his stead. When the case was heard in the Exchequer Chamber, this fact was prominently in the minds of the judges. How in all consistency could the action be allowed? Ascoughe J. was convinced that this was a plain case of Covenant; Case did not lie without misfeasance, which was absent in the case at bar: 'issint en nostre cas, si defendant ust retenu la terre en sa main sans feofment fait, donques le plaintif n'aura forsque bref de Covenant; *jeo entend tout un cas quand le defendant fist feoffment a un estranger et quand il retient la terre en sa main.*' This was doubtless the conclusion of strict logic; but a majority of the judges thought the action would lie.[1] The motives which impelled them to this conclusion are interesting.[2]

1. The defendant had paid his money; he could not get it back again, nor had he any means of compelling a conveyance of the land at common law. He, therefore, had a strong 'moral' right, which it was difficult for the common law to ignore. It is not certain, though highly probable, that the chancellor recognized such a right at this time; at all events he ultimately held that in such case the vendor stood seised to the use of the purchaser. Jealous of the fast encroaching jurisdiction of chancery, the common law judges were forced to strain every effort to give relief to a plaintiff under such circumstances.

2. But even if the purchase price were not paid, there was a powerful analogy in the law relating to chattels. From the

---

[1] This cannot be treated as a decision, for the case was adjourned.
[2] For an able statement, upon which I have drawn largely, see Holdsworth, iii. 338 ff.

remark of Fortescue C. J. in this same year,[1] it appears that
in the case of sale of a chattel for a fixed price, the vendor
had at once his action of Debt for the money, while the vendee
might maintain Detinue for the chattel.   By a curious logical
inversion, Newton C. J. applied this to land : '. . . quand le
plaintif avoit fait plein bargain ove le defendant, maintenant
le defendant purra demander ceux deniers par bref de Dette
et *en conscience et en droit* le plaintif doit avoir la terre,
mesque la propriete ne peut passer en luy par ley sans livere
del' seisin.   Donc ceo serra merveillous ley q'un bargain
serra parfait sur que l'un party serra lie par action de Debte
et q'il serra sans remedie envers l'autre.'[2]   The words 'in
conscience and right' come as a strange echo from the
chancery.

It is not difficult to detect a flaw in Newton's argument.
Inasmuch as the property in land could not pass without
livery of seisin, there was no *quid pro quo* to support Debt
against the purchaser.[3]   The analogy with the sale of a chattel
was far from perfect.   But law is something more than a sport
for logicians, and its development has not always been consistent and harmonious.   Fallacious or not, this argument had
its effect ; the courts, in struggling to give wider scope to the
action of Assumpsit, disregarded logic and looked at facts.

By the time of Henry VII it became established that
a breach of undertaking by conveyance to a stranger was an
actionable deceit.[4]   The gap between misfeasance and non-
feasance was practically bridged for good and all, when in
1504[5] it was decided that if money were paid for an undertaking, and nothing were done, case in the form of Assumpsit
would lie.   But a limitation was imposed upon the action ;
Assumpsit did not lie for all non-feasances, but only when the
plaintiff in reliance upon the defendant's promise had incurred
a detriment, as, for example, by parting with money.   In the
beginning of the sixteenth century there is thus found an

---

[1] Y. B. 20 H. VI. 34. 4 ; see *supra*, p. 32, note 2.
[2] Y. B. 20 H. VI. 34. 4 (*ad fin.*).
[3] See Ames's criticism, H. L. R., ii. 11, n. 6.
[4] Ames, H. L. R., ii. 13.   [5] Keilw. 77, pl. 25.

action which will lie upon parol contract. The subsequent history and development of the action lies outside the limits of this essay.

To summarize : Assumpsit made its appearance about the middle of the fourteenth century. The presence of the undertaking in the delictual action was occasioned by the limited notion of delictual liability. Used at first in cases of misfeasance alone, the action was extended after a prolonged struggle to breaches of undertakings by non-feasance. This was accomplished first in trespass on the case ; the limitation which was ultimately imposed on Assumpsit was reached through Deceit. But Assumpsit in 1504 still remained a delictual action in the theory of contemporary jurists. There was no theory of consideration ; the question of gratuitous promises had not arisen at all. The promise was not definitely recognized as the basis of the action till later. It then became necessary to frame a test whereby the enforceability of promises might be determined, and that test was found in the doctrine of consideration.

SECTION V. SUMMARY

We have now to make a brief review of the situation of contract in the common law during the fifteenth century. Assumpsit need not be considered, for it did not become available as a contractual action till 1504. Covenant was useful, but it had no application except to contracts under seal. There remain, then, Account, Detinue, and Debt. From what has been said, it must be obvious that the influence of the first two on the law of contract was very slight. Debt was the contractual action *par excellence*, for all that it gave to the term contract a very limited significance. The 'real contract' was enforced at common law, but all parol agreements which failed to come within its scope went remediless.

If we look for a moment to what the common law did not do, the need for equitable intervention becomes the more apparent. It is somewhat difficult to find a satisfactory scheme of classification which will emphasize this point. The one which follows is open to criticism as a logical division ; but it is hoped that it may to some extent bring into prominence the 'gaps' in the common law.

I. *No remedy is provided by the common law.*

  1. Particular contracts.

    (1) Contracts to convey land.

      Whether or no the purchase price was paid, the common law afforded no means of compelling conveyance, nor of obtaining damages for failure to convey (unless the promise were under seal).

    (2) Marriage settlements.

      A promises to give B £50 if B will marry his daughter. It was ultimately settled that Debt would lie, but it is very doubtful if it was available in the fifteenth century. If the promise were to make an estate of land, there was no common law remedy.[1]

    (3) Executory contracts for the sale of chattels.

      There was no action to recover damages for the breach of such a contract.

    (4) Indemnity and Guarantee.

      A surety could not be held if he bound himself by parol. Parol promises 'to save harmless' (i. e. promises of indemnity) did not support an action.

    (5) Agency.

      The contract of agency received very slight recognition. Debt was the only action which could lie against the principal on the contract by his agent, and in such case the principal must always have received *quid pro quo.*

  2. The particular contracts mentioned do not exhaust the list ; they are chosen merely as conspicuous examples. In short, there was no action whereby one might obtain damages for the breach of an executory parol contract. The large class of contracts which ultimately found support from Assumpsit were left without a remedy.

  3. There were certain relations in which parties might stand toward one another that did not fall within the class of express contracts. From such a relation an obligation might arise,

---

[1] Of course this refers to a *parol* promise.

which natural justice would regard as enforceable, but which was not sufficiently recognized by the common law. As examples we may note contributions between persons liable for the same debt ; or contributions between partners.

II. *Theoretically the law provides a remedy, but it fails in the particular case.*

1. This might arise from difficulties of pleading or proof.

(1) Transactions out of England.

Even if a contract were of such nature that the common law afforded a remedy, the remedy failed if the contract were made out of England. To bring an action at law the venue must be laid in some English county ; this of course was impossible where the transaction took place abroad.

(2) Action against a feme covert.

A married woman could not be held by her contracts at common law. This might present a difficult situation, e. g. see IX. 472, considered *infra*, p. 100.

(3) Actions by one partner or executor against another.

One executor could not sue another at common law ; nor could one partner hold another to account. Partnership, so far as relations between partners is concerned, was largely ignored by the common law.[1]

(4) Loss of an obligation.

If an obligation were lost, stolen, or destroyed, the obligee lost his right of action.

(5) Assignment of a chose in action.

A chose in action could not be assigned at common law so as to enable the assignee to bring suit.

(6) Actions against personal representatives.

Personal representatives could not be held liable for the debt of the deceased, unless it were proved by a deed. Generally speaking, death terminated all liabilities.

---

[1] Fitzherbert states that one partner might bring Account against another. F. N. B. 117 D. I do not know of any cases in the Year Books which support this statement ; on the other hand, one partner frequently filed a petition in equity against his co-partner, alleging that he had no remedy at law. And see Langdell, Survey of Equity Jurisdiction, H. L. R., ii. 242 ff.

2. Again, it might arise from limitation within the action itself.

(1) In Debt.

(a) A benefit conferred on a third party at the request of the defendant would not support Debt in the fifteenth century.

(b) If it was not definitely agreed how much one should have for a chattel sold, or for work done, Debt would not lie. The *quantum meruit* and *quantum valebant* counts never gained a foothold in Debt,[1] nor were they recognized in Indebitatus Assumpsit till 1609.[2]

(2) In Detinue.

(a) When Detinue was brought on a bailment the requirement of privity was strictly enforced. If it were sought to charge some one else than the bailee, his possession must be connected with that of the bailee.

(b) Detinue did not enable the bailor to recover damages for misuse of the thing bailed.

III. *The remedy at law is insufficient.*

1. Recovery of specific chattels.
   The common law afforded no remedy by which the delivery of a specific chattel could be compelled. The defendant in Detinue could always discharge himself by paying the assessed value of the chattel.

2. Specific performance.
   There was no means of compelling specific performance of a contract, and yet in many cases damages proved an inadequate remedy.

IV. *The remedy at law is difficult or ineffectual.*

1. Taking accounts.
   The action of Account was a clumsy method of obtaining an accounting. Common law process and procedure were inadequate to secure the desired end.

2. Set-off.
   A defendant might have an adverse claim against the plaintiff, but he could not make use of it at common law by way of set-off.[3]

---

[1] Ames, H. L. R., viii. 260.   [2] Ames, H. L. R., ii. 58.
[3] 1 Spence, 651.

V. *Strict interpretation of the contract under seal.*

This topic is somewhat out of place in the present classification, but it is worth while to point out the defects in the law of obligations.

1. Duress, fraud or failure of consideration could not be alleged by way of defence against a deed.

2. Payment, unproved by an acquittance, was not a defence.

3. If an obligation were executed for a specific purpose (not appearing on its face), the fact that the purpose had been accomplished did not afford any defence to an action by the obligee.

4. A condition by parol could not be pleaded against an obligation absolute on its face.

5. An obligation could not be varied by any subsequent parol agreement.

Such were the defects in the law of contract as it existed in common law in the fifteenth century. The question therefore remains: How far were these 'gaps' supplied by the relief granted to litigants in equity?

CHAPTER III

THE DOCTRINE OF CONSIDERATION

THE history of parol contracts raises two distinct problems: (1) How did parol contracts become actionable at all? (2) How did consideration become the test of the enforceability of such contracts? Before it is possible to classify agreements and determine what are enforceable and what are not, it must be first settled that a contract will support an action. Any classification or generalization is a matter for later consideration. In consequence, nothing but confusion will result if we fail to observe the historical sequence of these two problems.

Now the answer to the first question is to be found in the history of Assumpsit. Starting as an action on the case, it was extended after the struggle of a century from cases of misfeasance to cases of non-feasance. Throughout this struggle there appears no theory of contract, nor was it apparent even that the judges considered the promise as the basis of the action. The delictual origin of the action overshadowed its development. The result is that at the beginning of the sixteenth century Assumpsit has in fact become an action to enforce parol contract, but such an achievement is not realized by contemporary lawyers. The reason is to be found in the principle upon which the action was allowed. A detriment to the plaintiff was an essential condition to its use; or, stated differently, a breach of promise supported an action when, and only when, it could be regarded as a *deceit* to the *plaintiff*. There was still a very strong element of tort in the theory of the action.

Some time in the sixteenth century another principle obtained a foothold. Men begin to speak of *consideration*, of promises as made in consideration of some act or forbearance. The early history of this doctrine is wrapped in obscurity. We

do not know how or when it made its first appearance, and
there is much dispute as to its source. But we do know that
the first use of the word at common law was in the action of
Assumpsit, and that ultimately it became settled that no
promise was enforceable unless it were made upon a valid
consideration.

To-day in the interests of logic it is deemed advisable to
resolve every consideration into a detriment to the promisee.
Such a definition, however, does not meet the situation in the
sixteenth century. The word was then of wider use than it is
to-day; for when we now speak of consideration, only
a *valuable* consideration is meant.

Historically, consideration seems to have meant any motive
or inducement which was sufficient to support a promise.[1] It
included such diverse species as (1) a benefit to the promisor,
(2) detriment to the promisee, (3) a moral obligation, (4)
natural love and affection. All of these are not found in
Assumpsit, but it would be a mistake to confine the doctrine
to that action. The *quid pro quo* which was essential to
Debt became ultimately absorbed by the wider idea. Now
in a certain phase, namely as a detriment to the promisee,
consideration bears a striking resemblance to the original
limitation in Assumpsit, the detriment to the plaintiff. But
the question remains, Is this more than an analogy? Is there
any historical connexion between the detriment to the plaintiff
in Assumpsit, and the detriment to the promisee into which
consideration was ultimately resolved? This is the crux of
the matter. We may therefore notice three principal theories
of the origin of consideration.

I. ' The requirement of consideration in all parol contracts
is simply a modified generalization of the requirement of *quid
pro quo* to raise a debt by parol.'[2]

This is the theory advanced by Mr. Justice Holmes. But
there are great difficulties in the way of its acceptance.

---

[1] Salmond, Anglo-Am., iii. 331.

[2] L. Q. R., i. 171. And see Holmes, Common Law, 258 ff. Mr. Justice
Holmes endeavours to connect the requirement of *quid pro quo* in Debt
with the secta, and transaction witnesses. For a criticism of this see
P. & M., ii. 214, n. 4.

(1) It assumes that the doctrine started from a narrow basis and became widened. Originally a benefit to the promisor, consideration came to embrace the notion of detriment to the promisee. But there is no evidence that this is what happened. Consideration as a rule of contract made its first appearance in the action of Assumpsit, and not in Debt. If this theory be correct, then the basis of one action must in some way have become the basis of the other. From the sharp line which was always drawn between Debt and Assumpsit, it seems in the highest degree improbable.

(2) The consideration in *indebitatus assumpsit* was not a modification of *quid pro quo*, but identical with it.[1]

(3) The idea of consideration as a detriment to the promisee never appeared in Debt; though repeated efforts were made to extend *quid pro quo* to cover detriment.[2]

For these reasons we must reject this theory. It fails to take recognition of the wide idea embraced in the word consideration ; it requires a transformation of *quid pro quo* which was never effected.

II. Another theory is put forward by Professor Ames in a brilliant series of articles in the Harvard Law Review.[3] He there identifies consideration with the detriment to the plaintiff upon which the action of Assumpsit was founded. This theory has a certain decided advantage. It shows a regular and consistent development in Assumpsit culminating in the evolution of the principle of consideration from within the action itself. So far as the Year Book cases are themselves concerned it seems impossible of refutation. But the theory is open to the following objections :

(1) It assumes that consideration is identical with the detriment to the plaintiff. As we have already pointed out, there is a strong analogy between consideration when resolved into a detriment to the promisee and the limitation fixed in the action of Assumpsit. But this analogy does not mean that the principles are identical. It is submitted that Professor Ames has not demonstrated this identity beyond peradventure.

---

[1] Ames, H. L. R., ii. 18.   [2] Salmond, Essays, 222.
[3] H. L. R., ii, pp. 1 and 53. See also H. L. R., viii. 252–64.

The principles may be extremely close to one another, and yet have no historical connexion.

(2) It does not account for all the species of consideration, such as moral obligation, for example. A moral obligation is no longer a consideration, but it was once. Moreover, a precedent debt was recognized as a valid consideration in *indebitatus assumpsit*. It is difficult to see how a precedent debt can by any contortion be twisted into a detriment to the plaintiff.

(3) This theory rests upon the assumption that the principle of consideration was a creation of the common law pure and simple. So keen is Professor Ames to emphasize this point that he is led to make certain unwarranted assertions with regard to equity. Not only does he contend that 'in equity . . . a remediable breach of a parol promise was originally conceived of as a deceit',[1] but he goes on to say that 'chancery gave relief upon parol agreements *only* upon the ground of compelling reparation for what was regarded as a tort to the plaintiff or upon the principle of preventing the unjust enrichment of the defendant'.[2] We shall take pains to examine both of these statements later on; it is believed that neither of them is correct. If, on the other hand, the Chancellor did exercise a general jurisdiction over parol contracts in the fifteenth century, if in fact he did evolve a principle upon which promises were held binding, it is surely fatuous to suggest that he borrowed this principle from the common law, which did not possess a general contractual action[3] till the sixteenth century. Furthermore, if parol contracts were so recognized in equity, that alone throws considerable doubt upon the correctness of this theory.

(4) It should be noticed, finally, that all the early cases in Assumpsit involve a specific undertaking. There is no recognition of agreement or a bargain as such. Indeed, it was found necessary in Slade's case to resolve that every contract executory imported an Assumpsit. That is to say, the fact of agreement did not of itself 'raise' any undertaking. In

---

[1] H. L. R., ii. 15.   [2] H. L. R., viii. 257.
[3] That is, an action applicable to parol contracts generally.

consequence we are forced to the position that originally every enforceable contract took the highly technical form of an undertaking. But does this seem a natural way in which a contract should arise? Men make informal agreements or ' accordes ' without troubling to incorporate them into a particular form. I venture to suggest that there were many such agreements which fell without the scope of undertakings; that, in fact, the theory which relies upon the ' undertaker ' fails to take account of many formless agreements which were the common experience of everyday life.

For these reasons we may question the theory advanced by Professor Ames. We can, however, state our objections with more effect after examining contract in equity.

III. Still another theory is advanced by Mr. Salmond.[1] He refuses to admit that the doctrine of consideration was identical with the detriment to the plaintiff in Assumpsit. Rather does he think that it was not 'a logical development from within the action at all, but was a ready-made principle imported *ab extra* '.[2] Now if we go back to the first cases in which Assumpsit lay for non-feasance, we find that the detriment to the plaintiff assumed one particular form.

He had parted with money on the strength of the defendant's promise, and that money had been received by the defendant. If, therefore, we shift our point of view, what on the one side appears to be a detriment to the plaintiff may on the other side be regarded as a benefit to the promisor. The theory that a promise is actionable because the promisee has incurred damage by relying upon it is essentially delictual. From the standpoint of contractual theory, a promise should be actionable if there were a sufficient ground for making it, regardless of whether or no the promisee had suffered damage from its breach. But in the specific case we are considering, the two principles amount to different ways of looking at the same thing. A promises to make an estate of lands to B for £50. B pays the money, but A fails to make estate. B has suffered a detriment, because he has parted with £50 on the strength

---

[1] Salmond, Essays in Jurisprudence, Essay No. IV.
[2] *Id.*, p. 212.

of A's promise. On the other hand, there was a sufficient inducement for A's promise, namely the payment of £50. Mr. Salmond's contention is this: Somewhere outside the common law the principle was evolved that a promise was binding if there were a ' legally sufficient motive or inducement for making it '.[1]

Now the promises which were first enforced in Assumpsit were only such as had a legal inducement; for the promisor had always obtained a direct benefit by the payment of money. It therefore became possible that the one principle should be substituted for the other. In short, the doctrine of consideration, already evolved, was thrust into the action of Assumpsit from without ; and its entrance into the action was facilitated by the strong analogy which it bore to the limitation already engrafted on Assumpsit. This ' introduction of a foreign principle ' breaks the logical continuity of the development ' of the action.

This theory is certainly plausible. But it leaves two questions unanswered :

(1) How and when did consideration gain its entrance into Assumpsit if it came from without ? This Mr. Salmond does not answer satisfactorily. Indeed, it is doubted whether this question can be answered at all. The reports do not show effectively the manner of appearance of consideration. In fact the doctrine is at first shrouded in mystery which it is very difficult to pierce. But if consideration was somewhere recognized as a principle before it was adopted in Assumpsit, the presumption that it was introduced from without becomes very strong. We therefore ask:

(2) Whence came the doctrine of consideration ? Mr. Salmond asserts that it had become established in equity. This is the weakest point in his argument. He can produce few cases; he is compelled to reason from inference. An occasional hint from the Year Books, and a brief quotation or two from contemporary writers, are all he has to offer. This, it must be admitted, is not very convincing.

---

[1] Essays, p. 213.

Mr. Salmond is not to be blamed for this defect, for he had no access to the materials whence proof might be drawn. But it is at this very point that our real inquiry begins. The burning question, which has been largely ignored, is this: What evidence is there that parol contracts were enforced in equity, and if they were enforced, upon what principle or principles did the chancellor act? To this inquiry the second part of the present essay is devoted.

PART II

CONTRACT IN EQUITY

CHAPTER I

INTRODUCTORY

EVERY one who is familiar with the records of the fifteenth century is aware of the activity of the court of chancery. Aside from matters of grace which were thought to be properly within its purview, the court was exercising a wide influence upon the development of the substantive law. Not even the freehold was sacred from its interference. A long series of protests in Parliament[1] bear testimony to the encroachment of the chancellor upon the sacred precincts of the common law, and as most of these complaints emanated from the Commons, they were, no doubt, the work of common law attorneys who resented the intrusion of another court.[2] Here and there in the Year Books appear references to the competition of chancery; Fairfax J., in a well-known remark,[3] urged pleaders to pay more attention to the action on the case, and thereby lessen the resort to the subpoena. In fact, there can be little doubt that the eagerness displayed by certain judges to extend Assumpsit from misfeasance to non-feasance was prompted by the strong desire to retain jurisdiction that was fast slipping away.[4] There is thus abundant extrinsic evidence of the interference of the chancellor within what was regarded as the domain of the common law.

---

[1] These protests begin in the reign of Richard II and continue at intervals for more than a century.

[2] Kerly, History of Equity, 37 ff.

[3] 'Et issint jeo vous conselle que estes pledes et donque les Sub paena ne seront my cy soventment use come il est ore, si nous attendoms tiels actions sur les cases et maintenoms le Jurisdiction de ce court et d'autres courts.' Y. B. 21 Ed. IV. 22. 6.

[4] See 1 Spence 243, note *b*.

Hitherto, however, the precise nature of the chancellor's jurisdiction in contract has been largely a matter of conjecture. Investigators have quoted *Doctor and Student*, passages from the *Diversity of Courts*, and other interesting texts. These do not carry us very far. The language of the text writers is not always free from ambiguity ; furthermore, our inquiry is not satisfactorily settled by the opinions of even the most trustworthy contemporaries as to what could be done in chancery. The actual pleadings are available, and before we can attempt to say anything definite, it is necessary to examine them.

Unfortunately, only a small fraction of this material exists in published form. In the two volumes of the Proceedings in Chancery a number of selected petitions are printed, and in the tenth volume[1] of the Selden Society publications Mr. Baildon has presented an interesting collection of cases. We find among these a few cases relating to contract, but they scarcely do more than rouse our curiosity. Moreover, it is questionable whether the material so far published adequately represents the great bulk of the petitions that are preserved. In consequence it seems desirable to go back to the original records.

The material which is the basis of this part of the investigation is found in the collection of petitions in the Public Record Office catalogued under the title, 'Early Chancery Proceedings'. This collection includes all the petitions addressed to the chancellors from Richard II to the early years of Henry VIII, so far as they have been preserved. The petitions are divided into 377 bundles containing an estimated total of 300,000 cases. Obviously it is impossible for one person to make an adequate examination of so vast a number of cases. All that one can hope to do is to make as representative a selection as possible.

Before describing the method followed in making such a selection, a few words may be said with regard to the petitions as a whole. Even a cursory examination shows

---

[1] This volume contains all the petitions in Bundle III, and a few others selected from miscellaneous bundles.

that the province of chancery was not definitely settled in the
fifteenth century.   Theoretically, appeal is to be made to the
chancellor only where there is no remedy at law, but this
allowed a very wide latitude to the chancellor's discretion,
and in fact, if he chose to assume jurisdiction in a particular
case, there was no means of preventing the use of the subpoena.   Equity might enjoin a plaintiff from prosecuting an
action at law, but the King's Bench or Common Pleas had no
process to restrain a petitioner from bringing suit in chancery.
We do not mean to say that relief was given in every case in
which it was sought, but it is apparent that there was a general
belief that in equity wrongs which escaped the common law
courts would be remedied.   'Nullus recedat a Curia Can-
cillariae sine remedio',[1] exclaimed a chancellor when a legal
technicality was urged against the subpoena in a particular
case.   This maxim cannot be applied literally ; it is, however,
very interesting as indicating the attitude of chancery, an
attitude which helps to explain the presence of so great
a variety of cases.

No doubt in many of the early cases the petitions were
experimental ; at all events some of the alleged causes of
action are so fantastic that they read strangely to modern
eyes.   The chancellor is asked, for example, to restrain the
defendant from using ' the craftys of enchantement, wychecraft
and sorcerye', whereby the petitioner ' brake his legge and
[his] foul was hurte'.   We are scarcely surprised to learn that
under such circumstances ' the comyn lawe may nouzt helpe'.[2]
Another petitioner alleges that he has been injured by the
evil practices of the defendant who ' par divers artez erroneous
et countre la foy Catholic, cestassavoir socery, . . . ad sustretez
la ewe de une certeine pounde de mesme cesty Suppliaunt
deinz la close avauntdit en graunde parde et anientisment des
bestez esteauntz pastez deinz mesme le close'.   After failing
in an action of trespass this disappointed litigant concluded
that the loss of water by sorcery was 'une mater de conscience',
and so he prayed for a subpoena.[3]   Again, injury has been

---

[1] Y. B. 4 H. VII. 4. 8.   [2] 1 Cal. Ch. xxiv.
[3] XII. 168.   For another petition seeking relief for damage caused by
alleged sorcery, see XII. 210.

done to the 'Kinges foul called an Estrich', and a petitioner demands compensation.[1]   One is tempted to dally longer over these delightfully ingenuous petitions, but they do not concern us here, except in so far as they indicate the diversity of causes heard in chancery.

The cases involving contract represent only a small proportion of the Chancery Proceedings.   Bills which sound in tort are very common,[2] and together with those in which the cause of action is purely equitable (e. g. breaches of trust, &c.), they make up the majority of the petitions.   There remains a residuum of cases in contract, and it is these which require our attention.

Naturally it is impossible to consider even this restricted class of cases in its entirety.   Two principles of elimination were therefore adopted.   First, I have confined myself very largely to the earlier bundles.   What we chiefly wish to know about equity is how far it enforced contracts before the common law obtained a rival remedy in Assumpsit.   Consequently the fifteenth century is the most important period, and we look with particular interest at the first half of it.   None of the petitions which are cited in the remainder of this study are of later date than 1485, and most of them are much earlier. In other words, they all antedate the appearance of Assumpsit by at least twenty years.   Secondly, such cases in contract as present purely equitable doctrines have not been considered. Within the two limitations mentioned, I have attempted to present a selection of cases which is characteristic of the whole body.[3]

---

[1] XI. 227.

[2] e. g. *Briddicote* v. *Forster*, 1 Cal. Ch. iv : LXVIII. 44 (10 S. S. 123) ; a bill against a surgeon for damage due to misfeasance.   The petitioner says he cannot bring an action at law ' par cause de graunde mayntenance encountre le dit suppliant en ycest partie '.

[3] The specific bundles which I have examined are as follows : Bundles IV to X were examined with great care ; in fact I looked at every case. After that I relied more largely upon the catalogue, looking only at such cases as seemed to involve contract.   In this manner Bundles XI to XX were examined.   Bundles XXI to XXVI were omitted ; but I examined Bundles XXVII to XXXI, XXVIII to XXXIX, XLI, XLIV, LIX, LXVIII to LXXI.   By studying the catalogue with care I was able to select petitions from different periods of the fifteenth century, and in consequence

The word ' cases ' has been used in referring to this material, but such a description is scarcely appropriate. For the most part we have only the complainant's petition; the answer and other pleadings do not often appear. Probably this is due to the practice, which prevailed for a considerable time, of not recording the defendant's answer in writing. When the defendant appeared, he was examined *viva voce* by the chancellor,[1] but no record was made of it. In the later cases we find defendants putting in answers in writing and sometimes the pleadings continued, and there was a replication from the complainant and a rejoinder by the defendant.[2] Largely, however, we have to be content with hearing only one side of a case.

While this dearth of answers is unfortunate, the petitions suffer from a defect even more lamentable. Very few of them are endorsed with judgement. Mr. Baildon[3] estimates the percentage of final decrees recorded to be about $9\frac{1}{2}$ per cent. of the total number of cases, an estimate which I am inclined to think too high if one is to judge the Chancery Proceedings as a whole. This, however, is not vital. The question of the authority of these petitions is, on the other hand, very important. If a petition is unendorsed we cannot determine whether or no relief was granted in that particular case. Are we therefore precluded from drawing an inference at all? I do not think so. A petition endorsed with judgement is assuredly the best evidence, and luckily we are able to present endorsed petitions which cover a variety of cases. But we can go beyond this. Where there are numerous petitions based upon the same or a similar state of facts, it is submitted that it may be reasonably inferred that relief sought was granted. Such evidence is not final, but it has a high persuasive value. While we do lament the absence of indorse-

they represent the attitude of the different chancellors throughout the greater part of the century.

[1] See 10 S. S. xxvii.

[2] e.g. XIX. 59, 56, *Cases*, pp. 199, 202.

[3] 10 S. S. xxix, note 1. This estimate does not, of course, pretend to apply to all the Chancery Proceedings. It was based upon the selected petitions in the Cal. Ch. and 10 S. S.

ments, we must take the material as it exists and make the most of it.

So much for the material upon which our study is based. We may now turn to the cases in contract. We use the term contract in its largest sense so as to include obligations under seal as well as parol agreements. While our main interest lies in parol contract, the attitude of the chancellor toward sealed writings is not without interest. Moreover, it throws a reflex light upon agreement itself. Attempts were made to discharge sealed instruments by verbal agreements. Deeds were sometimes conditioned or otherwise modified by parol. Such transactions raise interesting questions which could not be answered if we were to limit ourselves to parol agreements alone. The principles upon which the chancellors acted can best be elucidated from as wide a consideration as possible of the treatment of contract in equity.

One preliminary question may be briefly noticed before we outline the method to be followed in this inquiry. Why did petitioners desire to bring a case before the chancellor? Did equity afford any advantages not possessed by the common law? The following points may be noted:

1. In concluding our survey of the common law we had occasion to point out certain agreements which did not support an action. The total absence of a legal remedy drove many litigants into equity.

2. Even where a remedy was provided at law it might fail in a given case. The cause of such failure will concern us later. We may note here, however, that the common allegation, 'no remedy at law,' covered a multitude of infirmities in legal procedure. This was carried to such an extent that wager of law by the defendant was recognized as a valid ground for appealing to equity. In an interesting case in 1432, a petitioner prayed that he might have the assistance of the chancellor in recovering goods bailed. He could bring Detinue, but if he did so the defendant would acquit himself on oath. The chancellor took jurisdiction and ordered the defendant to return the goods.[1]

[1] XI. 427a, *Cases*, p. 187.

3. Chancery offered decided advantages of which litigants were always eager to avail themselves.

(*a*) Chancery process was speedy, and the trial itself was not subject to the delays which beset an action at law.

(*b*) Remedies were obtainable in equity which did not exist at law, e. g. specific performance of contract.

(*c*) The common law would never compel, and in some cases would not permit, parties to testify. In chancery the defendant could always be examined.

(*d*) It was possible to join several causes in the same suit in equity. We find a petitioner alleging a variety of claims against one defendant in the same bill,[1] and, if we may believe the writer who makes bold to unfold the practice of the High Court of Chancery, several plaintiffs ' for different and severall causes' might join in one bill against a defendant, while a single plaintiff might bring a bill against ' diverse Defendants for severall and different causes'.[2] We do not go so far as to say that equity took jurisdiction because a petitioner had several claims against a defendant; but, at any rate, if any one of them gave jurisdiction to the chancellor, the others might be included in the bill.

We may assume, therefore, that whenever possible a case was brought before the chancellor. What has been said so far is only by way of introduction. There remains now the vital part of our study which is concerned with the examination of contract in chancery in the fifteenth century. This falls into three parts:

I. The scope of equitable jurisdiction in contract.

II. Chancery process and procedure.

III. The theory of contract in chancery.

---

[1] e. g. IV. 94 (Relief against an obligation which was paid, joined with a claim against the defendant by a bill unsealed); VI. 211 (To secure an accounting for moneys received and to recover charters bailed); IX. 147 (To recover payment due on a sale of land and to stop suit on an obligation); XI. 4 (To recover goods and chattels, and to recover payment for land sold). Such cases are of frequent occurrence. Many more might be cited.   [2] Choyce Cases, 4.

CHAPTER II

THE SCOPE OF EQUITABLE JURISDICTION
IN CONTRACT

THE purpose of this chapter is to show the extent of the jurisdiction of chancery in contract. As the scheme of classification of the petitions is not strictly analytical, I wish to say something by way of explanation. Equity is not an independent and self-sufficient system of law. It has built itself into and round another system, and if the common law should be swept away, equity would be left, so to speak, suspended in the air. We cannot, therefore, find a principle of classification within the chancery material itself. In consequence, one of two things might have been done. The petitions might have been divided according to the types of contract which they present; or we might have found our basis of division in the causes of the failure of remedy at common law. Neither of the methods has been followed exclusively; rather have we attempted to use both, and in consequence the scheme adopted is open to criticism.

Before saying anything in attempted justification we may outline the method followed. In Section I are collected some petitions of a miscellaneous character, which are brought in equity for some reason not concerned with the subject-matter of the case. These petitions have one element in common. They concern cases for which in theory the common law did provide a remedy. In Sections II to V the common law actions are clearly paralleled. Thus, in considering obligations under seal, and the recovery of debts in chancery, we follow closely the actions of Covenant and Debt. Again, in the petitions for recovery of specific chattels and the petitions brought against vendors of personalty, the parallel is with the action of Detinue. The remaining sections (VI–XII) are concerned entirely with parol contract, and herein the petitions have been grouped according to the subject-matter of the agreement and the nature of the promise.

It will be obvious that these sections are not co-ordinate, nor are they mutually exclusive. The divisions cross each other, and there is a certain amount of unavoidable repetition. This is a grave defect. However, this method, whatever its logical deficiencies, has made possible what could not have been accomplished in any other way. It enables us to do three things:

1. To examine the various reasons assigned for bringing a petition in equity.

2. To contrast the treatment of similar types of cases at common law and in equity.

3. To classify the cases involving parol contract (for which there was no remedy at law), according to their subject-matter. Symmetry has been sacrificed for what seemed practical utility; I hope the cost is not too great.

Section I.—Petitions brought in Chancery despite the existence of a Remedy at Common Law in Theory

The Prior and Convent of Mountgrace and their predecessors had been seised time out of mind of a rent. The defendants (lessees) always paid the rent regularly, '. . . yitte nowe late by the space of two yeres the said . . . (defendants) . . . of ungodly disposition refuse to pay hit saying that your seid besechers shuld noo landes ne rentes have there but if they would come and dwell þeruppon and kepe hospitalitee'. In consequence the petitioners pray the assistance of the chancellor, '. . . consyderyng that your saide besechers be but poore symple menne and not enhabited in that contre neiþer havyng knowlege [nor] favor, nor being of power to sewe þe law agaynes þayme'.[1] The case is plainly one of Debt, yet the petition is brought before the chancellor because of the weakness and lack of power of the petitioners.

This appeal is typical of many others. The disorganized

[1] XIX. 92.

state of the country induced by the struggle between the Houses of Lancaster and York, the damage wrought by robbers and freebooters [1]—in brief, the failure of the ordinary courts to carry out justice because of extraordinary conditions—all these stand forth vividly in the chancery petitions. There is a remedy at law theoretically, but it fails because of the poverty of the petitioner, or the power and influence of the defendant. Juries were packed and bribed, officers of courts were overawed and induced not to serve writs ; in fact, there were times when the judicial system of the country was reduced to chaos. Under such conditions parties took their cases to chancery, alleging in bitter truth that there was no remedy at law. Nor is this all. Common law process was slow, and there were many inevitable delays. Merchants [2] who were only temporarily in England, or soldiers in service abroad, could not always await the beginning of term, nor risk the perils of continued essoins on the part of the defendant.[3] The remedy, if it be remedy at all, must be speedy. So multifarious are the grounds of appeal that it becomes difficult to classify them. We shall attempt, however, to bring them under certain heads. It should be remembered that in all the following cases there is supposedly an adequate remedy at law. The chancellor is not providing a new remedy, nor enlarging the scope of the substantive law. For an extrinsic reason he takes jurisdiction. This may be due to :

1. *The Parties.*

(1) The king or persons who represented him might always bring their case before the chancellor. It was not necessary to allege that there was no remedy at law; the king might choose his own court and appear indifferently in the Common Pleas or King's Bench, or before the chancellor.[4] But the

---

[1] e. g. VII. 119.

[2] In III. 16 (10 S. S. 10) the petitioner asks for speedy relief in collecting a debt, because he cannot stay 'ad longam prosecucionem'. And see VII. 119 (Petitioner, a 'merchant estraunge', cannot remain in England to suffer the delays of law).

[3] e. g. VI. 175 (Petitioner, being in the service of the Count of Salisbury, cannot stay in England to bring suit at law) ; VII. 25 (The delay of the common law is alleged as the reason for coming to equity).

[4] In Y. B. 39 H. VI. 26. 36 it is held that as the plaintiff was a grantee

personality of the king was extended in various ways. The
defendant by refusing to pay a debt hinders the payment of
the king's rent; again, he is stated to be a 'comond Wyth
Drawer of the kynkes custume out of Ingland'.[1] The
petitioner appeals to chancery, alleging that the king is
interested.[2]

(2) A clerk in chancery could not be sued against his will
in the common law courts.[3] If suit were thus brought against
him he might remove it to chancery by a supersedeas.[4] So,
too, a clerk might begin suit before the chancellor, though he
had a remedy at law.[5]

(3) An alien plaintiff could not sue in the ordinary courts.
The chancellor (at all events in conjunction with the Council)
took jurisdiction of cases where one or both parties were
aliens.[6]

2. *The place in which the transaction occurred.*

(1) It seems, though there is little authority on the point,
that a petition could be brought in equity where the agreement on which it was founded was made within the chancellor's
jurisdiction, namely, within the royal palace of Westminster.[7]

(2) Contracts abroad : The common law did not take jurisdiction of contracts made out of England.[8] Thus, where the
petitioners seek to recover money lent in France, they say,

of the king, he might bring an action at law or sue in equity. This is stated
to be a privilege of the king.

[1] XV. 237.

[2] For a collection of cases where the ground of appeal is that the pleas
were supposed to concern the king, see 10 S. S. xxiii–iv.

[3] Except for felony, or if a freehold were involved. Choyce Cases, 38.

[4] 'Par cause que le dit John Owgham est une del Chauncerie, il avoit
une supersedeas hors del Chauncerie solonc le privelege de mesme le lieu.'
IV. 76, cf. Y. B. 3 H. VI. 30. 15. In an action of Debt counsel for the
defendant 'vient et mist avant un Supersedeas rehersant come le privelege de le Chancery est que nul q'est officer ou minister de le Chancery ne
soit my emplede hors de le dit Place de nul ple que sera move, s'il ne soit
de pleint de terre ou de treason ou de felony, encontre sa volonte ; et pria
que le Court surcesse '. The supersedeas was allowed. See also Y. B.
37 H. VI. 30. 15, and Choyce Cases, 78.

[5] VI. 299, *Cases*, p. 177 (An ordinary case of Debt).

[6] 10 S. S. xlii; III. 4 (S. S. 3) ; III. 16 (10 S. S. 10) ; VII. 71 (Appeal
on another ground); VII. 196 (*semble*).

[7] III. 3 (10 S. S. 2).

[8] e. g. Hertpol in Y. B. 32–3 Ed. I [R. S.] 377 : 'jugement si de receyte
ou de contracte fet en Hyrland deyt ceyns respondre '.

'... a cause que les ditz obligacions furent fait a Caleys et non pas en Engletere, ils ne sachent en quel Countee d'engletere, ils purront prendre leur accion pur trier la dite some'.[1] The difficulty, which was procedural (it being impossible to lay the venue in an English county), was later overcome by a fiction,[2] but in the fifteenth century many obstinate debtors availed themselves of the technical defence at law. For example, the plaintiff, being in Rome, there lent the defendant £4, upon promise of ' hasty payment ' as soon as they returned to England; but after their return '... the said Abbot (defendant) knowing utterly that your said besecher can have no remedy agenst hym by the lawes of this land for as muche as ... the said money was lent by yonde the see and not wythe in the Realme ...', refused to pay.[3] Appeals on this ground are frequent.[4] Many of these petitions relate to obligations[5] made abroad, but there are others which concern more general transactions.[6] In two cases appeal is made to equity to introduce evidence of an agreement made out of England by way of defence to an action at law.[7]

---

[1] LXIX. 131.

[2] The fiction consisted in the use of a *videlicet*. See Tidd's Practice (8th ed.), 430.

[3] LIX. 38.

[4] Thus in XXIX. 317, the petitioner says, '... for asmuche as the seide bargeyn was made in the parties of beyond the see and not Within this Realme, your seide bisecher hath no remedie by the comone lawe of this lande, but onely by supplication afore your good and gracious lordship in the Court of Chauncery'.

[5] Obligation made at Calais: VI. 71; VII. 71; VII. 226. In VI. 161 the petitioner asks the chancellor to give him relief against an action brought at common law on an obligation made in Rouen; he alleges two reasons, first that the obligation is in fact satisfied, secondly ' que la dite obligacon feust fait es parties ou la comune ley D'angletere ne purra avoir iurisdiccon '.

[6] Account: 2 Cal. Ch. lxv; Debt, XII. 51 (Petitioner says, '... for the said duytees growing by certeyn contracte made by yonde the see ... [he] ... hath no remedy ... by the Commune law of ᵭis land ...'); Petition against a factour in regard to transaction in Prussia: XVI. 427; Suit for expenses incurred abroad at the defendant's request: XIX. 295 ('... for as moche as the saide expenses and costs were done oute of this lande your seide besecher faileth remedy atte comune law '); Assignment of goods made abroad: LIX. 124.

[7] Agreement made in Spain: XLIV. 253; Transaction at Calais: LIX. 294 (Petitioner says it is not pleadable in bar at law ' by cause it is so not matter triable wyth in this lond ').

3. *Inequality of Parties.*

The weakness of the petitioner on the one hand, or the strength and power of the defendant on the other, brought many cases before the chancellor.[1] 'Your heart and hand must be ready for the relief of the poor', exclaimed Lord Chancellor Hutton in an address to the sergeants;[2] and in a tract relating to the office of the chancellor, the court is thus described: ' It is the refuge of the poor and the afflicted ; it is the altar and sanctuary for such as against the might of rich men, and the countenance of great men cannot maintain the goodness of their cause.'[3] That these were more than a set of good adages is witnessed by the petitions themselves. We may group them in two divisions:

(1) Poverty of the petitioner.

These appeals are often framed in piteous terms. ' Poor fadyrless children' bewail the fact that they cannot afford the expense of a common law action;[4] a convent has ejected the petitioner from his lease, and he is ' by the meane of the same puttying oute so enpoverisshed where thrugh he is noun-sufficient in goodes to mayntene hys accion at the comune lawe . . .'.[5] Common law writs were expensive luxuries, and if the petitioner was reduced to poverty, he thereby lost his remedy. The denial of justice was substantial, if not theoretical. Hence came the appeal to equity.[6]

---

[1] ' Inequality of persons is cause to hold suit here (i. e. in chancery), although otherwise the matter be determinable properly at the common law.' *Green* v. *Cope*, Hill. 9° Jac., Choyce Cases, 47.

[2] Sanders, ii, p. 1035 (cited 1 Spence, 387).

[3] Lord Ellesmere: Office of Lord Chancellor, 21 (Holdsworth, i. 206, n. 6). It may be that this tract is erroneously ascribed to Lord Ellesmere. See Pollock, Expansion of the Common Law, 70.

[4] XIX. 20.

[5] XXIX. 321.

[6] In the following cases the petitioners allege poverty as the ground of appeal to chancery: 1 Cal. Ch. xiii; 1 Cal. Ch. xxx; 2 Cal. Ch. xii; III. 114 (10 S. S. 40); III. 93 (10 S. S. 47); III. 91 (10 S. S. 76); IX. 342; X. 308 (Petitioner ' ys so pouere that he hath not where of to sewe þe comone lawe'); XI. 84; XI. 213; XVI. 438 (10 S. S. 134); XIX. 480 (' for asmoche as your said besecher hath lost his goodis be yonde þe see . . . (he) . . . is nat of power to sue þe comune lawe . . .'). In XI. 358, the defendant is described as ' havynge grete habundance of Richesse', whereas the petitioner is ' but a pore man nouzt yn power to sue the comune lawe agenst hym '.

(2) Maintenance and power of the defendant.

The system of common law courts, depending as it did upon a jury and many petty officials, was one of which a rich and unscrupulous defendant might readily take advantage. The case was tried in the particular county in which the transaction took place, and it was easily possible to corrupt the officers of the courts or to overawe a jury. Defendants made use of the influence of their family and friends[1] to procure decisions favourable to themselves and to obstruct justice. The petitions repeat this charge with a wearisome monotony. The defendant 'is riche and mayneteined by strength and your seid besecher hath sued many wryties atte comyn law and he canne get noun served'.[2] 'Howsoever the seid suppliant would sue against the said William Clopton at common law, he can never come to his purpose, because of the great maintenance of the said William in those parts.'[3] The petitioner attempted to bring Detinue, but such was the influence of the defendant that the sheriffs refused to serve the writs.[4] Sometimes the petitioner was himself threatened and oppressed so that he did not dare bring suit at law ;[5] 'nulle n'oise pursuer envers luy come le commune ley demande par cause de sa grante maintenance'.[6]

Bribery and corruption likewise were alleged against defendants. For example, the petitioner brought suit against one Albright Yanson de la Wyke before the bailiffs of Yarmouth, but the gentleman of that engaging name succeeded in greasing the palms of the officers of the Court, for our artless pleader remarked that 'because that the sayd bailyffs lofe and cherisshe the sayd Albright, they wil not gyfe iugement accordyng to the truth of the matter as faith and conscience will'. The petitioner prayed that the bailiffs might be brought into

---

[1] '... les ditz Johan et Thomas sont si grandz de consanguineteez, alliancez et amistez en lour pays, qe le dit suppliant n'auera mye droit deuers eux par ascun pursuite a la commune ley...' III. 82 (10 S. S. 48). In III. 41 (10 S. S. 34) it is alleged that the defendant is 'si riche et si forte d'amys en pays la ou il est demourant' that the petitioner can never recover against him.

[2] XII. 205.   [3] VI. 156 (10 S. S. 111).

[4] XII. 56.

[5] See III. 58 (10 S. S. 31); III. 60 (10 S. S. 33); III. 65 (10 S. S. 26).

[6] III. 22 (10 S. S. 11). To the same effect, XI. 84.

chancery by subpoena, '. . . to be examynet of these premisses so that be your discrecon ryght mey be done to all
parties, for the luf of god and in the way of charite '.[1]

Space forbids the inclusion of further excerpts from these
petitions. They bear eloquent testimony to the difficulties
which beset an action at law in the fifteenth century. We
cannot state the relative proportion of the chancery petitions
which were based on the misconduct of the defendant, but
they are sufficiently numerous to form a large and distinct
class.[2] We feel reasonably sure that the chancellor did intervene. The number of appeals leads one to suspect this; and
furthermore, we have one petition endorsed with judgement.
An action of Debt was brought on an obligation against the
petitioner. The defendant caused ' a panell to be retorned of
suche persons of his affynyte which woll here no evydence for
the part of yor seid Orato^r . . .' Appeal was made to the
chancellor, who granted an injunction, restraining the defendant from prosecuting his action at law until the case could
be heard in equity.[3]

4. *Failure of common law process.*

(1) Inability to serve a writ on the defendant.

A defendant by constantly moving about could hold
common law process at bay. There appear to have been
many of these elusive persons, who avoided their just debts by
keeping away from the place in which they were contracted.
One petition sets this forth in so naïve a manner as to deserve
quotation: Adam, Prior of Tutbury, borrowed £160 of the

---

[1] XVI. 573.

[2] The following petitions, in addition to those already cited, allege the
power and maintenance of the defendant as the reason for appeal to the
chancellor : V. 65 (Petitioner brought Replevin, but the action failed ' par
cause de la graunde puissance . . . et subtile confederance ' of the defendants); VI. 92 (in nature of Detinue); VI. 156 (10 S. S. 111); VI. 140
(Detinue) ; VI. 165 (Detinue) ; VII. 219 (another reason as well alleged) ;
X. 181 (Debt ; petitioner is unable to have any writ served against the
defendant because of the 'favour that he hath of officers in that countre . . .') ;
XI. 84 (Detinue on a bailment ; the defendant ' hath so grete power and
mayntenaunce in the said contree that the saide pouere Wydowe (petitioner)
is of non powere to pursue the comone lawe agenst hym . . .') ; XXIX. 410
(Relief against an action of Debt which is like to go against the petitioner
because of the defendant's maintenance).

[3] LIX. 242 (LIX. 243 is the defendant's answer).

petitioners and bound himself in four obligations, but on the day of payment he refused to satisfy them. Then, say the petitioners, 'le dit Priour est home aliene neez et engendrez et de lieger conscience, issint que si les ditz suppliantz voillent conceyver envers le dit Priour ascun accion a la comune ley, il est divers foitz alauntz outre la meer et diverse foitz ad protections et en diverses foitz le dit Priour est expectant et demourant en divers lieux priveleges issint que les ditz suppliauntz ne purront mye executer la comune ley envers luy a graund damage et arrerisement des ditz suppliantz s'ils n'ount vostre tres gracious eide et socour en celle partie '.[1]

Despite the patriotic avowal of the complainants in the petition already instanced, we find that debtors of domestic nurture developed a capacity of movement not inferior to that of the 'home aliene neez et engendrez '. Some defendants refused to appear at all ;[2] others, who were never ' continuelment demourant en nul lieu ',[3] moved rapidly from county to county or at the critical moment went abroad.[4] The subpoena was superior to the common law writ. It was easier to serve ; it was not limited by county boundaries ; it could be obtained very speedily. It was not remarkable, therefore, that despairing creditors took refuge in equity.

(2) Privileged Places.

There were numerous ' privileged places ' in England in which a common law writ would not run. The defendant, says one petition, has departed to 'place privileged and seyntwary where your besechers can no remedy have by þe comune lawe . . .'[5] Into these numerous special jurisdictions

---

[1] IX. 324.

[2] X. 76 (Petitioner attempted to bring Debt, but the defendant refused to appear, though he had acknowledged ' before notable persones ' that the debt was due).

[3] LXVIII. 228.

[4] e.g. in III. 71 (10 S. S. 70) it is said that the defendant 'soi absent et voidit de lieu en autre issint q'ele nulle recouere ne remedie vers luy ent puisse auoir par commun ley. . .'; VI. 168 (The defendant purposes to leave the jurisdiction and the petitioner ' de luy n'avera recovere solonc le processe de ley . . .').

[5] LIX. 106. In XI. 211 it said that the defendant 'hath enhabite hym in suche a place priveleged that the kynges write renneth not . . .'

or franchises it was possible to follow a defendant by
subpoena.   The council had power to issue writs into such
jurisdictions,[1] and apparently this same power was exercised
by the chancellor.   At all events we find petitions addressed
to the chancellor in which a subpoena is prayed against
defendants, who are in Wales,[2] in the franchise of the Abbot
of Whitby,[3] or in the county palatine of Chester.[4] Whether or
no these cases were heard before the council we are not
prepared to say ; but at all events the petitioners did expect
and claim relief in chancery.

In concluding we may advert to a question which is somewhat perplexing : Did the chancellor proceed upon principles
of equity and conscience in deciding these cases ? Mr. Spence,[5]
relying upon the authority of Lord Ellesmere, asserts that in
the exercise of his ordinary or common law jurisdiction the
chancellor could not advert to matters of conscience.   Now
the so-called common law jurisdiction is usually considered to
be that exercised over cases in which the Crown or a clerk in
chancery was a party.[6] It may be, though of this I am not
convinced, that in exercising this jurisdiction the chancellor
followed the common law.   There is practically no authority
on the point, but I should like to call attention to the remark
of the chancellor in a case in 1469.

A subpoena [7] was brought against three executors, of whom
only one appeared.   It was urged that he should be compelled
to answer, but to this the chancellor was unwilling to agree ;
the three executors together represented the estate of the
testator, and that the answer of one should bind the other two

---

[1] 1 Spence, 330.   [2] XI. 402.

[3] '. . . also for as muche as the . . . (defendants) . . . dwellen within the
Franchise of the Abbot of Whitby, . . . (petitioner) . . . may have no
manner of writte for to be executed agenst thaym after the cours of the
comune lawe of this land . . .' XIX. 471.

[4] The petitioner brought Debt on a recognizance, but the defendant has
betaken himself 'into count palyse in Chestourshire and in other places
priveleged with his goodus and catels and no lond hath at the comyn lawe
so that the seid beseecher may not have execution of the seid summe . . .'
IX. 475.

[5] 1 Spence, 337.

[6] This is only a part of the common law jurisdiction. See Coke, 4 Inst.
79, and 1 Spence, 336.

[7] The nature of the case does not appear from the report.

would, he said, be *contrary to conscience.* In the course of the discussion, Pigot, representing the complainant, instanced what he thought was a pertinent analogy. If an attachment, so he argued, were sued against several clerks in chancery as executors, and one appeared, he would be forced to answer. To this the chancellor replied : ' Cel attachment doit ensuer le nature d'action al comen ley, et issint n'est cel Subpoena,' &c., ' en l'attachment jay ij powers, un come judge temporal, et autre come Judge de conscience, car s'il appiert a moy sur le matter monstre en le attachment que conscience est en le matter, jeo adjudgera sur ceo come judge de conscience,' &c.[1]

In the hypothetical case the clerk would appear as a defendant and not as plaintiff ; and we do not know the precise ground upon which jurisdiction would be assumed. However, the chancellor declares that on an attachment,[2] which partakes of the nature of an action at common law, he may decide on principles of conscience. This is an interesting and important declaration. It seems to throw doubt upon Lord Ellesmere's statement, at least so far as the court of chancery in the fifteenth century is concerned.

However, even if it be granted that in cases in which clerks in chancery and the Crown were concerned equity followed the law, there still remains that large class in which the poverty of the complainant, the power of the defendant, &c., or the fact that the transaction took place abroad, brought the case before the chancellor. The petitions, one and all, demand relief in accordance with reason and conscience ; they are framed upon exactly the same lines as those upon which the chancellor granted relief not obtainable at common law. Are we to believe that reason and conscience were exhausted in conferring jurisdiction ? Must the chancellor admit all the technical defences available if the action had been brought at law ? Though matter of conscience arise, must it be ignored ? In the absence of any endorsed case it is difficult to tell. I venture, however, to suggest that the chancellor decided

---

[1] Y. B. 8 Ed. IV. 5. 1 (p. 6).
[2] An attachment was a writ issued against a defendant who, after service of the subpoena, did not appear at the time fixed. 1 Spence, 370.

these cases on his own principles wherever they conflicted with a rule of law. The court which gave relief in the face of a technical legal defence, such as wager of law, would not be likely to withhold such relief as accorded with reason and conscience, no matter upon what specific ground it assumed jurisdiction. Any other conclusion seems to run counter to the principles and practice of the chancellor.

SECTION II. PETITIONS RELATING TO OBLIGATIONS UNDER SEAL

In examining the doctrines of chancery with regard to obligations under seal we shall not consider defences which are purely equitable, as, for example, fraud. Without doubt, from early times equity granted relief against sealed writings procured by duress[1] or induced by fraud[2]; there is much talk of false obligations and feigned acquittances. In a case which may be noticed as typical, a petitioner besought the aid of the chancellor, because the obligor had 'feyned acquitaunce' to bar a just debt; he prayed that the defendant (obligor) might be brought into chancery 'for to be examined in þis matiere and þere for to answer in þe same and to receve þat þe court shall award'.[3] But, though the multiplicity of these appeals tempts one to examine them further, our real interest lies in those cases in which equity definitely met the law in its own field and supplemented or altered the stricter legal doctrines from principles of reason and conscience.

The specific topics to be considered are as follows:

I. Cases in which the obligation is satisfied but the obligor has no acquittance.

II. Simple (i. e. unconditional) obligations which are conditioned by parol.

---

[1] Ancient Petitions, No. 14806 (10 S.S. 127); 1 Cal. Ch. xliv; IV. 6; V. 118. Payment procured by duress was good ground for the chancellor's intervention. Thus where one by duress of imprisonment constrained another to pay a debt already satisfied, a confident appeal was made to equity to recover the second payment 'come conscience et bon foy requiert'. XI. 23.

[2] III. 3 (10 S.S. 2); V. 64; VI. 117; XI. 257.

[3] XI. 257.

III. Obligations executed for a specific purpose which has been accomplished.

IV. Variation of an obligation by parol.

V. Inquiry into the consideration of sealed instruments.

I. *Obligation is satisfied but still retained by the obligee, and obligor has no acquittance.*

' There is a general maxim in the law of England that in an action of Debt sued upon an obligation the defendant shall not plead that he oweth not the money, ne can in no wise discharge himself in that action, but he have an acquittance or some other writing sufficient in the law, or some other thing like, witnessing that he hath paid the money ; that is ordained by the law to avoid a great inconvenience ... that every man by a nude parol and by a bare averment should avoid an obligation. ... And yet ... [the law] ... intendeth not, nor commandeth not, that the money of right ought to be paid again, but setteth a general rule, which is good and necessary to all the people, and that every man may well keep, without it happen through his own default. And if such default happen in any person whereby he is without remedy at the common law, yet he may be holpen by a subpoena . . .' [1] So speaks the Student in the famous dialogue. There is abundant external evidence that many suitors were appealing to the chancellor to be ' holpen by subpoena ' ; for the frequent recourse to the subpoena excited the envy and indignation of the defenders of the common law. An irate serjeant complains bitterly of the interference of the chancellor, who, he says, ' regarding no law but trusting to his own writ (*sic*) and wisdom, giveth judgment as it pleaseth himself and thinketh that his judgment, being in such authority, is far better and more reasonable than judgments that be given by the king's justices according to the common law of the realm '.[2]

The chancery pleadings afford ample proof that the rigid common law rules regarding sealed instruments were counter-

[1] Doctor and Student, i. 12.
[2] A Replication of a Serjeant at the Laws of England to ... certain points in the Dialogue. Doctor and Student (ed. Muchall), 347.

acted by the chancellor's intervention. So innumerable are
the appeals that it is impossible to take note of them all.
They appear in the earliest records preserved, and the stream
continues unabated to the end of the Early Chancery Proceedings. The chancellor was giving ear to the unwary, the
simple people, the 'fatui',[1] who through ignorance or carelessness, or because they reposed confidence in the honour of the
obligee, paid their debts but took no acquittance. 'He so of
his innocencye and for such confidence as he had to the said
Henry (obligee and defendant) left his obligation in his hand ',[2]
exclaims one complainant who repented him of his folly, after
making payment. The obligee in this case had promised to
deliver the obligation, but time passed, his memory grew dim,
and he so far forgot himself as to bring an action of Debt in
the Mayor's court in Bristol. The complainant was in dire
distress; he knew he would be compelled to pay again; he
felt it was against all law and conscience, nevertheless, as he
related in his petition, he knew he was helpless at law: 'your
said pore besecher can not make any barre in the lawe . . .
for *that it is his dede which shall be demed his foly* . . .'[3] He
asked, therefore, that the defendant (the obligee) be brought
before the chancellor by subpoena, and that a writ of Corpus
cum causa issue to the 'Mayor and Bailyffs' of Bristol.
Thereby he might accomplish two things: he could stop the
action at law, and obtain an examination of the defendant
under oath. Unfortunately this petition is not endorsed; we
cannot say' definitely that the relief sought was granted, but
so numerous and repeated are these appeals in exactly similar
circumstances that the presumption is very strong in the
complainant's favour.[4] Furthermore, the chancellor definitely
recognized such a situation, for he said: 'Si on paye un duty
d'un obligation et n'ad escript, *ceo est bon conscience*; et

---

[1] 'Deus est procurator fatuorum.' Y. B. 8 Ed. IV. 4. 11.
[2] XXIX. 406.
[3] *Id.*
[4] VI. 339; VII. 155; VII. 218 (Complainant is arrested and in prison);
IX. 94 (1441); IX. 190 (1442); IX. 214; IX. 215; X. 44; X. 168; X.
185; XI. 242 (1431); XI. 244; XI. 368; XI. 370; XI. 379; XV. 185;
XVI. 263; XIX. 116; XIX. 439 *b*; XXIX. 308; XXIX. 440. These are
merely a few selected cases out of many that might be cited.

uncore al comon ley nul barre.'[1] This simple state of facts is capable of almost infinite variation in detail without any fundamental change in the position of the parties.[2] Thus says one complainant :[3]

'Supplie tres humblement vostre povre orator, Robert Popyniay, que come il est grevousement sue et vexe par un William Newland, marchant d'everwyke a cause d'un simple obligacion fait a dit William par le dit suppliant ... nient obstant que le dit William est pleynement content et paie ... sicome devant vous par examinacion sera loialment prove.'

Nor need the payment necessarily be made by the debtor; it was just as successful if made by some one else in his behalf.[4]

Payment made to a testator was a good defence against an action brought by his executors on an obligation, although the payment could not be proved by specialty.[5] In this connexion we may note an interesting and important case which throws much light on the attitude of the chancellor toward obligations which were in fact satisfied by payment:

The complainant was bound in an obligation of 10 marks to one Alice Reme. She died, leaving the defendants her executors, whom complainant 'truly paied and full contented of the dewete of the seid obligacion'. In full trust that the executors would discharge him, he left the obligation in their hands; one executor died, and some years later the surviving executor, despite the payment made, 'not dredyng God nor th'offens of his own consciens,' brought suit in the Common Pleas on the obligation. The complainant, well knowing that

[1] Y.B. 7 H. VII. 10. 2.

[2] Appeal is made to the chancellor where payment was not according to the terms of the obligation, but was accepted by the obligee; e.g. by furnishing pipes of wine where (apparently) the obligation was to pay money. XII. 16.   [3] IV. 94.

[4] The complainant was bound to the defendant by an obligation. He journeyed up to London to purchase goods, where unluckily the defendant (obligee) met him, caused him to be arrested, and would not release him, till complainant's wife paid the debt. Afterwards the complainant asked for an acquittance, which was refused, and after a brief interval the defendant began suit on the obligation at common law. The complainant seeks general relief. VII. 273.

[5] VI.197; IX. 83 (1431); XI. 46; XIX. 219; XIX. 123 (The defence brought forward by an executor). Naturally these cases are not so numerous, but they are sufficient in number to establish the point.

payment would be no defence at common law, filed his petition
in the chancery, alleging that it was 'contrary to all reason
and gode conscience' that he should be compelled to pay
twice, and yet he was 'without remedy be the Comen Lawe'.
He asked for a subpoena requiring the executor to bring in
the obligation to be cancelled, and that he might be enjoined
from proceeding further at law.[1] The defendant in his answer [2]
set up the usual technical defence with which most answers
as a matter of practice began : that the matter alleged in the
bill was not sufficient to put him to answer ; then he proceeded
to deny that payment had ever been made, which he held
himself 'redy to averre as this court will award'.   The petition
is endorsed [3] with an order for an injunction to the defendant's
attorney, restraining him from further prosecuting any action
at law, until the matter could be heard and determined in the
chancery.   What the ultimate finding of fact was, we have no
means of knowing ; but there is small doubt that if the complainant could prove the truth of his bill, the chancellor would
order the obligation to be cancelled.[4]

Sometimes in the prayer of the petitions complainants ask
that the obligee be compelled to bring in his obligation to be
cancelled ; more often the prayer is general, the complainant
trusting to the chancellor's discretion.   The main thing was to
get the creditor into the chancery, and have him examined
upon oath.   A careful and rigid examination, coupled with
such evidence as the complainant himself might introduce, was
bound to disclose the facts of the case.   The petitioner usually
offers to support his case by further testimony.   'Si come
devant vous par examinacion sera loialment prove,' [5] 'Si come
par proves suffisauntz,' [6] are phrases in constant use.   One man
alleges payment before 'several notable persons',[7] another is
ready to testify himself and bring in his friends, but he is
particularly eager to have the defendant examined, and prays
that after such examination right may be done him as reason
and conscience require.[8]

---

[1] LIX. 227, *Cases*, p. 231.
[2] LIX. 228, *Cases*, p. 232.   [3] LIX. 227, *Cases*, p. 231.
[4] Cf. LIX. 285, *Cases*, p. 232 ; XXIX. 13, *Cases*, p. 214 ; where the chancellor, being satisfied that the obligation should not be enforced, ordered
it to be cancelled.   [5] IV. 94.
[6] VI. 339.   [7] XIX. 116.
[8] '. . . et sur ycell examinacion de feare droit en cest partie a dit sup-

'Reason and conscience' is a thing of great flexibility; indeed, in this rough and ready intervention of the chancellor there is observable a desire to isolate each case and decide it on its merits. It was against reason and conscience that a debtor should have to pay the same debt twice ;[1] and on such ground the chancellor intervened. But this process of reasoning applies equally well where a debt has been *part* paid as where it has been paid in full; and it is not surprising to find that suitors appealed to the chancellor in such situations. In an example, selected as typical, the complainant was bound by obligation in 45s., of which sum he had paid 34s. 4d., but had no acquittance therefor. The obligee brought an action of Debt for the whole sum of the obligation, and, being without remedy at law, the petitioner appealed to the chancellor and asked for a Certiorari.[2] So, too, a debtor who has lost his acquittance,[3] a surety who is being sued on an obligation, when the principal debtor has satisfied the debt,[4] one who had an acquittance, but delayed so long in introducing it into evidence that it cannot be received,[5]—all these appeal with confidence to the chancellor. A little transaction which often created difficulties for the guileless debtor was responsible for appeals to equity. It seems to have been not uncommon that a debtor, for 'further security', should bind himself in double the amount of the actual debt ; he might pay the debt, and still the creditor, armed with his sealed writing, could collect the full sum named in the deed ; for the common law received such evidence as conclusive. The debtor's only resource was in the subpoena.[6] It would be rash to assert that

pliant come bon foy et conscience demandent, pur dieu et en overe de charite . . .' VII. 33.

[1] Thus, exclaims one petitioner : '. . . For oon duetee, withoute youre good grace, your forsaide besecher is leke to make ij° paiementz which were gretly agenst conscience.' IX. 459.

[2] X. 220, and see IX. 133 (1439); X. 175 ; XI. 46.   [3] VII. 92.

[4] X. 94 (Original debtor had an acquittance but has gone 'beyond the sea', taking the acquittance with him); X. 128 ; XIX. 257.

[5] IX. 459; in which complainant says that ' processe of the same accion (i. e. action of Debt on the obligation) is so ferre forthe that for defaute that the forseide acquytauncez were not shewid nee leyd in due tyme that by the comone lawe nowe they mowe not be resseved '.

[6] VI. 6; VI. 160 (An obligation for £10, which had been paid, was retained as security for a further loan of 50 shillings); VII. 33 ; XV. 236

in all these cases relief was granted. I have stated them to show the nearly universal appeal made to equity, where an obligation or the intent thereof was partially or wholly satisfied, and yet the obligor was helpless. For in all these cases he would have sought a defence at common law in vain.

We turn now to other classes of cases. The obligation is simple, but a condition has been engrafted upon it. In the first case there is an express condition, but it is not available at law because it is parol ; in the second there is no express condition, but one is implied from the circumstances, namely, that the obligation was executed for one specific purpose, and for that purpose alone.

II. *The obligation is simple (unconditional), but a condition is annexed by parol.*

Obviously the condition might assume various forms. It might require, for example, the doing of some act by the obligee, before the obligation should be effectual, that is, speaking roughly, the condition might be a condition precedent. Few examples of this species of condition are presented by our material.[1] Again, the obligation might have been conditioned for the performance of some act by the obligor. This represented a common situation in the fifteenth century. Bonds were given in surety to make an estate of lands, to secure the payment of rent, for the performance of some act ;[2] and a prudent person would insist on having a clause of defeasance inserted in the obligation itself, or a separate defeasance bond. Judging from the numerous applications to equity, there were many persons who through ignorance or inattention neglected to take this precaution. They bound

(Obligation of 12 marks in security for debt of 6 marks. The debtor paid the 6 marks, but did not secure the obligation, and the obligee is bringing suit to recover 12 marks). And note V. 110 (A bond for £40 was made to secure a debt of £20. Before the debt was due the obligee brought suit on the bond ; the obligor was cast into prison and compelled to pay £30. He appeals to the chancellor to recover the excess payment of £10 and also damages for his imprisonment).

[1] XV. 231 ; XIX. 249 ; LIX. 122 (The obligee is bringing suit without having performed the condition).

[2] e. g. to secure performance of a covenant, which was to say masses for the soul of a certain person : VII. 79 ; to resign a church to the obligee : IV. 90.

themselves in an unconditional obligation; the only condition
lay in the oral agreement between the parties. Petitioners
describe such a condition variously as 'rehersed by words',[1]
'rehersed by language',[2] 'saunz autre condition forsque par
parole';[3] the condition, says another, 'n'est pas de recorde
en l'enscript mes solement par bouche'.[4] The chancellor,
not regarding a deed as of superior value, and being restricted
by no stringent rules of evidence, was able to regard the
transaction as a whole. There seems no question but that he
admitted evidence of a parol condition[5] to controvert a sealed
instrument, absolute on its face. Here is a typical case :[6]

Complainant took to farm the 'Frank chappel de Steres-
brigge' of the defendants, paying 12 marks a year in rent.
In security he bound himself to defendants in a simple obligation 'saunz autre condicion forsque par parole'. The parol
condition was that he should pay the rent and bear all charges
connected with the chapel. He avers performance of the
condition; nevertheless the defendants (i. e. the obligees)
'ount grevosment sue le dit suppliant par force del obligacion
avantdit, a graunde enpoveresment et perpetuel destruccion
del dit suppliant s'il n'eit vostre graciouse eide celle partie'.
In relief complainant asks that writs may issue to bring defendants before the chancellor '... et sur ceo *eux examiner
del faisaunce del obligacion* avant dit et d'ordeigner due remedie
al dit suppliant solonque vostre tres sage discrecion ...'

I regret that I am unable to present any cases of this class
which are endorsed, but the appeals are not infrequent,[7] and

---

[1] XIX. 249. [2] XVI. 450. [3] V. 143. [4] VII. 79.
[5] Even where the obligor had not performed the condition, but stood
ready to do so, he appealed to the chancellor. X. 259 (The obligation
was bailed on condition, and the obligee's executor obtained it from the
bailee by force).
[6] V. 143.
[7] Accord (with principal case) IV. 20; IV. 28; IV. 90; IV. 139; IX.
37; IX. 147; XV. 231; XVI. 408 (Relief against an action of Debt on a
bond, contrary to a defeasance, of which complainant can make no use, as
it is in the obligee's possession); XVI. 410; XIX. 279; LIX. 113; LIX.
122. These few cases scarcely give an adequate notion of the generality
of the appeal to the chancellor. They are typical of many others. And
see LIX. 285, *Cases*, p. 232, where an obligation executed for a specific
purpose (i. e. condition implied) which had been accomplished was ordered
to be cancelled. *A fortiori* the obligation should be cancelled if the
condition was express.

the claim to relief is fully as valid as any that might come before the court. The relief sought is to have the defendant (obligee) before the chancellor, and compel him to show why the obligation should not be cancelled,[1] or 'wy he wol not deliver the seid obligacion as consciens and good feith requyreth'.[2] That powerful weapon of the chancery, the examination[3] of the defendant, could be used with deadly effect; and once the real position of the parties was ascertained, an order could be made which would accord with the demands of 'reason and conscience'.

III. *Obligation executed for a specific purpose.*

In these cases there is no express condition; yet it is understood that the obligation absolute on its face is really executed conditionally, the condition being implied from the circumstances under which it is given. We cannot illustrate this better than from a case which is endorsed with judgement, so that there can be no doubt as to the decision :[4]

John Merfyn and William Clyfford agreed to enfeoff one Agnes in certain lands; and 'to the intent' that this feoffment should be made, bound themselves in a simple obligation to Geoffrey and William Hamond. The obligors died, and after their death the petitioner, as executrix of John Merfyn, caused an estate to be made to Agnes, 'according to the trewe intent of the makyng of the seid obligation'. Nevertheless the obligees not only refused to deliver up the obligation, but proceeded to bring suit upon it in the king's court 'callid the Comon place'. Petitioner appealed to the chancellor, asserting that this suit was against conscience, and praying for general relief. The obligees were brought in by subpoena, and examined under oath. Upon examination they admitted that the obligation was made for the intent specified in the petition, and that the intent was performed; whereupon the chancellor ordered that the obligation should be delivered to the petitioner to be cancelled.

The obligation did not disclose the purpose for which it was executed, but from an examination of the defendants the chancellor was able to gather the nature of the whole pro-

---

[1] IV. 90; IX. 37 (*semble*, obligation to be cancelled).
[2] XVI. 450.   [3] XVI. 410.
[4] LIX. 285, *Cases*, p. 232.

ceeding. The obligee had only a technical right to enforce his deed; isolating the case, and considering it on its individual merits, the chancellor concluded that it would be against reason and conscience as well as contrary to the intent of the obligation that it should stand good; hence the order. To turn to another case:[1]

Complainant agreed to enfeoff one Katherine in certain lands; in surety for the performance of the agreement, his uncle was bound, and complainant in turn bound himself to his uncle by a statute merchant to the intent ('al intent') that he should be saved harmless. The statute merchant bore no condition. Complainant enfeoffed Katherine; subsequently his uncle died, and the statute merchant came into the hands of an executor who is bringing suit against the complainant on the obligation, despite the fact that the purpose for which it was made has been accomplished; complainant asks for a writ against the executor, commanding him to appear before the chancellor with the obligation, and that the chancellor give 'remedie en ceste partie come la bon foy et conscience demandent'.

Appeal was made to the chancellor where a bond was given as a surety, though it bore no evidence of this on its face,[2] where the intent of the bond was to take seisin of land,[3] where a bond was bailed as security for a loan,[4] where an obligation was made to warrant peaceable possession under a lease.[5] The latter cases are not endorsed with judgement, but the principle upon which the chancellor acted in the first case cited applies equally well here.

IV. *Variation of a deed by a subsequent parol agreement.*

In the cases already considered, the whole agreement could only be ascertained by reading the obligation in connexion with the condition, express or implied. But there is a further

---

[1] IV. 69, *Cases*, p. 172.   [2] VI. 229.
[3] VIII. 12 (1450).   [4] VI. 122.
[5] XI. 90 (Complainant leased his church to X for one year, and in security that X should be in peaceable possession executed a simple obligation, which was delivered to X. X remained in possession for a year, ... took the profits and died. Now the obligation has come into the hands of his executors, who threaten to sue complainant, though the purpose for which the obligation was made is accomplished. Complainant asks for general relief).

possible situation: the agreement may be complete and in writing under seal, and at a *later* time the parties may agree by parol to modify or abrogate the contract as expressed in the writing. It is not a question, then, of explaining a sealed instrument by further evidence: the deed did represent the intention of the parties at the time it was made: it is complete in itself. What has really happened is that another contract has been made; can it be introduced in evidence? To-day one who sought to use such evidence would doubtless find himself in difficulties with the 'parol evidence rule'; in the fifteenth century he would have been helpless in the king's court. In equity, however, rules of procedure and practice had not taken hard and fast shape; and it is possible that relief would be given in that quarter. With this in mind, let us examine three cases, which present different aspects of this situation.

A 'bargaine'[1] was made between Roger Denys, a 'Free-mason' of London, and defendants, that the said Roger should build 'l'esglise et le steple de la . . . ville de Wyburton'. The precise terms of the contract were reduced to writing, and incorporated in an obligation under seal. The mason was to receive £190 for his work. Subsequently 'bargaine ceo prist saunz especialtee' between the same parties: Denys was to build twelve corbels in the church, and make certain alterations in the steeple, for which work, in as much as it was beyond the requirements of the original contract, he was to be paid 'a taunt come il expenderoit entre la faisaunce de le dit overaigne outre le primer covenaunt'. Apparently this sum was not fixed by the parties, but four masons of freestone estimated it at 100 marks. Defendants later refused to pay this additional sum. Denys asserts in his petition that he can have no action against them 'par brief de covenaunt ne en autre manere' at common law. Covenant, of course, would not lie on a verbal promise; but it is a little puzzling at first to see why Debt could not be brought. However, there is nothing to show that there was any statement as to how much the mason should have had for his work: the sum was indefinite;[2] and secondly, any attempt to prove the parol

---

[1] This case does not really represent the modification of a deed by parol. The new agreement was in fact a new contract. I have put the case here, however, because it represents a kind of borderland.

[2] 'A promise to pay as much as certain goods or services were worth

agreement would be met by the introduction of the deed, behind which a common law judge would not go. At all events Denys filed a petition in equity, and asked that the defendants be summoned 'de respoundre a les premisses'.[1]

Complainant bought 'certeyn Bales of Wode' of one Thomas Clement, and bound himself in an obligation of £27 by way of payment. Clement warranted the woad to be according to sample, but it proved inferior ; upon discovering this, complainant went to Clement and threatened to bring an action of Deceit. An agreement was then made that complainant should pay only the actual value of the woad, and this 'payment' was to take the form of dyeing cloth for Clement. Complainant did the work, Clement was satisfied and promised to deliver up the obligation, but shortly afterwards he died. The obligation came into the hands of his executors, who refused to give up the obligation 'as gode faith and conscience wold', and brought an action upon it. Complainant appealed to the chancellor.[2]

An obligation of 10 marks was made in payment for a 'last of rede heryng'. Before the day of payment it was agreed 'bi trete' between the parties, that the obligor should have 'longer day of payment of the said x mark if...(he) ... coude fynde other suerte to be bounde therfor...' The sureties were found, and bound themselves, but the obligor incautiously left the original obligation in the hands of the obligee, who is now bringing suit against the obligor, though the sureties 'have trewly kept every day of the secunde obligacion'. The obligor appeals to the chancellor, praying that the obligee may be compelled to deliver up the original obligation and to withdraw his suit.[3]

With regard to these cases we may note the following points :

(1) The original contract was under seal ; the subsequent and modifying agreement was by parol.

(2) In each case the complainant has altered his position on the strength of the defendant's promise ; in the first case he did additional work, in the other he has in fact satisfied the

would never support a count in Debt.' Ames, H. L. R., viii. 260. When later it became the practice to declare in Indebitatus Assumpsit though no price had been fixed by the parties, we see a departure from principle. Ames, *loc. cit.*

[1] VII. 104, *Cases*, p. 177.   [2] XV. 5.
[3] XVI. 444.

obligation, though not according to its terms.   He has a plain
moral right to the relief he seeks.

(3) The defendant occupies a strong position, but its strength
lies purely in technicalities.   If these be brushed aside, and
the plain equities of the individual situation regarded, the
obvious right of the case is with the complainant.

What did the chancellor do in such a situation?   A categorical answer is impossible from the limited evidence
available.[1]   The difficulty of the complainant in each case
was due to the fact that he had neglected from ignorance
or carelessness to avail himself of his legal rights, and
this was one of the notorious grounds on which equity took
jurisdiction.[2]   But we can state this only as a strong probability.

V. *Inquiry into the consideration of sealed instruments.*

We come now to the final class of cases : those in which the
obligor never obtained the benefit for which he executed the
obligation.   In modern phraseology, the consideration has failed.
The situation becomes plainer from a practical example.
Richard Cordie purchased a house and forty acres of land of
Thomas Rose.   He bound himself to the said Thomas in an
obligation, by way of payment, but shortly after going into
possession, he was ousted by the lord of the manor ; nevertheless Thomas is bringing suit against Richard on the
obligation, ' sur quele grevaunce le dit Richard n'ad mie
remedie al le comune ley ', wherefore Richard appeals to the
chancellor.[3]   Again, an obligation was made in payment for
land under a marriage contract, but the land was never conveyed ; complainant comes to equity, for 'by way of conscience
. . . the said obligation [ought] to be void because the said
William (the obligee) perfourmed not his covenant '.[4]   So, too,
where an obligation was made for the price of woad, which the
vendee subsequently refused to deliver.[5]   Examples might be

---

[1] I do not mean to imply that I have exhausted the evidence.   The
catalogues of the Chancery Proceedings indicate that there were numerous
appeals of this nature.   But limitations of time have prevented me from
examining all of them.

[2] See Vinogradoff, L. Q. R., xxiv. 381.   [3] IX. 405 (1440), *Cases*, p. 183.
[4] XIX. 38.   [5] X. 195.

multiplied,[1] but these are sufficient for illustration. The same situation may assume various forms, but in the end we come back to this: the obligor has received nothing, but despite this the obligee, relying on his sealed instrument, is bringing suit against reason and conscience. The failure of the consideration is total; the enforcement of a deed under such circumstances would be inequitable. If equity cancelled an obligation where the purpose for which it was made had been accomplished, is there any reason to doubt that it gave aid in these cases? Though we have no positive evidence from any indorsed petition, it is confidently submitted that complainants had good reason to expect relief from chancery.

Section III. Petitions for the Recovery of 'Debts'

If the common law provided any remedy which was adequate and effectual, it would seem to be Debt. The scope within which it acted was clearly recognized and defined; it was an action in very general use. We may therefore be somewhat surprised to find that many appeals are made to chancery to recover money due for the sale of goods, for services rendered, &c.—cases in which there is obviously a *quid pro quo*, and upon which Debt ought to lie. The period we are considering, however, is the fifteenth century. Debt had not yet attained its full stature, and Indebitatus Assumpsit was a thing unheard of. The problem before us is this: Did equity to any extent usurp the field of Debt, and did it provide a remedy in analogous cases though none existed at common law? The cases to be considered therefore fall into two groups:

I. Cases in which the common law in theory provided a remedy (i. e. by way of Debt).

II. Cases where there is no remedy at law.

---

[1] e. g. X. 54; X. 59 (Obligation made in payment for fruits of a church which obligor was never permitted to receive); XIX. 4 (Acquittance made on promise to pay a debt—debtor after receiving acquittance refuses to pay); IX. 64; *idem* XIX. 410.

I. *Cases in which the law theoretically provides a remedy.*

We find numerous cases before the chancellor, in which no reason for the appeal is set forth in the petition. Clerks of chancery claimed the use of the subpoena as of right; and the mere allegation that one was such a clerk seems to have sufficed.[1] Other cases are more puzzling. Goods are sold and the price fixed; it appears to be a plain case of Debt, and yet the petitioner confidently comes to equity, without troubling to allege any reason for so doing.[2] We are somewhat at a loss to account for the jurisdiction.[3] It is more usual, however, to find some specific ground of appeal set forth in the petition. These grounds are interesting and worthy of note.

1. As we have already seen,[4] the poverty of the complainant, or the great power and maintenance of the defendant, often explains the presence of the case in equity. Nor was common law process always effective; there were light-footed debtors who moved rapidly from county to county, and the only means of fixing the attention of such vagrants seems to have been a subpoena.[5] Furthermore, one transaction might include several elements. Land might be sold, and a bond executed by the vendor to ensure conveyance. If after the land was conveyed, the vendee refused to pay the price and still kept the bond, the vendor's position at law was awkward. If he brought Debt for the purchase price, he could not at the same time recover the bond, and if it were simple (as often happened),

---

[1] e.g. VI. 299, *Cases*, p. 177. Complainant describes himself as 'un des clerks del Chauncellerie nostre Segnur le Roy'; the simplicity with which he states his case is noteworthy. The 'luy doit et luy detient' recalls the count in Debt. And see IV. 76 (where the defendant is a clerk).

[2] XI. 454. Defendant 'bargaynyd and bought' of complainant certain hops and garlick. It was agreed that there should be made 'billis indented and inselyd be the parties aforseid of and for the certeynte and fulfillyng of the bargayn', in trust of which complainant delivered the goods. The price was fixed, and it seems that Debt would lie. Complainant, however, appeals to the chancellor, without alleging any reason.

[3] See XI. 8 a, *Cases*, p. 185. Complainant, who is seeking to recover rent due on a parol lease, asserts that he is without remedy, because he has 'no writyng to ground him apon at the comyn lawe'. It is not clear why Debt would not lie in such case.

[4] *Supra*, p. 78.   [5] e.g. IX. 324. *Vide supra*, pp. 80–1.

it would still be hanging over him. If, however, he could bring the vendee before the chancellor, he might recover the purchase price and at the same time obtain an order for the delivery and cancellation of the bond.[1] The defence against the bond was purely equitable ; the claim for the price was recognized by law ; but in the early chancery jurisdictions, which had no set limits, there is good reason to suppose that the two might be combined. Once equity assumed jurisdiction on any ground, it disposed of the whole matter.

2. In Debt, the debtor could always wage his law. Early in the fifteenth century[2] we find creditors asking for a sub-poena, because if Debt is brought the defendant will acquit himself on oath. ' A cause que le dit John (complainant) n'ad null especialte . . . le dit William (defendant) soy purpose de gager sa ley '[3], exclaims one petitioner, who adds that in consequence he has no remedy by the common law. There is pretty good evidence that relief was granted. Witness this case :[4]

Two were indebted to complainant ' in certain sums of money w^t oute specialte '. They refused to pay, and complainant, knowing they would wage their law ' agens faithe and good conscience ', sued to the chancellor, and writs were issued ; one debtor appeared, was examined and made agreement with complainant, but the other could not be found. Therefore complainant now appeals again, and asks for a writ against the defaulting debtor.

185197

Evidently the debtor who appeared would not have come to agreement, unless he feared compulsion.

Even where the petitioner had already brought his action at law and it had failed for the above reason, he was not barred in equity. Indeed, the *actual failure* of the attempted legal remedy is sometimes stated as the specific reason for coming to equity. The defendant did his law that ' he owed your seid besechers ne peny . . . where of your seid besechers have notable witnes and profes of þe contrarie . . .',[5] recites a petition. Always the complainant makes offer of further

---

[1] See IX. 147, where this is the relief sought.
[2] At least as early as 1413, in all probability. See VI. 85.
[3] VI. 85.   [4] IX. 335, *Cases*, p. 182.
[5] XVI. 386.

proof of his just debt, often by parol evidence, sometimes by way of examination of the debtor. He is convinced of the inherent justice of his case; all he desires is that the whole matter may be heard in chancery.

In the above cases, equity is plainly appropriating to itself the jurisdiction of the common law. We pass now to situations which fell outside the range of common law actions. Naturally these are the commoner cases.

II. *Cases in which no remedy is provided at law.*

John Paynell sold 'xix balettes of wode for a certein sume of moneye' to 'Mald, the wyf of Robert Hynde'. Mald apparently traded by herself, for it is stated that she 'paieth daly to other diverse merchants and fulfilleth the covenantz that she maketh with hem, her husband not pryvy therto, ner entermetyng of the hous ner the occupacion ther of...' Complainant cannot hold the husband, for he was not a party to the contract and there was no specialty. If he should bring Debt[1] against Mald she would allege that she 'is no sole marchant and under covertour de Baron'. He has parted with his goods, he cannot recover against the husband, nor the wife, nor could he successfully join them, at common law. In this dilemma he appealed to the chancellor and prayed for a subpoena against Mald.[2] We do not know what relief, if any, was granted. The situation is typical of many presented by the technicalities of early common law. We shall now attempt to classify the cases and consider them in groups. It is to be remembered that in all these cases the complainant is in equity because even in theory the law cannot assist him.

1. The debt is proved by an obligation which has been lost or destroyed.

At common law a deed so far absorbed the debt of which it was evidence that it became the debt itself. It would

---

[1] By custom of London a *feme covert*, trading by herself in a trade with which her husband did not intermeddle, might sue and be sued as a *feme sole*. Pollock, Contracts (7th ed.). 83, citing Bacon, Abr. Customs of London, D.   [2] IX. 472.

follow logically from this that the loss or destruction of the obligation meant the loss of the debt, and such was the rule. Equity, however, showed no particular respect for the seal. As we have seen, evidence of payment was admitted against a deed, though not supported by specialty. By parity of reasoning, a creditor who had lost his deed, but still had good and sufficient proof of his debt, ought to obtain relief in equity. We are not therefore surprised to find appeals such as the following:

Complainant, as executor of one Anne Hay, seeks to recover £12 due from the defendant for goods sold. The defendant bound himself by an obligation, which was delivered to Anne, but complainant cannot find it, 'which the seid Richard (obligor) knoweth right wele and how be it he knoweth also right wele that he delyvered unto the seid Anne the seid obligacion in her lif as for his dede and dutie, and that he never contented her nor any other in her name any peny of þe same dutie as he hath many tymes confessed . . ., yet he wol in no wise make contentacion of þe seid money by cause he knoweth wele that your seid Oratour can not fynde the seid obligacion.' As complainant is without remedy at law he comes to the chancellor and prays for relief.[1] Defendant in his answer denies all the allegations of the complainant.[2]

Again, where an obligation was taken by persons unknown from the obligee,[3] and the obligor 'noght wᵗ seyng the seide dette, exscuteth hym by the seide obligacon, as apereth by record of her plee a fore the Justice of the comyn place', the obligee comes to the chancellor and prays for a subpoena. Appeal is made because an obligation has been lost,[4] or stolen,[5] or has been burned[6]; in all these cases complainants come forward and pray aid, because they are without remedy at law. The obligor, sure of himself so far as common law process is concerned, refuses to pay. It should be noted that the complainant always alleges the cause for which the obligation was made, as for goods sold, or services rendered, &c.:

[1] LIX. 212.   [2] LIX. 211.   [3] X. 160.

[4] XI. 160. This is a good example and is reported in full, see *Cases*, p. 186.

[5] 'The which obligation was taken away from your seid besecher by persons to hym unknowyn in the troublouse season.' XXVII. 68.

[6] LXVIII. 49.

likewise he is ready to prove to the satisfaction of the chancellor that a just debt exists.[1]   The situation in equity is the same as if there had been no deed at all; the primary question is, what are the facts of the particular case? If the defendant is withholding something that in right and conscience belongs to the complainant, there is every reason to suppose that the chancellor will not let a mere technicality of law obstruct justice. We have no petitions here endorsed with judgement; but the general trend of reasoning in equity lends support to the view that relief was granted.

2. Transactions abroad.

We have already adverted to the fact that the common law did not assume jurisdiction over contracts made out of England. In consequence, if a debt arose from an obligation made abroad, or from money lent or services rendered out of England, the action of Debt would not lie. In such cases petitioners appealed to equity.[2]

3. Actions against executors.

The action of Debt did not lie against the executors of the debtor, unless the debt were proved by specialty; for by the theory of the common law in any case where a debtor might wage his law, no recovery was allowed after his death, as the personal representatives could not acquit themselves on oath of the debt of the deceased. This arbitrary though logical rule was provocative of much hardship, for most executors stood staunchly on their legal rights;[3] in any such case the creditor's only possible relief was by the subpoena. After Assumpsit supplanted Debt, it was doubted whether it lay against any one save the original debtor; indeed, the right of

---

[1] e. g. XIX. 410. The defendants were bound to complainant in an obligation of £20. Afterwards it was 'accorded' between the parties that the defendants should deliver to the complainant 'moevabble goodes, catelle and money' to the value of £20, and thereupon the complainant made and delivered to defendants an acquittance. Now the defendants will not deliver the goods, and if complainant sues at law, they will stop action by the acquittance; yet the debt in equity and conscience is not discharged. The prayer is for general relief.

[2] This has already been considered, *supra*, p. 76.

[3] In X. 289, the complainant says that the defendants (executors) refuse to pay their testator's debts, because they know they cannot be compelled so to do at law.

the creditor against the personal representative of the debtor was not definitely settled until 1612.[1] From the following cases there is at least a strong presumption that the chancellor anticipated the common law by nearly two hundred years.[2] The cases are chiefly those in which the petitioner would have had an adequate remedy at law except that death intervened. For example:

One John Faireman, 'pur certeinz infirmitez quy il avoit,' retained the complainant 'pur estre son fisision et luy faire d'estre seyn de son maladie'. It was agreed that five marks should be paid for the cure. The complainant 'par son diligent labour fist le dit John seyn de son dit maladie', but before the five marks were paid, the patient was inconsiderate enough to die. His executrix appears to have entertained some scepticism as to the efficacy of the cure; at all events she refused to pay the 'fisision', and he made petition in chancery and prayed for a subpoena.[3]

The petitioner seeks to recover the price of merchandise sold to the defendant's testator. He says that 'of grete trust and confidence that your seid Oratour had to the same John (the testator), he neither toke ne had obligacion ne other writyng for the same dueteez'. The testator died before the day of payment, leaving the defendant, his widow, his executrix. Complainant often asked defendant for the debt, and though 'ther been comyn to the handes of the seid executrice godes that were of the seid testatour sufficiant to pay and content all his dettes, legatez, and other ordynarie charges, yet that to doo (i.e. pay complainant) the same executrice utterly hath denyed and yet doth, In which case your seid Oratour hath noon remedie by the comone law but oonly by this Courte of conscience'. He prays that defendant may be ruled to do what reason and conscience require.[4]

Complainants make much of their helplessness because they have no specialty. One says he has 'none escript obligator nor none oder mater by þe ywych ye sayd John (defendant), executour, may be charged to pay ye said x marc as executour

---

[1] *Pinchon's Case* in Ex. Ch. 9 Co. Rep. 86 *b*. See discussion in Pollock, Contracts (7th ed.), 202, Note G.
[2] See VI. 20 (*c.* 1425), *Cases*, p. 175.
[3] XII. 248.　　　　　　　　　[4] LIX. 103.

at ye comone law '.[1]   Another laments that he has no deed, but only 'his (i. e. the debtor's) worde'[2] for payment, and he is dead.   Land is sold, and the price 'parentre eux (i. e. the parties) accordee saunz ascun seurte eu de dit William (vendee) par obligacion ou en autre manere sinon par simple contract',[3] and as death has intervened the simple contract is of no avail.   We might multiply instances, but those which have been quoted show the typical method of appeal.

There is a further question.   Was it enough to show that the testator would have been liable for the debt had he lived ? Apparently not; the complainant must go further and prove to the court that the executors have assets of the testator sufficient to pay his debts.   The frequent appearance of such allegations[4] leads us to suspect this; and certainly it would be contrary to all the principles of equity to charge an executor in his own goods for his testator's debts.

Unhappily, I cannot present any cases endorsed with judgement; so, as before, we must fall back upon inference.   The reason for intervention is plain.   The debt should justly be a charge upon the debtor's estate ; the mere accident of death ought not to defeat so just a claim.   The constant application for subpoenas against executors leads irresistibly to the conclusion that the chancellor granted relief.[5]   Our conclusion is, moreover, supported by the declaration of a chancellor reported in the Year Books: 'si on n'ad ascun escript et son

---

[1] XI. 275.   See IX. 40; XI. 237; LIX. 93 (' no specialty in writyng '); also cases cited, *infra*, note 5.   This is a very common allegation.
[2] XXX. 18.   [3] XI. 79.   And see VI. 20, *Cases*, p. 175.
[4] Thus one petitioner says that the executors have 'in their handes goodes sufficiaunt of the said testatour and more . . .' XV. 234; and see XI. 99 ; XIX. 103 (Executors were enfeoffed of land for the purpose of paying debts).
[5] It was impossible for me to take down all the cases even in the bundles which I have examined.   The following are thought to be representative: VI. 20, *Cases*, p. 175 ; VI. 71 (for goods sold: only part of the price paid) ; VII. 136 (money lent and goods sold); IX. 134; IX. 153 (payment for land); IX. 221; IX. 337; IX. 430; IX. 431; IX. 434 (for a horse sold); X. 178; X. 268 (on parol grant of testator) ; X. 289; XI. 79; XI. 237; XI. 275 (executor of vendor *v.* executor of vendee) ; XI. 413; XII. 248; XV. 234; XVI. 385; XIX. 103; XXX. 18; XXX. 50; LIX. 60; LIX. 93; LIX. 103.   Appeal is made even where there is no executor or administrator, but the defendants have taken the intestate's goods out of the manor with the intention of defrauding the creditor: V. 102.

debtor meur', nul remedy per le comon ley; et uncore icy per ce Court in conscience il aura remedy.'[1]

4. No definite sum has been agreed upon.

Goods might be sold or services rendered without any stipulation as to the precise amount of payment. Thus tithes were sold, and it was agreed that buyer should pay 'selonque le prys que greynes furent comunement venduz'[2]; again, an agreement was made that the defendant should assume control of the plaintiff's lands and pay over the excess in yearly value beyond £6 10s.[3] In either case, evidence would have to be introduced to fix the amount which was due.

Such situations resulted from many informal agreements. Thus, to take the case of services rendered, note the following:

> Complainant was 'reteyned with Thomas, Abbot of the Church of Malmesbury to thentent to labour and sue for one William Stevenes of Mynty, Bondman to the seid Abbot, whych was endyted of felony a fore the Justices of peas...' The Abbot promised to recompense complainant of all costs and expenses and to pay him for his labour. Complainant sued out a Corpus cum causa, and Stevenes was taken 'to bayll', but later made escape; and for this default, complainant had to pay heavily. Now the defendant (the Abbot) refuses to pay, and complainant says he has no means of recovery at law.[4]

This case is typical. It appears to have been common to request a person to undertake certain work, and promise to pay for all expenses incurred as well as to give a suitable reward.[5] Necessarily, the amount to be paid could not be definitely agreed upon beforehand.

---

[1] Y. B. 7 H. VII. 10. 2.   [2] IX. 452.   [3] XXXI. 120.
[4] XIV. 1.
[5] e. g. An Abbot appointed the complainant his 'procuritour ... de pursuer en la noune de dit Abbe diverses materes et causes devaunt noster seynt pier le pape en la courte de Rome'. He promised to pay the expenses, and also reward the complainant. The work was done, and then the Abbot refused to pay. VII. 292.

Again: A letter was sent to complainant while at Rome, requesting him to purchase 'un bulle de grace que est appelle un pluralite'. Promise was made to pay the costs, &c. Complainant obtained the bull and sent it

The petitions cited fall within the fifteenth century ; indeed, one may possibly be as early as 1391.[1] Complainants state with uniformity that they have no remedy at law. Is this true ? The only common law remedy available would have been Debt, which lay only for a sum certain. The uncertainty of the amount precluded the use of that action. However, the complainant has done the work, and it has not been done officiously, but at the request of the defendant. In later times, Indebitatus Assumpsit would have come to the rescue ; it is submitted with some confidence that the chancellor afforded relief much earlier.

5. The promise to pay is implied.

This may be considered a corollary to the principle in the cases just considered. Goods are sold, but there is no promise to repay ; services are rendered on request under the same circumstances. I am able to present only two petitions, but they are of great interest :

Complainant was 'factor et attorne en la faite' in Prussia to the defendants. Defendants purchased certain merchandise in Prussia, and for default of payment it was seized by the vendors, whereupon the defendants sent a letter of attorney to complainant 'luy requirant de pursuer pur la recoverer' of the merchandise. He did so and incurred great expense ; when he returned to England he 'allegea la dite lettre d'attorne en son accompte et demaunda estre aloue de toutz les despenses et costages faitz solonque la fourme de dite lettre...'; which defendants refused to allow.[2]

Where a complainant is seeking to recover the price of goods taken, he sets up his case thus[3] :

'Also the said Robert Saxby toke of your seid besecher

---

back to England ; but the defendant refused to pay the costs. XI. 328 (c. 1431).

See also: X. 325 (Complainant 'hath effectually spedde a prorogacian of a pluralite' at defendant's request : there was a promise to pay the costs) ; XIX. 295 (Suing to the king at defendant's request : promise to pay costs) ; LIX. 169 (Complainant was requested by the defendant to secure certain writings in Spain : promise to pay expenses and give a 'resounable reward for his labour ').

[1] VII. 292. Addressed to the Archbishop of York.
[2] IX. 223 (1435-6).   [3] XI. 573.

iiij bowe staves w^t oute any price or payment mad be twene hem . . .'

'Also Peers Wympryngham and John Skandylhy, bailyffs of Grimesley toke of your seid besecher w^t oute liveraunce or paiement made vj bowe staves.' Complainant says he is without remedy at law.

The promise is implied from the circumstances of the case. It was precisely this situation which was met in the seventeenth century by allowing the 'quantum meruit' in Assumpsit. Surely it is not without significance that an attempt was made to secure the same kind of a remedy in equity in the early fifteenth century.

6. Benefit conferred on a third party.

A benefit conferred upon a third party at the request of the defendant would not support Debt[1] in the period which we are considering. However, it was made the basis of appeals to the chancellor. Thus we find complainants making appeal where they have ransomed a prisoner,[2] paid over money,[3] or said masses for the soul of one deceased,[4] at the request of the defendant.

7. Assignment of debts.

The common law regarded the relation between creditor and debtor as an intensely personal one; in consequence, the right of action which arose from such relation could not be assigned either by act of the parties or by operation of law.

---

[1] The dictum of Moyle J., in Y. B. 37 H. VI. 9. 18, did not become established law till after the fifteenth century. See Ames, H. L. R., viii. 262–3.

[2] XLIV. 272 (Defendant promised to pay complainant £20 if he would deliver one B out of prison in 'the mount seint Mighel'. Complainant delivered B, but defendant refused to pay. He asserts that there is no remedy at law).

[3] XI. 361 (Money paid to a third party at the defendant's request). XV. 248 (X borrowed a certain sum of Y, leaving in pledge jewels of greater value than the debt. Later he desired a further loan, and Y, being unable to lend the money himself, desired complainant to advance it to X, and expressly 'undertoke to youre seid besecher that he shulde be paied truly'. Complainant made the loan; subsequently X repaid both loans to Y, but Y never paid complainant. Y is dead, and complainant asks for relief against his executors).

[4] VII. 79 (Perhaps it is stretching a point to treat a departed soul as a third party).

To a certain extent this notion was modified [1] by allowing the personal representatives to recover the debts of the deceased ; but, as we have seen, the common-law judges showed great reluctance in allowing any corresponding right *against* the representative of the debtor. At all events, it was a settled rule of law that a chose in action was not assignable, at least not so as to enable the assignee to sue in his own name. This rule was the logical outgrowth of the conception [2] above referred to, and was strictly enforced throughout the history of the common law. If the assignee wished to bring any action at all, he must bring it in his assignor's name.[3]

The practice in equity was otherwise. Among the earliest petitions preserved, we find assignees seeking to recover in their own names debts which had been assigned to them :

1413 (?) [4] : Defendant owed X £50. X, desiring to compensate complainants for injuries done them, wrote a letter under his seal requesting defendant to pay over the £50 to complainants. X died, and defendant refused to comply with the request. Complainants, having no remedy at law, pray for a subpoena.

1432 [5] (probable date): X was 'fermour' to Y, paying for seven years £35. Y by letter under his seal assigned the £35 to complainant. X died and his executors (defendants) refused to pay. Complainant says he has 'nothyng to shewe in especiall save such bokes of a Countes', but no 'mater to recuver atte comene lawe '.

1432 [6] (probable date): Freight for wine was assigned to complainant when he purchased the ship in which the wine had been transported.

---

[1] Mr. Ames (Anglo-Am. iii. 581) says that this was not a modification ' since the representative was looked upon as a continuation of the *persona* of the deceased '. But, if this statement be correct, Debt should lie *against* as well as *for* the personal representative. The very reason alleged for not allowing Debt against the personal representative (i. e. that only the original debtor could wage his law) seems to reflect the intimate personal relation between creditor and debtor.

[2] Coke's explanation (*Lampet's Case*, 10 Co. Rep. 48 *a*), that the origin of this rule is attributable to the desire to discourage maintenance and litigation, is effectually disposed of by Mr. Spence (2 Spence, 850).

[3] The Year Book cases are carefully analysed in Pollock, Contracts (7th ed.), Appendix, Note F.

[4] VI. 141. Addressed to the Bishop of Winchester. The date cannot be fixed with certainty.

[5] IX. 337.   [6] X. 74.

1432[1]: Debts assigned to complainant 'in recorde of the Mayre of Caleys'. Afterwards the debtor in London 'a fore worthy men knowleged the dewete and payment ther of to be made to your seyde suppliaunt'. Nevertheless he refused to pay.

1432[2]: As security for a loan from complainant, X delivered (bailla) two obligations to him, by which W. and T. were bound to X, the intention being that payment be made to complainant. To this W. and T. agreed at X's request; X died, leaving no property; W. also died. Defendants (W.'s executor and T.) refused to pay complainant, who is without remedy at law.

1450[3]: Defendant was indebted to complainant's father in 10 marks 12 shillings. The father died and his executrix 'graunted the seid x marc xij s. to your seid besecher for parcell of his fynding at London'. Defendant agreed to pay complainant and did pay part of the debt, but afterwards refused to pay the rest. Complainant asks that the defendant may be compelled to pay.

It is impossible to determine whether it was necessary that the debtor should agree to pay the assignee. In only two of the above petitions is any such agreement expressly alleged. Nor is it apparent whether or no any 'consideration' was required for the assignment; it seems probable that at this time it was not. Some three hundred years later it was assumed as common knowledge that an assignment of a chose in action was valid in equity without any consideration.[4] The petitioners in each case claim the debt as belonging to them in reason and conscience.

From cases of assignment are to be distinguished those of substituted agreement, that is, where a new liability is substituted for the old. This is what we should now describe as novation, but it did not exist at common law before Assumpsit was allowed on mutual promises.[5] We may note two early cases in equity.

[1] XI. 47, *Cases*, p. 186.
[2] X. 17, *Cases*, p. 184. Cf. with this the statement in Y. B. 15 H. VII. 2. 3.
[3] XIX. 151.
[4] 'And first it was admitted on all sides, that if a man in his own right be entitled to a bond or other *chose in action*, he may assign it without any consideration.' *Lord Carteret* v. *Paschal*, (1753) 3 P. Wills. 199. The remark is *obiter*. As to the ultimate requirement of valuable consideration, see Spence, Eq. Jus. ii. 852.   [5] Ames, Anglo-Am. iii. 584.

1475[1]: One Harry Denne owed complainant £8. Defendants at the request of Denne 'became dettours and promysed to pay your said Oratour . . . the said summe of viij li. at a certeyn day . . ., uppon trust onely of which promyse your seid Oratour acquitted and discharged the seid Harry Denne of the viij li. and toke them dettours for the same . . .' Now defendants, contrary to conscience, refuse to pay and complainant has no remedy at law.

1475[2]: K. was indebted to complainant in £10. She desired complainant to accept her son (the defendant) as debtor in her stead. Defendant, at the request and desire of K. ' made feythfulle promysse before sufficiant Recorde to content, satisfie and pay . . .' the said £10. ' Upon truste of such promysse to have ben trewly fulfilled . . .' complainant discharged K., and took defendant as debtor. He now refuses to pay, and complainant is without remedy at law.

In conclusion, a word may be said about the relief sought. It is obvious, of course, that the creditor wishes to recover his debt; sometimes he asks for the specific sum,[3] sometimes that the defendant may be compelled to pay what is due.[4] More often the relief is asked in general terms, namely that the debtor may be compelled to do what reason and conscience require.

SECTION IV. PETITIONS FOR THE RECOVERY OF PERSONAL PROPERTY

We have already noticed the narrow scope of the action of Detinue as it appears in the early Year Books. Detinue ' sur bailment' was the commoner form of the action; Detinue ' sur trover' was used indeed in the fourteenth century, but it did not become a form of action in general use till the next century. It is believed that no small amount of pressure was exerted by the interference of chancery; and that the ultimate development of a right *in rem* at common law, in favour of the owner of a chattel, was hastened by a jealousy of the encroaching equitable jurisdiction.

---

[1] LIX. 57.   [2] LIX. 75.   [3] VII. 292.
[4] X. 325; XV. 32 (Alternative relief; land was sold, and the prayer is that the defendant be compelled to pay the price or make relivery of the land); XXIX. 18.

In the fourteenth century the disseisee of a chattel had the following remedies: If there were a bailment he might bring Detinue, but in such a case only against his bailee or some one in privity with him. If he brought Detinue 'sur trover' he must show how the chattel came into the defendant's hands; the allegation that the defendant casually found the chattel had not yet become a fiction. Under certain circumstances Trespass would lie, but it sounded only in damages. In no case was there any common law process for compelling the return of a chattel.

There was thus good opportunity for the chancellor to intervene, as the legal remedies were far from satisfactory. Even where Detinue would lie, we find complainants appealing to equity, alleging that because of the defendant's maintenance and power,[1] or the refusal of sheriffs to serve writs[2] the action at law failed. Wager of law is set forth as a reason for coming to chancery. This appears from an interesting case of which the chancellor took jurisdiction.[3] In fact, in many petitions no reason for application to the chancellor is assigned. The petitioner simply states his case, claiming that the defendant has property which belongs to the complainant, and which reason and conscience require should be given up.

The situation will be plainer from several illustrative cases:

c. 1405[4]: X, before going to Normandy, placed his charters in a box and delivered them to the defendant to be kept. X died, and complainant (his heir) asks that the defendant be compelled to deliver up the charters. It is not asserted that there is no remedy at law.

1421-2[5]: Petitioner is the heir of Richard le Scrope. He seeks to recover charters affecting his inheritance, which 'a les mayns de William Mayhewe sont devenus'. *Endorsed:* The defendant is ordered to bring the charters into court.

---

[1] VI. 92; VI. 140; XI. 84.
[2] XI. 56 (Detinue was brought, but it failed for this reason).
[3] XI. 427 a, *Cases*, p. 187. The petition is endorsed with judgement.
[4] IV. 46.
[5] IV. 158, *Cases*, p. 174. The presence of the case before the Chancellor may be due to the fact that the petitioner was in the wardship of the king. But there were many similar appeals where there was no such reason: e.g. V. 63 (1418); VI. 22; VI. 94 (A widow seeks to recover charters in hands of her late husband's executors); VI. 140 (though here 'maintenance' of defendant is alleged); VII. 174; IX. 417.

1413–1426[1]: Petitioner, before leaving England, put his charters and jewels in a box, and left them in his house. The defendant came to his house, during his absence, to stay with his wife, and treacherously secured the charters. In such a situation petitioner was in a difficulty at law. Detinue would not lie, and Trespass would only give damages.

1432[2]: Complainant bailed goods to defendant in security for a loan of 20 shillings. He repaid the loan and requested defendant to redeliver the goods. Defendant promised to do so, but afterwards sold them to a stranger. *Endorsed:* Order that complainant should recover his goods.

After 1432[3]: X, a foreign merchant, delivered certain goods to defendant at Colchester, to be delivered to him, or his attorney on demand. X gave a letter of attorney to complainant giving him power to receive the goods, but the defendant refused to deliver them. X is being sued for debt by creditors in London, and complainant cannot pay these debts, because he cannot recover the goods.

1438[4]: Edmund, 'Erle of Dors', delivered by the hand of his servant an 'ouche of gold with dyvers precious stonys in hit set' to Gilis, wife of William Norton, in pledge of £20 which he borrowed from the said Gilis. It was agreed that the ouch should be redelivered on payment of the loan. The ouch was worth 100 marks, and the bailee and her husband refused to deliver it up when the complainant tendered the £20, but 'the same ouche hath solde and aloyned'. Complainant asks the chancellor to give him relief as 'by the comyn law ther ys no remedye for the seyd Erle to recover the seyd ouche'.

1439–1440[5]: Petitioner, probably as an arbitrator, was in possession of an obligation. Defendant came to him and asked to see the obligation; 'and whenne he (i. e. defendant) hadde yt, he held yt and wolnot giffe it agayne'. Petitioner attempted to recover by Detinue, but failed,[6] and therefore comes to equity for relief.

---

[1] VI. 175. Petitioner, however, alleges as his reason for coming to equity, that he is in the service of the Count of Salisbury and hence cannot remain in England to sue at common law.

[2] XI. 427 *a*, *Cases*, p. 187. Cf. VI. 327, and IX. 109, where an obligation was delivered up by a bailee in violation of the terms of the bailment.

[3] XII. 262.   [4] XII. 206.   [5] IX. 132, *Cases*, p. 180.

[6] He could not allege a bailment, nor could he bring Detinue 'sur trover'; for the allegation of loss by finding was still traversable at this time. The defendant's act constituted a trespass, but the action of trespass afforded no real relief in such a case.

Lack of space forbids the inclusion of further cases. With these, however, as illustrations, we may proceed to summarize our conclusions :

1. Only in chancery could a plaintiff obtain the relief which met the requirements of the case, namely an order for the re-delivery of the chattel sought.[1] Equity of course acts *in personam,* and consequently its only means of carrying out the relief was by decreeing that the defendant should give up the chattel in question.[2] It is true that in one case we do find it ordered that the ' plaintiff do recover his goods ' (' quod predictus Thomas recuperet bona infrascripta ' [3]). This decree is certainly curious, and can scarcely be interpreted literally. It seems to show two things : *first,* that decrees in chancery had not yet assumed absolute and definitive form ; *secondly,* that the chancellor meant simply that his decision of the case was in favour of the complainant, and that he would use such process as lay within his command to make this decision effectual. A contumelious defendant might conceivably refuse to comply with the order and go to prison rather than carry it out. But in the majority of cases appeal to chancery would succeed in its purpose. At all events, equity in the fourteenth century afforded a remedy for the recovery of a chattel which did not exist at law till the nineteenth century.[4]

2. Though the chattel had been bailed, it was not necessary in equity to connect the defendant's possession with that of the bailee ; want of privity did not bar the subpoena.[5]

3. But it was not necessary to allege a bailment, nor to decide the manner in which the defendant obtained possession of the chattel. Apparently, it was enough to show that the complainant had the right (at least a moral right) to recover, and that the defendant in reason and conscience should give

---

[1] Or to bring it into court. IV. 158, *Cases,* p. 174.

[2] ' Equity . . . acts only *in personam,* never decreeing that a plaintiff recover a *res,* but that the defendant surrender what in justice he cannot keep.' Ames (History of Trover) Anglo-Am. iii. 436.

[3] XI. 427 *a, Cases,* p. 187.   [4] *Supra,* p. 33, note 3.

[5] VI. 175. And see especially VI. 245 (10 S. S. 113). See also XXVII. 390 (10 S. S. 150).

up possession.[1]   Thus the fact that a charter affected one's right to land was ground for recovery.[2]

4. Though the owner were effectually divested of possession, as by a tort, he was not barred from enforcing his claim to recover his property in equity.[3]   At common law his only remedy was by way of damages ; but it seems that the chancellor would enable him to follow his property into whosesoever hands it came.[4]

In brief, the chancellor, untroubled by any complex theories or any technicalities of procedure,[5] endeavoured to do substantial justice in the individual case. It is difficult to estimate accurately the extent of the use of the subpoena in the recovery of personal property ; but from what has been said already it will appear that the influence of chancery in shaping the law of movable goods must have been considerable.

SECTION V. SALES OF CHATTELS. PETITIONS AGAINST VENDORS

The petitions brought against vendors on the sale of a chattel fall into two classes. The petitioner is asserting a claim: (1) for non-delivery of the chattel ; (2) for breach of warranty.

1. *For non-delivery of the chattel.*

In ordinary cases there would seem to be a plain remedy at law. If the purchase price were paid, or the buyer's sealed obligation for the price delivered,[6] Detinue would lie from early times. The buyer's right was extended in 1442 or

---

[1] Cases, *supra*, pp. 111–12.   And see III. 111 (10 S. S. 81) ; VI. 94.
[2] IV. 158, *Cases*, p. 174.   [3] IX. 132, *Cases*, p. 180.
[4] VII. 119 (Complainant had woad on the high seas.   It was seized by robbers and taken to Cornwall, where it was delivered to the defendant. Complainant appeals to the chancellor for a subpoena against the defendant).   See also III. 20 (10 S. S. 12).
[5] Cf. X. 151 (One executor endeavours to obtain an obligation from a co-executor.   The defendant [the co-executor] refused to take any part in the administration of the estate, and yet would not give up the obligation.   No suit could be brought at law, ' because ðat ðe said John was made executour in the fourme aforseid . . .')
[6] The right to bring Detinue where a sealed obligation was delivered was recognized in 1344–5: Y. B. 21 Ed. III. 12. 2 (per Thorpe).

thereabouts, so that he could claim the specific property though he had not paid the price; for Debt and Detinue were regarded as reciprocal remedies.[1] Why then should a vendee appeal to the chancellor? There seem to be the following reasons:

(*a*) The vendor might have sold the chattel to third parties, in which case it would be useless to bring Detinue. The only remedy then is by way of damages for the loss of the bargain, and that is what the petitioners claim.[2]

(*b*) Again, if the vendor had no title in the goods at the time of the assumed sale, there would be nothing upon which to base a common-law action. Thus, where one who sold wool had no title to it, the vendee appealed to the chancellor, saying he had no remedy at law because ' the proprete of the said wolles vested not in your said suppliant ', for the ' said wolles were not the said John Adam's (the vendor) at the time of the bargain '.[3]

(*c*) The transaction might not be a sale of specifically ascertained property, but an agreement to provide articles of a certain kind by a certain date. Failure to deliver would be a breach of contract; the basis of the action would be the vendor's non-feasance. This appears to have been the ground of appeal in one very interesting case.[4]

2. *For breach of warranty.*

From early times a vendor was held liable for breach of an express warranty in an action of trespass on the case. We have two petitions brought on the same ground in chancery. The reasons for appearing in equity are interesting:

XI. 512. Woad was sold and warranted merchantable. It proved to be unfit for use. Nevertheless, complainant is being sued at law for the price, and he has no defence at law. He wishes to set-off his loss from the breach of warranty against

---

[1] 20 Hen. VI. 35. 4 (per Fortescue C.J.).

[2] VII. 201; XLI. 262 (In this case there is a further reason for coming to chancery. The vendor agreed to sell his tithes to the complainant, *in case he sold them at all*. Thus it was not a true contract of sale; moreover, the property was not definitely ascertained, so that Detinue would not lie. Complainant seeks to be recompensed for his loss by this breach of ' Covenant ').

[3] LIX. 185, *Cases*, p. 230. [4] XX. 39, *Cases*, p. 211.

the claim for the price; he therefore comes to the chancellor and prays for a Certiorari, to have the whole case heard in equity.

XXX. 33. Defendant sold cloth, warranting it to be 'trewe marchaunt', &c., but it turned out to be 'motthetyn and rat byten'. Complainant sought to hold the defendant in an action at law, but he 'wold not abide answer in the Kynges Court'; therefore appeal is made to equity.

This affords an excellent illustration of equity supplementing the common law. But the theory upon which the relief was given is not that there is a *quid pro quo*, nor a detriment to the plaintiff. On the contrary, petitioners emphasize the fact that the defendant made a promise or a bargain and did not carry it out. In other words, the claim for relief is based on breach of contract.

SECTION VI. SALES OF LAND. PETITIONS AGAINST VENDORS

Actions against Vendors on Contracts to convey Land.[1]

The cases now under consideration possess especial interest; for it was in this phase of contract that equity developed a remedy peculiar to itself, which never existed at law: specific performance of contract. Specific performance and the injunction remain two enduring features of equitable jurisdiction which persisted in full vigour into modern times, and are indeed conspicuous to-day. Specific performance did not create, strictly speaking, a new substantive right, but it was a new and advantageous remedy. We should, however, observe that it was invented before the common law regarded parol contracts as enforceable; indeed, we hope to show that the chancellor exercised a wide jurisdiction over contract in the fifteenth century where there was no remedy at law. Nowhere is this more conspicuous than in the petitions brought against vendors for non-performance of contracts to convey land. The gist of the action is in each case non-feasance; the vendor has done nothing and refuses to act at all. No action lay at law

---

[1] Further cases of petitions to compel the conveyance of land are considered in Section VII, *infra*, pp. 123 ff.

until Assumpsit was formally recognized in 1504, and at that time the payment of the purchase price was a condition precedent to bringing the action. Moreover, it was necessary to show that the vendor has expressly undertaken to convey the land; Assumpsit did not originally lie upon a promise or bargain as such.

The discussion falls into three parts : first, the conditions which were necessary to bring the subpoena; second, the parties in favour of whom, and against whom it would lie; third, the relief granted.

1. *The types of cases in which the subpoena is brought.*

There are two features characteristic of the cases brought before the chancellor. In the first place, the agreements are always by parol. If the complainant had a deed, there was a ready common law action in Covenant; it was the lack of any such writing which is most frequently alleged as the reason for appealing to chancery.[1] But secondly, and this is most interesting, we note that the agreements are often very informal. For, while a complainant might allege that the defendant undertook or covenanted to convey land,[2] this is not the usual practice. The common statement is that there was an agreement or bargain, or that the defendant 'sold' the land to the complainant. Petitioners do not take pains to incorporate the facts into any peculiar form of statement; they present informally the terms of an informal agreement, and it is the fact of agreement upon which particular stress is laid. This circumstance seems of such importance that I venture to state one example at length.

One William Serle came to Robert Ellesmere (petitioner) and said that he had certain 'termes' of land to sell. Petitioner wished to see and examine the evidences of title before any bargain was concluded; in consequence, it was agreed that

---

[1] e. g. complainants describe the transaction as 'par parolle saunz escript' (XI. 109); 'by mouthe without writyng' (XI. 485); 'upon covenaunt without writyng' (XIV. 3), &c.; and conclude by declaring that in consequence they are without remedy at law. Thus, says one, 'your saide suppliant hath no specialty of þees covenauntez . . . so þat þe comone lawe gevof no remedie in þis partie' (XXXIX. 52). This is a typical allegation.

[2] i. e. in the form in which plaintiffs later counted in Assumpsit.

he should come to Serle's house and look over the documents. On the day appointed, petitioner came with George Horton, 'a man of Counsell', who read through the 'evidences' and found them to be satisfactory. Several other people were present, and after some discussion an agreement was reached, and William Serle 'rehersed' the bargain to one of the by-standers. Petitioner then stated the terms of the agreement to George Horton, who turned to William Serle and said 'Be ye accordeth in the maner as Robert here hath rehersed', the answer was in the affirmative. Afterwards all went together 'To the Swan beside Seynt Antonyes and there they dronke to gederes upon the saide bargayn atte the coste of the saide Robert Ellesmere'. The agreement was that the petitioner should have the 'termes' for £40; and the parties were to meet subsequently when the price should be paid and a deed made, &c. At the time specified the petitioner offered pay-ment, but Serle refused to seal the writing or deliver up the evidences. In consequence, petitioner has lost his bargain, and, as he has no writing of the agreement, is without remedy at law. He prays for a subpoena directed to Serle, and general relief.[1]

The importance of cases of this type lies in the fact that by reason of the very informality of agreement, they were for a long time unenforceable at common law. Yet it is believed that such represent a large number of the ordinary transactions of daily life. The parties were not skilled in the technic of law; but they made a bargain in their own simple way. It was not only fortunate, but necessary, that some one should give protection to such compacts.

There is a still further question. Was it enough to allege a mere bargain, or must the petitioner go further and show that he had suffered damage by relying upon the defendant's promise? In other words, has one of the parties altered his position on the strength of the agreement? There is at first sight some indication that this was so. A most obvious way

[1] XIX. 354 a–354 e, *Cases*, pp. 204–207 (consisting of petition, answer, replication, and three depositions). Cf. XVI. 412, *Cases*, p. 198, which is on all fours with the principal case. There was an agreement to sell land, but 'be cause there was no clerk nor lerned man there to make upp their dedes accordyng to the sayde covenauntes, It was appointed and accordid betwixte the saide parties that at a certaine day by them assigned they shuld have met and paied the furst paiement and made upp here dedes'. Defendant refused to make the deed, though complainant tendered the price agreed upon.

in which a complainant might have changed his situation was by payment of part or the whole of the purchase price. In the majority of the petitions I have examined this was the case ;[1] it is often alleged as ground for relief.[2] If anything had happened which strengthened the complainant's position, he did not fail to emphasize it. Thus we find it alleged that the petitioner has spent money on the land in making improvements,[3] sometimes even at the defendant's request [4]; again, that the petitioner was put in possession and has subsequently been ousted,[5] or that by reason of holding possession he has been distrained of rent by the chief lord.[6] These are aggravating circumstances which cry aloud for intervention. They represent the strongest grounds of appeal to the chancellor.

There is, however, no conclusive reason for believing that even payment of price was a prerequisite to bringing the subpoena. In fact there are indications which point the other way. We know that at a later date an unpaid vendor might be held a trustee for the purchaser.[7] Finally, there are numerous petitions in which it is not asserted that the price is paid, though the complainant usually adds that he stands ready to pay it.[8]

In conclusion, we may note that in none of the petitions is an appeal made where there was not, in fact, a consideration for the agreement. No attempt is made in these cases to hold the vendor on a bare promise.

[1] Purchase price is paid: IV. 96, *Cases*, p. 173; VI. 58; VI. 176; X. 184; X. 263; XI. 109; XI. 178; XI. 485; XII. 175; XIV. 3; XV. 222; XIX. 101 ; XIX. 340 *a*–341; XIX. 404 *a*–404 *b*, *Cases*, pp. 207– 208; XXXIX. 53; LIX. 86. Part of purchase price paid : IV. 100, *Cases*, p. 173 ; IX. 207 ; IX. 409; X. 323; XI. 537 ; XIV. 16; XVI. 377; XVI. 645 ; XIX. 59–56, *Cases*, pp. 199–203 ; XXVII. 16 ; XXVII. 83; XXVIII. 227 ; LXX. 148.

[2] e. g. complainant says, 'nient contresteant le paiement devant maynes' the defendant will not make estate. IV. 100, *Cases*, p. 173.

[3] This, in addition to payment of the purchase price : IV. 96, *Cases*, p. 173; XV. 222; XVI. 377.

[4] XXXVIII. 160 (Complainant was in possession of an inn under a parol lease, and expended money thereon at the defendant's request).

[5] IV. 126; XXXI. 189 (Parol lease).

[6] XIV. 3 (The vendor had no estate save in the right of his wife,—and yet complainant, as ostensible owner, was compelled to pay the rent to the chief lord).

[7] Maitland, Equity, 251.

[8] Purchase price not paid: IV. 126; VII. 219; IX. 443; XV. 19; XVI. 347; XVI. 412, *Cases*, p. 198; XIX. 354 *a*–354 *e*, *Cases*, pp. 204–207.

2. *The parties in favour of whom, and against whom the subpoena lay.*

It seems that rights under the contract might be assigned either by act of the parties, or by operation of law. We find petitions brought by heirs [1] and executors, [2] and by a widow [3] to whom her husband assigned his rights in the land purchased on his death. On the other hand, actions are brought against heirs [4] on the contract of the deceased, where the vendor covenanted for himself and his heirs, and against an abbot's successors [5] where they were expressly bound in the original grant. Whether or no the heir would be liable if he were not expressly included in the contract, we are not prepared to say. But the subpoena was not limited to the original contracting parties. It lay against the feoffees [6] to the use of the vendor to compel them to make conveyance, and even against third parties [7] who had maliciously induced the vendor to break his contract. In the last case, the prayer is that the third parties, as well as the vendor, should be brought before the chancellor to say why an estate should not be made according to the agreement.

3. *Relief Granted.*
(*a*) Specific performance.

It is obvious that there are many cases in which a contract

---

[1] VI. 176 (Complainant is 'prochein heir a dit Nicoll', the purchaser, who is dead. Purchase price was paid; still defendant has sold to a stranger 'encountre droit et bon conciense'); XIX. 404 *a*–404 *b*, *Cases*, pp. 207–208 (Petition by heir. Land sold to petitioner's father; price paid. Now defendant refuses to make estate to the heir after the father's death. In the answer defendant denies that the land was ever sold).

[2] Action by executors, XIX. 101 (Defendant, vendor, was permitted to remain in possession after the purchase price was paid. Vendee died, ordering by his will that the land should be sold. Complainants, executors, have sold the land, but defendant refuses to make estate).

[3] IV. 126 (The widow was in possession, though the price was not paid. She was ousted by the vendors).

[4] XXVII. 83 (In this case part of the price was paid to the heir. This may be a material fact).

[5] XV. 222 (Complainant had paid part of price, had entered into possession, and spent money on the land).

[6] X. 184; XIV. 16; XIX. 59–56, *Cases*, pp. 199–203; XXVIII. 227.

[7] XV. 222 (The vendor by the 'steryng and procurement' of X and Y refused to make estate. Petitioner prays for writs against X and Y as well as the vendor. The chief defendant was not really the vendor, but his successor).

to convey land is broken and damages do not afford an adequate remedy to the disappointed vendee. The land, for some reason, possessed a peculiar value to him ; he may have been ready to pay more than the market price. At all events, what he wants is the land, and not some attempted monetary compensation in its place. Complainants do not always ask in so many words for specific performance,[1] but that such is their real desire may be gathered from the case set out in the petition. We observe, for example, this interesting petition which was brought about 1433 :

Complainant is Chancellor of the University of Cambridge. The university had determined to found a new college, and in consequence an agreement was made between the defendant and complainant that the Chancellor should 'have a place . . . (of the defendant) adioynyng on every side to the ground of the seyd Chaunceller and universite ', and that in exchange the defendant should have ' a noder place therfor lyeing in the sayd toun '. The place to be given in exchange was, according to the petitioner, of greater value. Complainant spent money in endeavouring to carry out the agreement, but the defendant 'of self wille and wythoute any cause ' refused to do his part. The relief sought is that the defendant may be compelled to do 'that trowth, good feith and consciens requiren in this caas'.[2]

The land in this case was especially desired by the university because of its location ; no other piece of land nor any amount of damages would be an indemnity for the loss of the bargain. Furthermore, what damage could be assessed? For the petitioner's own statement, the actual value of the land sought was less than of that offered in exchange. No jury, supposing that there were an action at law, could estimate the damages. Specific performance alone would give relief.

Again, it is a common practice to ask for subpoenas against the feoffees to the use of the vendor as well as against the vendor himself.[3] Where this occurs in connexion with a

---

[1] e. g. complainant asks that the defendant be required to show why he will not make estate : XVI. 645. And see IX. 135 (An agreement was made to exchange benefices. Petitioner is ready to perform his part, but defendant refuses. Relief: 'to sette due remedie for the seide bysecher as reson woll').

[2] XXXIX. 55, *Cases*, p. 221.   [3] P. 120, n. 6.

prayer for a general remedy, we are forced to conclude that the petitioner seeks specific performance and not damages. Otherwise there would be no point in bringing the feoffees before the court. It seems probable, then, that in the majority of cases the petitioner was seeking to compel the vendor to perform his part of the contract, even though he asked merely that he should be compelled to do what reason and conscience required.

We may now turn to the more interesting cases in which performance of the contract is specifically asked for. We find such petitions as early as the reign of Richard II,[1] and by the fifteenth century they have become comparatively common. In the reign of Henry VI there are decrees awarding specific performance, so that we are sure that the chancellor did grant such relief at least as early as the middle of the fifteenth century.[2] The situation of the parties where this relief is demanded is not materially different from that in cases where it is not. However, in all save three of the petitions I have examined, the complainant had paid the whole or a part of the purchase price,[3] but it does not appear that this was essential; sometimes the part of the price advanced, the 'earnest money', was very slight as compared with the price as a whole. The complainant alleges that he has paid part of the price and stands ready to pay the rest, but he does not stress the pre-payment as an especial reason for carrying out the contract. Apparently, it was left for the chancellor to determine whether or no the circumstances of the case demanded a fulfilment of the agreement. Specific performance of an agreement to lease is asked as well as of an agreement to convey.[4] Finally, we should note that in some petitions an attempt is made to obtain the land, though the vendor had already conveyed it to another.[5] The chancellor could not,

---

[1] *Wheler* v. *Huchenden*, 2 Cal. Ch. 2 ; III. 103 (10 S. S. 78). The date of the latter petition cannot be fixed with certainty. It lies either between 1396 and 1399, or between 1401 and 1403.

[2] XXV. 111 (10 S. S. 141), A. D. 1456 ; 2 Cal. Ch. 27 (where the decree is called an award).

[3] Price paid : X. 184 ; XIX. 59–56, *Cases*, pp. 199–203 ; XIX. 101. Part of price paid : IX. 207 ; X. 537. Price not paid : IX. 443 ; XXXI. 189 ; XXVIII. 160.   [4] XXXI. 189 (Parol lease) ; XXXVIII. 160.

[5] X. 184 (Prior conveyance to another 'to disceyve your seide poure

of course, set aside a conveyance; but it is possible that he might require the feoffees to re-convey to the original purchaser.

(*b*) Damages and Rescission of Contract.

On the other hand, complainants appeal to the chancellor where the vendor has put it out of his power to fulfil the contract, as by conveying to a third party.[1] Or again, it may be that the vendor had no estate in the land which he assumed to sell,[2] or the contract may have failed from some other reason.[3] These are cases in which the claim is plainly for damages; but most frequently the complainant is asking that the agreement be rescinded, and that he be restored to his former position. Thus, where the price has been paid, the petitioner asks to be recompensed therefor;[4] or if he has spent money on the land,[5] or has been compelled to make payments,[6] he seeks to recover what he has expended. He asks to receive what equity and good conscience require; in other words, that he may be requited for the loss he has sustained by reason of the defendant's breach of his agreement.

SECTION VII. PROMISES MADE IN CONNEXION WITH MARRIAGE (MARRIAGE SETTLEMENTS)

We have here to consider, not the contract of marriage itself, but promises made, as we should phrase it to-day, in consideration of marriage. Needless to state, these agreements are by parol. The proper form at common law would have been to incorporate the 'accord' in a deed, when the promisee would have had a ready action in the form of Covenant. But only too often the arrangement was made 'without endenture of covenaunt made of the same',[7] and there was no remedy at law unless the promise had been to

---

Oratour...' Subpoenas asked against the vendor and feoffees to whom he had conveyed the land). And see XIX. 59–56, *Cases*, pp. 199–203 (an interesting case with four pleadings).

[1] X. 163.   [2] XIV. 3.

[3] III. 34 (10 S.S. 59). In this case it became impossible to carry out the contract, and complainant asks to be restored to his former position.

[4] X. 163 (Defendant has conveyed to a third party, and petitioner seeks to recover the price paid); XIV. 16; LIX. 86.

[5] XVI. 377.   [6] XIV. 3 (To recover rent paid to the chief lord).

[7] XX. 4.

pay money. If one promised or granted another £10 if he would marry the promisor's daughter, would Debt lie? This question is the subject of endless debates in the Year Books. At first, it is thought that a promise so intimately connected with marriage must be enforced, if at all, in the ecclesiastical courts; later, the judges fall to considering the problem of *quid pro quo*.[1] Despite many dicta to the contrary,[2] it can hardly be regarded as firmly settled that Debt will lie on such a promise until the reign of Elizabeth.[3] There was a decided inclination to allow the action in the fifteenth century; but for one reason or another the chancellor did assume jurisdiction of these cases,[4] perhaps because of wager of law in Debt.[5] Furthermore, if the promise were to make an estate of lands (and in the petitions such are the more frequent), the promisee or beneficiary must find relief in equity or not at all.

The discussion deals with three points: (1) circumstances under which application is made to chancery; (2) the person who brings the subpoena; (3) the relief sought, and the ground on which it is demanded.

1. *Circumstances under which application is made to chancery.*

These petitions reveal an interesting, if rudimentary, form of marriage settlement. The agreement is entirely informal and by parol. This can be better appreciated from a case which happily sets forth the facts with some detail:

A marriage was arranged between Richard Dryffeld and Denys, daughter of Thomas Sele.[6] Dryffeld, the petitioner, states that William Brampton, the defendant, made the 'contracte of Marriage by his owne pursuyng by twene the seid Richard and Denys'; but this is denied by the defendant, who asserts that the said Richard 'laboured to þe seid Thomas, faþer of þe seid Denys ... of his owen desire willing to have her to wife'. At all events it was agreed that the

---

[1] Holmes, Common Law, 268.
[2] e.g. Danvers J., in Y. B. 37 Hen. VI. 8. 18.
[3] See Ames, H. L. R., viii. 262; *Applethwaite* v. *Northby*, Cro. El. 29.
[4] e.g. XVI. 334 (Petitioner says he has no remedy at law; this is repeated in most of the other cases); XVI. 386, *Cases*, p. 197; XXVIII. 299, *Cases*, p. 213; XXIX. 254; LIX. 65; LIX. 132–3, 137–9, *Cases*, pp. 227–230; LXXI. 7–8, *Cases*, pp. 233–234.
[5] XVI. 386, *Cases*, p. 197.   [6] LXXI. 7, *Cases*, p. 233.

parties interested should meet and discuss a settlement.
Brampton, as cousin of Denys, represented her. The petitioner
asked for twenty marks 'wᵗ the seid Denys'; to which
Brampton answered, 'in the name of þe seid Thomas and his
frendes þat yf þe seid Richard wold have þe seid Denys to
wyf that he and all the frendes of þe seid Denys wold make
hir worth x marc in money and in godes.' Dryffeld agreed
and the marriage took place.[1]

The promise in this case was made directly to one of the
parties to the marriage ; but, as other petitions show, it might
have been made to his father in his behalf. Especially is this
true where the person in whose favour the promise was made
was the daughter.[2] A and B agree that A's daughter shall
marry B's son, and B promises A that he will make an estate
of lands and tenements to the son and daughter on the
marriage. Thus :

Agreement ('accorde') was made between petitioner on the
one side and John Drayton and his son on the other, that
the son should marry petitioner's daughter, and that after the
marriage, John Drayton should make an estate to the son
and daughter and their heirs. The marriage took place, issue
were born, and the son died, 'le dit estat nient fait'. John
Drayton refused to make estate ; petitioner asks for a subpoena.[3]

The cases fall naturally into two groups :

(a) The promisor has received some substantial benefit in
return for his promise.[4] This is the result of a family arrangement. A's daughter is to marry B's son. B agrees to enfeoff

---

[1] The amount to be paid is in dispute. Petitioner contends it was 10
marks in money, and 10 marks 'in howsold'. Defendant in his answer
says it was 10 marks in money *and* household (LXXI. 8, *Cases*, p. 234).
[2] e.g. XV. 20 *a*-20 *b*, *Cases*, pp. 189-191 ; XV. 140 *a*-141, *Cases*,
pp. 192-194. [3] VII. 250, *Cases*, p. 179.
[4] III. 104 (10 S. S. 43) ; IX. 448 (Defendant was one of the parties to
the marriage) ; XV. 140 *a*-141, *Cases*, pp. 192-194 (Facts were in dispute ;
after petitioner brought his first petition a 'trete was taken', and arbitrators appointed ; one abitrator at defendant's instigation refused to attach
his seal to the award. Hence the second petition, No. 141) ; XXVIII. 52
(Petitioner paid defendant 160 marks ; he says furthermore that the marriage took place 'to the grete costagies' of himself) ; LIX. 132-3, 137-9,
Cases, pp. 227-230 (An action against the executors of the promisor. Petitioner failed to join all the necessary parties ; hence the second petition.
In the answer, the defendants make denial of facts alleged by petitioner) ;
LXIX. 98.

the son and daughter of certain lands on their marriage, 'for the whech marriage and estates to be made ',[1] A agrees to pay B a sum of money. B does not carry out his promise, and A brings a subpoena and prays relief. The marriage was not the sole inducement to the promise.

(b) The promise is gratuitous, that is, the promisor gains no direct benefit from making it. It is said to be made 'for the marriage', or, taking the petitioner's point of view, the marriage was made 'on the faith of' the promise.[2] These cases are more interesting and, so far as my observation goes, more numerous.[3] We have direct and convincing evidence that the chancellor did enforce such a promise.[4] Ordinarily, the promisor is the father of one of the parties to the marriage ; but there are petitions where there was no relationship connecting the promisor with the husband and wife for whose benefit the promise was made.[5]

2. *The person who brings the subpoena.*

Naturally, in the majority of cases this is the promisee, even though he were not a party to the marriage. The father claims damages or asks for specific performance on behalf of his son or daughter as the case may be. The promise was made to him, and his is the right to enforce it. But equity went beyond this. Not only did the subpoena come to the rescue of the promisee, but the *beneficiary* might use it.[6] He was not a party to the contract, but the contract was made for his benefit. This is a matter of great interest ; for we know that the beneficiary could not bring Assumpsit,[7] and that when Consideration came to be an accepted doctrine, it

---

[1] XV. 20 a–20 b, *Cases*, pp. 189–191 (Relief is prayed against the defendant and his feoffees ; 20 b is the answer of the feoffees, who aver that they are ready to make estate, so soon as certain matters in debate between petitioner and defendant are settled).

[2] IX. 401 (Petitioner says that he ' trusting to the faithful accorde and promys of the said William was maried to the seid Maud ').

[3] VII. 250, *Cases*, p. 179 ; IX. 401 ; XV. 116 ; XVI. 277 ; XVI. 334 ; XVI. 386, *Cases*, p. 197 ; XX. 4 ; XXV. 111 (10 S. S. 141) ; LIX. 65.

[4] XXV. 111 (10 S. S. 141) [Endorsed with order for specific performance].

[5] XV. 116 ; XXIX. 254.

[6] The beneficiary is the petitioner : XV. 20 a, *Cases*, p. 189 (Promisee and beneficiary are petitioners) ; XXVIII. 299, *Cases*, p. 213 ; LIX. 65 (Promise made to petitioner's father).

[7] *Crow* v. *Rogers*, 1 Strange 592.

was held that it must move from the promisee. But there is strong evidence that the rights of the beneficiary were protected in equity; we shall consider this more at length in discussing the principles upon which the chancellor acted.[1]

3. *The relief sought and the ground upon which it is demanded.*

(*a*) Relief.

For the most part the prayers are couched in general terms; the petitioner desires to have the defendant before the chancellor to show why he 'should not be content after promys made be twix them',[2] but he asks only that the defendant be compelled to do what reason and conscience require. Of course, what is really sought is specific performance; and thus we find it specifically asked that the defendant be compelled to pay the money[3] or convey the land[4] in accordance with his promise. At all events, there was an especial reason why the defendant should be compelled to carry out his promise in these cases. Specific performance was the only relief which was adequate. Often the petitioner, though the promisee, is not the beneficiary. Obviously he is not seeking damages, but rather asking that the beneficiary's rights may be protected. Judging the pleadings as a whole, we conclude that the petitioners are seeking to hold the defendant to his promise; and that the chancellor did grant an order for specific performance. In the interesting case[5] which is endorsed, it is noteworthy that the petitioner was content to set up the material facts, and trust to the chancellor; a decree for specific performance was made.

(*b*) The ground on which the relief is demanded.

Though, as we have seen, there is a class of cases in which the promisor has obtained a pecuniary benefit for making his promise, it is nowhere suggested that the promise should be enforced on that account. It is true that complainants allege that they have been put to expense on account of the marriage,

---

[1] *Infra*, p. 164.   [2] LXXI. 7, *Cases*, p. 233.
[3] LIX. 139, *Cases*, p. 230.
[4] XV. 20 *a*, *Cases*, p. 189 (The relief was prayed against the defendant's feoffees as well as the defendant).   [5] XXV. 111 (10 S. S. 141).

or that they paid money for the conveyance; but even in these cases stress is always laid on the fact that the promise was made 'for the marriage'. The facts of the case are such that there was a legitimate 'cause' for the defendant's promise; he made it deliberately, and has led the petitioner or beneficiary to act on the strength of it. Reason and conscience require that he should carry it out. In consequence, it does not matter whether the promisee or the beneficiary is the petitioner. A promise made to another in the interest of the beneficiary, confers a right in equity upon the latter, just as much as if it were made to him directly. There may have been another factor. In most instances the promisor is closely related to one of the parties of the marriage; that is, there is the element of blood and natural affection. But I believe that marriage alone was a sufficient cause for the promise, and there are petitions which support this.[1] Whether this may be so or no, it seems to be clear that a promise made 'in consideration'[2] of marriage, at least when the promisor was bound by ties of family to one of the parties to the marriage, was enforceable in equity in the fifteeenth century.

SECTION VIII. PARTNERSHIP

The cases considered in this section relate to arrangements of a humble nature; two people have simply put their stock of goods together to be managed for their common profit. The control of the property may have been in the hands of one partner, or of both, but one has kept all the profits and refuses to give the other his rightful share. The arrangement might be confined to one transaction. For example: A and B were taken prisoners in Brittany and lost all their goods. They bought a ship and goods of C, and B remained with C

---

[1] XV. 116 (Defendant promised to make an estate to R and S, petitioner's daughter, on their marriage; in consequence of the promise petitioner married his daughter to R); XIX. 347-346, *Cases*, pp. 203-204 (Defendant promised to pay J's debts when he married J); XXIX. 254 (Defendant in recompense for certain wrongs done to petitioner, promised to pay a certain sum of money for the marriage of E. There is no evidence that petitioner or defendant was related to E).

[2] I use the word without any technical significance.

' in plege' for himself and A, while A returned to England to sell the goods. It was agreed that A should come back to Brittany and pay C with the money received from the sale of the goods, the residue after that payment to be divided between A and B. There remained £17, but A refused to give B his share; consequently B asked for a subpoena against A.[1]

The example given is not, speaking strictly, a true case of partnership; for partnership implies a relation between persons carrying on a *business* in common with a view of profit.[2] It does, however, raise the same kind of question which is presented in the following petitions :

A was 'partyng felawe in biyng and sellyng in certeyn marchaundyse' with B. They both sold certain cloth to C, who was bound therefor in an obligation, which was delivered to B. By virtue of possession of the obligation, B received £10, but refused to give A his share, ' as right and consciens requireth.'[3]

A and B were pedlars and had their goods together for some six years. B has kept all the increase, and A cannot get any part thereof by common law, 'where by their covenaunt he shuld have the half'.[4]

A and B ' were possessed iointly' of certain fish which were to be sold 'to their bother use '. B sold the fish, ' and noon accompte ' will render to A.[5]

A and B had goods together to be used to their common profit. B, contrary to 'reason and conscience', converted the goods to his own use. B refuses to give A his share (a half of the profit, &c.).[6]

These examples are sufficient without more to show the kind of case which came before the chancellor.[7] Petitioners

---

[1] XI. 506; see also IX. 39 (A and B agreed that B should buy wood to their common use, A paying a part of the price. B sold the wood to C, and refused to give A his share of the proceeds).

[2] Cf. the definition in the Partnership Act, 1890 (53 & 54 Vict. c. 39), s. I (I).

[3] XXIX. 516.   [4] IX. 382, *Cases*, p. 182.

[5] XIX. 26, *Cases*, p. 199.   [6] XXVIII. 378.

[7] For other examples, see VII. 186 (Ship owned by A and B, but under B's management; B sold the ship and will not give A his share of the proceeds); IX. 131 (An agreement to share profits); XXVII. 84 (Ship owned by A and B ; A had the management of the ship and kept all the profits. B seeks to recover his share).

usually rest content with asserting that the goods were
held in common, to be employed to the use of both parties,
without alleging any express promise on the part of the
defendant to pay over the just share. The question, then, is not
one between the partners and third parties, but rather one of
accounting between themselves. No action at law met this
situation. One partner could not charge the other as factor
or receiver, for obviously there was no such relationship.[1] He
could not bring Debt, for he could not claim a share of the
profits as his sole property; moreover, a difficulty of pleading
stood in the way. One partner could not sue another at law
in a matter involving the partnership business. It was this gap
in the common law which was supplied by the chancellor's
intervention. The law could handle adequately matters
arising from dealings between partners and third parties; but
in questions which arose between themselves, chancery
assumed in the fifteenth century a jurisdiction which it retained till modern times.

The principle upon which equity acted is simple and plain.
The property was held jointly; even without an express
agreement the situation of the parties conferred upon each
a right to a share of the profits. This right equity enforced.

Section IX. Agency

The contract of Agency as we see it in the Year Books is
very rudimentary. By deed, one might appoint another to do
many acts in his name; but it is in informal agency, which
existed without speciality, that we are primarily interested.
Any such contract by an agent must find enforcement, if at
all, in the action of Debt; in consequence, it was limited by
the requirements of *quid pro quo*. Thus in all cases of sale to
an agent, it was necessary to show that the goods sold went
to the benefit of the principal. We read that an abbot is
chargeable on the deed of his monk made for goods furnished,
which went to the use of the convent; but it is to be noted

---

[1] Pollock, Contracts (7th ed.), 140 (citing F. N. B. 117 D), says one
partner might bring Account against another. But the principle upon
which this was allowed is not stated, nor are any cases cited.

that he is not charged as for the act of his agent. Unless it be shown that he obtained the benefit, Debt would not lie; and this means that the contract was unenforceable. Of the undisclosed principal or the doctrine of ratification we read nothing.

The chancery material does not present many petitions directly concerned with Agency, but we find that the contract received wider recognition than at law. If goods were sold to an agent, and went to the use and profit of the principal, the principal was chargeable.[1] But the chancellor went further than this. If one held out another as his agent, and he were generally so known, then the principal was bound to pay for goods or money furnished to the agent for his use. That is, the goods must be supplied to the agent for his principal, but it was not necessary to prove that the goods actually were received by the principal. Thus:

Petitioner at 'Brugges' delivered £100 to M, 'factour and attorney veryly knowyn un to John Warde, . . . to the use of his seid Maister, to be repaied agen at London'. M. made out a bill 'signed with his Masteres Mark', witnessing the loan 'after the cours of Merchaundice'. Warde, however, refused to pay; petitioner alleges that this is 'contrarie to the Cours of trewe Marchaundice' and prays for a remedy.[2]

This is a definite step in advance. M was held out as an agent; he was engaged in commercial transactions for his principal, and consequently from that fact the principal became liable. Moreover, we note the stress which is laid upon the phrase 'the cours of Marchaundice'. The whole fabric of commercial dealings rested upon the validity of such arrangements; and it was the chancellor rather than the judges who gave recognition to the claims of the 'lex mercatoria'.

[1] VII. 112, *Cases*, p. 14. Probably this case is in equity because the facts are so in dispute. Note that petitioner asks for a subpoena against the agent as well as the principal.

[2] XXVIII. 210, *Cases*, p. 178; XXIX. 317 (Goods were sold to Thomas Savage 'in the name of Roger Chedwyk . . . the same Thomas at that tyme beyng Factour and attourney to the same Roger . . . whiche Thomas occupied at that tyme all feates of marchaundises at Andewarp . . . as Factour and Attourney of the seid Roger, And so he there was taken and reputed . . .' Roger refused to pay, and the vendor appeals to equity).

But this is not all. One petition, at least, shows a recognition of the rights of an undisclosed principal. A's servant bought goods of B, using A's money. The servant died, and B refused to deliver the goods to A. A came to equity and prayed for a subpoena against B, alleging that the servant had acted in his behalf and made the purchase with his money.[1] It does not appear that B knew he was dealing indirectly with A. The undisclosed principal was unprotected at law till much later.[2] It is surely interesting that he seeks to obtain relief in equity at an earlier period.

Again, there is recognition of the obligation of the principal on a broader ground. A principal could be bound by the act of his agent, though the authority were given by parol,[3] and though that authority were given subsequent to the act. There is what appears to be a clear case of ratification. A son made an obligation assuming to bind his father. Whether or no he had authority at the time of making the obligation is not certain, but afterwards the father acknowledged and expressly sanctioned the son's act. The chancellor decreed that he should be held.[4]

SECTION X. GUARANTEE (SURETYSHIP) AND INDEMNITY

The petitions which we are to consider under this heading do not present such nice questions of discrimination between guarantee and indemnity as later arose in connexion with the construction of the fourth section of the Statute of Frauds.[5] The facts are simple, and the classification is not perplexing. Briefly stated, a contract of guarantee or suretyship implies a relation between three parties; the creditor can fall back

---

[1] VII. 201.

[2] See Holmes, History of Agency, Anglo-Am. iii. 392, citing *Scrimshire* v. *Alderton*, 2 Strange 1182.

[3] See XLIV. 163 (Relief on a 'promise to save harmlese', made by an agent for his principal).

[4] XXIX. 13-4, *Cases*, pp. 214-19.   There were other facts in the case, as will appear later in the discussion.   The 'bill' made by the son was merely in proof of the furnishing of goods; but it was allowed as a set-off against the father.   The son expressly says he acted throughout as agent (XXIX. No. 9).

[5] e.g. *Sutton* v. *Grey* [1894] 1 Q. B. 285 ; 63 L. J. (Q. B.) 633.

upon the promisor only in case the principal debtor makes default. In other words, the promisor's liability is contingent and secondary. An indemnity, on the other hand, is a promise to save another harmless from any liability through a transaction into which he enters at the request of the promisor.[1]

Neither guarantee nor indemnity were valid by parol at common law in the fifteenth century. Though there is evidence that a contract of suretyship might have been established without a writing in the Norman period,[2] it became settled by the reign of Edward III that a deed was necessary.[3] Indeed, it appears from an interesting case in the Eyre of Kent that resort was had to the clumsy method of making the surety a principal debtor by affixing his seal to the bond.[4] Certainly this would not have been attempted, had it been possible to charge him without writing. The common law therefore appears to have repudiated any nice distinction between primary and secondary liability. At all events, the parol contract of guarantee was not recognized till the time of Henry VIII.[5] Nor was indemnity a valid parol contract during our period.

We turn, therefore, with some interest to the petitions in equity. Those involving indemnity are quite numerous; I can present but a few relating to suretyship.[6]

1. *Contract of Suretyship or Guarantee.*

1443–1450.[7] One Lawrence Walker bought cloth of petitioner for £8, ' for whiche payment as woll and trewely to be made ... (defendant) . . . undurtoke and bykome borowe for the seide Lawrence, in as muche as the seide supliant nold nothur have

---

[1] Anson, Contracts (11th ed.), 74.
[2] See Holmes, Common Law, 260, citing Glanv. x, c. 5.
[3] Y. B. 44 Ed. III 21–3 (cited Holmes, Common Law, 264, n. 4).
[4] *Bokeland* v. *Leanore*, Y. B. 6 & 7 Ed. II. [S.S.] 9.
[5] Y. B. B. 12 H. VIII, Mich. pl. 3 ; 27 H. VIII, Mich. pl. 3 (cited Holdsworth, iii. 342, n. 4).
[6] This is not to be understood to mean that there were very few such petitions ; rather that in the limited time at my disposal I was only able to transcribe a few.
[7] XIV. 5, *Cases*, p. 188. Certain phrases in the petition seem to indicate that the defendant was primarily liable ; if that were so, this would not be a case of suretyship. However, reading the pleading as a whole, I interpret it as a contract of guarantee.

sold nor delyverode the seide clothe unto the seide Lawrence butt only uppon trust of the seide . . .' (defendant). £3 remained unpaid. The debtor has gone to 'strange places unknowen', and petitioner, having no remedy against the defendant at common law, comes to the chancellor and prays to 'have dewe remedy'.

c. 1475.[1] Petitioner sold kerseys to Thomas Ashley for £10; and for security of payment 'Thomas Goselyn at the time of the makyng of the said bargayn was and became suerte . . . (to petitioner) . . . and then graunted and promittid to the same William (petitioner) that if the seid Thomas Asshley paid not to hym the seid x li . . . that then the seid Thomas Gosselyn wold pay . . .' Petitioner is particular to state that he sold the kerseys trusting to Gosselyn's promise. Ashley paid £5 and then went to 'places unknowen', and Gosselyn refused to pay. Petitioner prays for a subpoena against Gosselyn. Gosselyn in his answer[2] sets up other facts, tending to show that the original debt is discharged.

We cannot draw strong inferences from two petitions. Two facts, however, should be noted. The creditor alleges in each case that he extended credit only upon the strength of the defendant's promise. Again, that promise was an important part of the original transaction. We observe, furthermore, that the petitioner has exhausted his remedies against the principal debtor before he turns to the surety. This seems to be of importance; for sureties did appeal to the chancellor because the creditor is seeking to hold them, when the principal debtors are able to pay,[3] or before the principal debt is due.[4] The remedy sought was a Certiorari. I believe that a parol contract of suretyship was recognized and enforced in equity, at least where the creditor could show that the defendant's promise was the inducement to the extension of credit to the principal debtor. On the other hand, equity was jealous of the surety's rights; his liability was strictly secondary, and he might use any defences open to the principal

---

[1] LIX. 140.

[2] LIX. 141. He also alleges that he became surety to petitioner only on condition that Ashley should find security that he should be saved harmless.

[3] XXIX. 462 (The surety was a joint obligor with the principal debtor. The creditor brought suit on the obligation at common law).

[4] LIX. 61.

debtor.[1] These promises were gratuitous. We note this in passing, but reserve it for later consideration.

2. *Indemnity.*

This represents a common arrangement. A desires a loan of money from B. B, however, is unwilling to give credit to A alone; in consequence, A goes to his friend C, and induces C to become jointly bound with him to B, at the same time promising to save C harmless as against B.[2] Or under similar circumstances C might become bound separately to B.[3] There are two distinctive features common to all these cases; C has become bound to B, not for his own duty but for A's; he became bound at A's instance, and relying upon A's parol promise to save him harmless.[4] This parol promise received no recognition at common law. I believe, for reasons that will be stated presently, that it was enforced in equity.

In the example above given, the promise to save harmless was express. But it need not necessarily have been so. Indeed, one petitioner, though he became bound at the defendant's instance and on the faith of his promise, puts his claim to a remedy on a broader ground; for he asks the chancellor to consider ' how that reson and good conscience wold that, sith your seid besecher was *for and by* the seid Thomas Oldebury (the defendant and promisor) *put in charge*, that the same Thomas should him *discharge*'.[5] In other words, requesting one to become bound in your behalf for your duty raises an implied promise to discharge him. And so we find petitioners relying upon the situation of the parties as their ground for equitable relief; the defendant may have promised expressly to protect them, but they do not allege any promise in the petition. The following extract from

---

[1] This I infer from LIX. 141, p. 134, note 2. And see XXXI. 82, *Cases,* p. 96.

[2] X. 207, *Cases,* p. 184 ; X. 242 ; XIX. 224.

[3] XIX. 91 ; XXXI. 116–17 ; LIX. 104 ; LIX. 123.

[4] Petitioners express this in various ways : X. 207, *Cases,* p. 184 (' at Instaunce and prayer of William Brompton . . . And opon ful promise to kepe him harmelesse ') ; XIX. 91 (Defendant promised ' on his faith and troueth to keep him harmless . . . for any suit or vexacon that should be hadde . . .') ; XIX. 224 (' by the steryng request and excitacion . . .').

[5] XIX. 204.

a petition is a fair example. Complainant thinks it sufficient to say that ' . . . where as your said besecher atte request and praier of on Thomas Mauleson was bound in on obligacyon of xvj li. iij s. x d. to on John Throkmorton, Esquier, and for defaute of nounpayment of the seid soum the said John sued your said beseecher . . . and now your said besecher hath content the party . . . and non parcell of the said soum his dute but dute of the said Thomas . . .'.[1]

Whether the promise were express or implied the defendant has received a substantial benefit. But we may go further; the promisor will be made to fulfil his promise even though it is gratuitous. If he induces one upon the strength of his promise to become bound for the duty of *another*, the chancellor will require him to fulfil his promise. This comes out in an interesting case, which is endorsed with judgement:

X sold certain goods to Y for £240. Complainants at the ' speciall instance and praier ' of Z became bound to X for the duty of Y. Z promised that they should be saved harmless. Z died ; X has taken an action on the obligation against complainants, and they are like to have to pay the sum. They therefore appeal to the chancellor and ask that defendants (Z's executors) may be compelled to protect them against X. Defendants in their answer [2] asserted that this was not a proper case for relief ; they then proceeded to deny the facts alleged in the petition. The chancellor, however, after ' good and ripe deliberation ', ordered that the defendants should ' acquit and discharge ' the petitioners against X for the sum, as alleged in the petition.[3]

---

[1] XVI. 440. In the following cases the petitioners allege that they became bound at the defendant's request, but no express promise to save harmless is set out : X. 186; X. 242; XV. 237.

[2] XLIV. 143, *Cases*, p. 224.

[3] XLIV. 142, *Cases*, p. 222. XLIV. 263 is a parallel case, but the petition is not endorsed. The defendant, late Prior of B., ' sent his owne servaunte . . . unto your seyd Oratours that they wull do at the Instaunce of the same late priour so myche to be seurte and undertake for on William Ecford . . . unto John Ellys of London, Mercer, for the some of [£5 13s. 4d.] and the same late priour grauntid be the same servaunt and messenger . . . to save them harmeles for the seyd some in peyne of xl li . . .' Petitioners became bound as sureties and had to pay the debt, after which they sent to the defendant ' for to content us (i. e. petitioners) acordyng to his promys and he denyth and bed us shewe owre specialte, and so we ar w^t owte Remady at the comon lawe of ony accion a yenst the same late priour for to be taken, wyth owte your gracious lordschip . . .' Petitioners pray for

There can be no doubt about the decision in this case. And reasoning back from this, we have strong reason to believe that relief was granted in the other cases. For if the chancellor held that one must fulfil his promise, where he thereby induced another to become bound for the duty of a third party, *a fortiori* he would hold him to his promise where the duty was his own. It is submitted with confidence that the contract of indemnity received clear recognition in chancery in the fifteenth century.

As the promise was to save the petitioner harmless, it became broken the moment suit was threatened or begun against the promisee. Payment of the obligation was not a condition precedent to bringing the subpoena. In consequence, the relief sought varies with the circumstances. Where the petitioner has been compelled to pay, he demands repayment of the sum,[1] and even of the costs sustained in defending a suit.[2] Where he is merely threatened with suit, or in the language of the pleaders, is being 'vexed', he asks that the promisor be compelled to fulfil his promise literally, that is, that protection be afforded.[3] We have seen that the chancellor might so rule.[4]

In conclusion, we may remark that the executors of the promisor were held to be bound by the promise, at least where they had in their hands assets of the deceased.[5]

SECTION XI. AGREEMENTS OF A GENERAL CHARACTER

The following cases, heterogeneous as they are, are connected by one common trait. The promise is for the performance of a definite act; the breach of the promise, with one or two exceptions, arises through failure to act at all. The agreements are all by parol, and are very informal in

---

a subpoena against the defendant, and such relief as accords with reason and conscience.

[1] IX. 411 (The obligee 'coarted the said bisecher by processe of lawe to contente him') ; X. 242 ; XIX. 224 (Petitioner has been ' arted to content' the obligee, and now demands repayment from the defendant) ; XXXI. 116–17 (Petitioner asks that defendant be compelled to pay) ; LIX. 104.

[2] XVI. 440.   [3] X. 207 ; XIX. 91 ; LIX. 123.

[4] XLIV. 142, *Cases*, p. 222.

[5] X. 186 ; XLIV. 142, *Cases*, p. 222 ; XLIV. 263 ; LIX. 104.

nature. None of the petitions is endorsed, and to that extent
the evidence is unsatisfactory. But no class of cases better
illustrates the wide scope of the chancellor's jurisdiction.
An agreement is made to deliver a letter or to transport goods.
For lack of formality it does not fall within the narrow range
of contracts enforceable by the common law. Yet these
contracts must have been very common. The absence of
a postal service and of any established system of common
carriers compelled the employment of private individuals.
Unless these could be held to perform their promises great
confusion would result. Herein there was scope for the
intervention of equity. I have attempted in a rough way to
classify the cases.

1. Agreements for Personal Services.

(a) *Promise to erect a building.*

The two following petitions recall many of the fifteenth-
century cases in Assumpsit, where it was sought to charge
the promisor for non-performance of his promise.[1]   The promisor has not begun the work and left it incomplete; he has
done nothing at all.   But there is one thing which differentiates
these petitions from their counterparts at common law: the
absence of any specific undertaking.   In the first case it is
simply said that an agreement was made; in the other the
defendant said that he *would* do a certain thing.   To distinguish the latter from an express undertaking may seem
captious, but the famous resolution in Slade's[2] case should
not be forgotten.

The church at K. had fallen into disrepair, and an agreement was made with the defendant 'q'il duist faire l'avaunt
dite esglise bien et covenablement estre fait, reedifie . . . et
reparaille'.   He was to receive 320 marks, of which 280 have
been paid; but nothing has been done, and the chancel of the
church is in such bad condition that it is like to fall at any
moment, to the great damage of the parishioners, the petitioners.

---

[1] e. g. Y. B. 2 H. IV. 3. 9.
[2] 4 Co. Rep., 92 a.   The judges thought it necessary to say specifically
that 'when one agrees to pay money or to deliver anything, thereby he
assumes to pay or deliver it '.

There is no remedy at law, and the chancellor is asked to grant relief.[1]

O. was in prison for non-payment of damages in an action of Waste, brought by petitioner for the burning of a mill. Defendant came to petitioner and said that if O. were discharged he would rebuild the mill at his own cost. Petitioner discharged O., but defendant has not built the mill, and still refuses to do so, 'contrarie to his seid promyse, good feithe and conciens'. Petitioner asks that he be . . . 'rewled and Juged as good conciens requyreth '.[2]

It is not perfectly clear whether the relief sought is damages or specific performance. Probably in the case of the church the parishioners were seeking to compel the defendant to fulfil the agreement. Even in modern times equity will decree specific performance of a contract to do work, under certain circumstances.[3] Whichever remedy were granted, relief would be afforded where there was no remedy at law.

(b) *Carriage and Delivery of Goods.*

The absence of any established system of transportation comes out vividly in the following cases. In each, goods have been entrusted to the defendant, to be conveyed to a certain place.

Petitioners are John Lakeham and Alice his wife. Lakeham was in prison in London, and sent to his wife, who was then at home in Sussex, asking her to bring his goods to London so that he might be 'socourid and holpe with his seide godes '. Alice, then, ' for the gret trust . . . that she had in on John Taylour, made covenaunt' with him to take the goods to 'Wynchilseye', whence they were to be taken to London by water. Taylour came and took the goods, promising to carry them to the destination, but instead took them to his own house, where they still are. Petitioners are destitute, and come to equity praying that they may ' be restoryd to there seide goodys '.[4]

' Acorde se prist' between petitioner and defendant that defendant should carry certain goods of the petitioner in a ship from London to Colchester. Contrary to the ' acorde' defendant took the ship to a place 'deinz la fraunchise de la

---

[1] VI. 21, *Cases*, p. 176.   [2] LIX. 114, *Cases*, p. 225.
[3] See Maitland, Equity, 239–40.   [4] XII. 84.

count d'oxenford', where the goods were seized 'par les officers le dit count', to the great damage of petitioner. He prays that defendant be made to find surety to recover the goods and take them to Colchester, as agreed.[1]

Petitioner delivered to defendant two horses and certain goods to be delivered to his wife in England. Delivery was never made, to petitioner's damage, for which he asks remedy.[2]

Petitioner 'fretta en la nief le dit John Dekene (defendant) ... xx ton de frument pur deliverer a burdeux (Bordeaux)'. Defendant discharged the grain at Plymouth, to the damage of petitioner in 'C li et plus', whereof he prays remedy.[3]

These are cases of misfeasance, and it is notorious that an action lay at law, where there was an undertaking. Why, then, are they in equity? Probably, in the first example, because the petitioner is in prison and in great poverty, which prevented his bringing an action at law. In the second, the relief sought is not damages, but that the defendant should find surety to carry out the accord, that is, in effect, specific performance. In the third, the contract was made out of England,[4] while, in the last case, there was no specific undertaking. The acceptance of goods for transportation seems in equity to have implied a promise to carry them to the intended destination. Such was not the case at law.

(c) *Special Services.*

As examples of what may be called special personal services, I have selected three petitions: A desires to send a letter to B; there is no regular post, and if the letter is to be taken some private person must be employed. C presents himself and promises to take the letter. He makes default.[5] There is no definite misfeasance, such as confronts one in the common law cases. Yet, as damage has ensued to A from

---

[1] X. 328.

[2] VI. 59. There was a further term in the contract: that defendant might keep the horses if he paid 10 marks. He never made such payment.   [3] XII. 181.

[4] It is alleged that there is no remedy at law, but no reason is assigned.

[5] XV. 52, *Cases*, p. 191. The case is complicated by other facts; namely, that the defendant was in collusion with persons who had received petitioners' goods. However, in the prayer, they seek to charge him for non-delivery of the letter, which seems to be the essential point. The claim for £1000 damages for the loss of goods valued at £500 is certainly strange.

the failure to deliver the letter, there ought to be some remedy. Again, A's servants are imprisoned abroad ; A goes to B, and agreement is made that B shall ransom the servants and deliver them out of prison. B receives forty marks, but does nothing. In consequence, the servants suffer, are 'distressez, stokkes et malement tretes', because the ransom is not forthcoming.[1] B, however, is at most guilty of a non-feasance. A would find cold comfort in seeking to charge him in Assumpsit.[2] In these two cases it is quite clear that there is no remedy at law. The third case is not quite so clear. A 'withheld with our sovereigne lorde þe kynge' one B to do service on the sea. B received his wages from A, but nevertheless deserted, which put A to 'right grete and notable Cost and losse of his gudes'. It is not perfectly obvious why A did not have an adequate remedy at common law.[3]

2. Agreements for the Compromise of Claims, &c.

Under this general heading I have put cases in which the parties made some arrangement with regard to a suit, or submitted themselves to an award.

(1) *Cases of ' award '*.

(*a*) Promise to 'stand by' an award :

A and B are in dispute as to their respective rights in certain lands. They are about to go to law, when 'by mediacon of frundis' the parties agree to stand by the award of certain arbitrators. The award is made: A carries out his part, or stands ready so to do, but B refuses. The common law, of course, afforded no means of compulsion, but A can present a strong case in equity.[4]

(*b*) Promise of arbitrators to make an award in a particular way :

Certain matters were in dispute between A and B, who agreed to submit to the award of defendants. Defendants

---

[1] XII. 201, *Cases*, p. 188.   [2] i. e. in the fifteenth century.

[3] XVI. 285 (1442). It may be that, as the cause of action was for desertion, the king would be regarded as interested. That would explain the presence of the case before the chancellor.

[4] X. 264 (Petitioner stands ready to perform his part, and has paid certain money to defendant); XV. 181 *a*–181 *c*, *Cases*, pp. 195–7 (Defendant in his answer says that the matter alleged is not sufficient to put him to answer ; petitioner replies that it is).

made promise to A 'apon their feith, trouth and honeste that
if they made ony awarde betwyxt the seid parties ... that
they should delyver the same awards in Wrytyng' to each
of the parties. A, giving ' full feithe And credence' to this
promise, became bound to submit to the award. The award
was made, but not in writing; and A and B fell into dispute
as to its terms, whereupon A requested defendants to commit
the award to writing at his cost 'according to their promise',
but defendants refused. A prayed for a subpoena and asked
that defendants might be compelled 'to delyver the seide
awarde in Wrytynge ... accordyng to their seid promyse or
else to make certayn reporte therof afore the Kyng in his
Chauncerye ther to be entrid of Recorde'.[1]

The defendant's promise was gratuitous, but it was the
inducement which led to A's changing his position. Moreover, great damage will ensue to A if the promise be not
fulfilled, because of the dispute about the terms of the award.

(2) *Agreements concerning litigation.*

A and B made an agreement that A should bring trespass
against B, and that B should appear in person or by attorney,
and plead as the counsel of A should wish; and after judgement A should release damages to B. The purpose of this
fictitious suit is not clear. A brought the action, B appeared
and pleaded as was desired, with the result that A obtained
judgement for £40. Afterwards A refused to release the £40
contrary to the agreement and ' encountre bon foie et conciens '.
B prays for relief.[2]

A had brought an action of trespass against B, for whom
C became surety. A promised B to 'take respyte and
sparynge of the callyng uppon the said action', till B had
gone abroad and returned. B went away, and now A, contrary
to his promise, 'calleth uppon the said accion,' and intends
to obtain judgement by default. C, the surety, appeals to the
chancellor and prays relief.[3]

(3) *Performance of a specific act, in general.*

This heading is not very happily chosen, but it may serve
to introduce certain cases not easily classified. The defendant
has promised expressly or by implication to do a certain
thing for the petitioner, and has refused subsequently to
do it.

[1] XXXI. 118.   [2] X. 163.   [3] XXXI. 82, *Cases*, p. 219.

A gave all his ' goodys and catelle' to B, to the intent that
B should furnish him with ' mete and drynke and cloth ' during
his life.   B took possession of the goods, but refuses to supply
A with meat and drink 'agens all good feith and concyense'.[1]
Again, A induced B to resign his prebend, promising to make
him sure of a pension of the value of the said prebend; B
resigned, and A refused to fulfil his promise.[2]

Agreement is made to procure a release on the payment
of 26s.; the money is paid, but the release is not forthcoming.[3]
A agreed to surrender a patent (Rangership of the New
Forest) so that B might obtain the same, if B would pay him
£20; B paid the money, A refused to surrender the patent.[4]
' Covenaunt and accord' was made between A and B that
A should surrender 'la garde de Stanke de Fosse deinz le
Counte D'everwyk', so that B might obtain the same, in
return for which B should make A sure of an annual pension
for life.   B stood ready to perform his part, but A would not
give up the ' garde'.[5]

In these cases we have the promise of the performance of
an act in return for money paid, goods delivered, or some
act performed or to be performed.   None of the promises are
gratuitous; there is clearly a consideration, but again, as the
defendant has refused to act at all, as the contract is to that
extent executory, the disappointed petitioner is remediless at
common law.

---

[1] IX. 162 (1438).   [2] XII. 197.   [3] XXXI. 374, *Cases*, p. 220.
      [4] LIX. 10.   [5] X. 276.

CHAPTER III

PROCEDURE AND PROOF

In considering the chancery procedure and method of proof I shall be as brief as possible. Both subjects have been considered at length elsewhere,[1] and in this connexion I wish only to introduce some statements from the petitions and Year Books.

I. *Procedure.*

The proceedings began by the bill or petition which was addressed to the particular chancellor who happened to hold the office, thus: 'A tres reverent piere en dieu et mon tres gracious Segnur, L'erchevesque d'everwyk et Chaunceller D'englitere.'[2] This title is written at the top of the petition, and in a rather large hand. Usually, the petitioner identifies the chancellor whom he is addressing by describing him as the Bishop of York or Canterbury, &c., as the case may be; this furnishes, generally speaking, the only means of determining the date of the petition. Where a chancellorship extended over a long period, or where a Bishop of the same diocese was chancellor at widely separated times, the problem of settling the period in which the particular petition falls becomes very difficult. For example, Thomas de Arundel, Archbishop of Canterbury, was chancellor in 1399; John Stafford,[3] Archbishop of Canterbury, was chancellor from 1443 to 1450. Now if a petition is simply addressed to the 'Archbishop of Canterbury', it may be very difficult to determine which Archbishop is meant, unless there chances to be some statement in the petition which in itself fixes

---

[1] e.g. Spence, Equit. Jurisdict. of the Court of Chancery; Kerly, History of Equity (Yorke Prize Essay, 1889).

[2] VII. 250, *Cases*, p. 179.

[3] John Stafford was chancellor from 1432 to 1450, but during the first eleven years he was Bishop of Bath and Wells.

a date.[1] Again, there are petitions addressed to the 'Chancellor of England' without any further description.[2]

The petitions are very much alike in form. They consist often of only one long and involved sentence which recites informally the wrong complained of, and concludes with a prayer for relief. Great particularity of statement was not required; 'en cest court', remarked a chancellor, 'il n'est requisite que le bille soit tout en certein solonque le solemnity del comon ley, car icy il n'est forsque petition, etc.'[3] The demand for relief is commonly in general terms, but it almost always comprises a request that the chancellor cause the defendant to come into chancery and be examined upon the matter alleged in the petition. The petitioner usually asserts in this connexion that he is without remedy at law. The following example is typical: 'Que please a vostre tres reverent paternite et gracious Seignurie, graunter brief direct al dit Mark (defendant) pur apparere devant vous a certein jour sur peyn par vous alymyter, d'estre examine de les matiere suisditz et sur son examinacion luy ensy iustifier et govourner que le dit Suppliant purra aver ceo qe reson et bon concience demaundent en celle partie, Considerant tres gracious Seignur que le dit Suppliant ne poet mye aver remedie en ceo cas a la comune ley, et ceo pur dieu et en œvre de charite.'[4] At the end of the petition are usually placed the names of the persons who stand as pledges (*plegii de prosequendo*) for the petitioner. This was occasioned by a statute of Henry VI,[5] which decreed that no writ of subpoena should issue until the petitioner had found sureties to satisfy the defendant for his damages in case the allegations made in the petition were not proven.

The Subpoena was the writ usually asked for, though we do find requests for a Certiorari or Corpus cum causa when it was desired to remove a suit from the common law courts, or to obtain relief from a judgement. In response to the writ the defendant appeared. At first he appears to have been examined at once orally; but at length the practice arose of

---

[1] Wherever petitions are endorsed, the date can usually be fixed from the endorsement.

[2] e.g. Bundles LXVIII–LXXV.

[3] Y. B. 9 Ed. IV. 41. 26.

[4] IV. 100, *Cases*, p. 173.

[5] St. 15 H. VI. c. 4.

putting in an answer in writing. The answer commonly begins by a protestation against the sufficiency of the bill, which is followed by a traverse of the chief allegations in the petition, and the defendant's statement of his own case. To the answer the petitioner might reply by replication, to which in turn the defendant might put in a rejoinder.[1] I do not know of any case in the Early Chancery Proceedings in which there are more than four pleadings, but there was nothing to prevent the parties from proceeding further.[2]

After examining the pleadings and hearing the evidence introduced by the parties the chancellor pronounced his decree. Probably this decree was made verbally, and in most cases no record was made of it. Chancery was not a court of record. In one case a chancellor said that it was customary in chancery to grant a certain kind of relief, ' car nous trovoms recorde en le chancery de tiels ' ;[3] again, the cancellation of an obligation is ordered to be 'inrolled on the record in chancery'[4] (*in Cancellaria . . . de recordo irrotulari faciat*). I do not know what these statements mean, unless they refer to the endorsements on petitions. Of a record as such there was none ; and, as has already been remarked, the endorsements are few and far between.

It is needless to say anything further of the kind of relief granted. That will be apparent from what has been said in the preceding chapter. Chancery of course acted *in personam* ; the only relief it could grant took the form of an order to the defendant. The court could not nullify a bond ; it might enjoin a defendant from bringing suit upon an obligation, but if he chose to be obstinate, it could do nothing except imprison him. The common law judges resented the use of the injunction, and in one memorable case they actually advised a plaintiff in an action at law to proceed to judgement in defiance of the chancellor's order, saying that if he should be imprisoned in the Fleet they would release him by writ of

---

[1] e. g. XIX. 59–56, *Cases*, pp. 199–203.
[2] In the case of *Hals et al.* v. *Hyncley*, the pleadings continued to a surrejoinder. Pike, Common Law and Conscience . . . , L. Q. R., i. 443.
[3] Y. B. 22 Ed. IV. 6. 18.   [4] XXIX. 13, *Cases*, p. 214.

Habeas corpus.[1] This is a threat which, so far as I know, was never carried out; in general, the intervention of chancery seems to have been successful.

II. *Proof.*

In the petition the complainant frequently offers to testify himself, or to introduce evidence in his own behalf, even going so far as to offer to prove his statements 'as this court will award'.[2] Payment is alleged in the presence of witnesses,[3] or it is said that it was made ' come certeinment par recordez des gentz dignes de foi et as quelx foi est done, devant vous sera monstre '.[4] Another complainant avers that his statements are true ' os the ful reverent fader in god, the bishop of Lincoln, in whos presence this covenaunt and acorde was made, wole recorde '.[5] In short, he takes pains to state that he has abundant evidence of the truth of his statements.[6]

In the matter of proof, a petitioner in chancery had one conspicuous advantage over a plaintiff at common law. This lay in the examination of the defendant under oath. We have noted that the petitions uniformly ask for an examination of the defendant, and it is common to find it alleged that the defendant has already admitted the case against him. Thus it is said that the defendant 'a fore worthy men hath knowledged the dewete and payment to be made to youre seyde suppliant',[7] or that ' þe seid John Loget (defendant) before notable persones hath knowledged þe seid x pound to be

---

[1] Y. B. 22 Ed. IV. 37. 21.
[2] XIX. 57, *Cases*, p. 202.
[3] XIX. 123.
[4] VI. 161.
[5] XXXIX. 55, *Cases*, p. 221.
[6] VII. 79 (' Si come mesme le suppliant par pluys notables et sufficiant homes de le dit paroche loialment purra prover ') ; XVI. 334 (' Accorde of mariage was taken and appoynted . . . in recorde and wittenesse of many thryfty gentilmen ') ; XIX. 345, *Cases*, p. 204 (' Heruppon my wife and I will swere uppon the sacrement that this is true that we swere and her-upon will bring . . . (six parties named) . . . and xx^{ti} good men mo to con-ferme this true that my wife and I will swere ') ; XXVIII. 210, *Cases*, p. 212 (Petitioner has a bill of a debt, 'testifying the same after the cours of Marchaundice') ; LIX. 212 (Petitioner alleges the defendant admits he owes money, ' as he hath many times confessed and seid unto divers per-sones which can and wol testifye the same '). In Y. B. 22 Ed. IV. 6. 18, reference is made to *two* witnesses against a matter of record. I do not think there is any significance in the number.
[7] XI. 47, *Cases*, p. 186.

dewe ... as it is above seid '.[1]   Petitioners even ask that the
defendants be examined ' et solonc lour respounse a doner iugement solonc ceo que loialte, foy et conscience demaundent ',[2]
and there is record of a decree which was based primarily
upon admissions made by the defendants in the course of
their examination.[3]   In this the chancery had a powerful
method for discovering the truth.

Perhaps the method of proof in chancery can be best seen
from one illustrative case.   The facts were extremely complicated, and as the case has already been considered [4] I shall
not restate them.   The defendant, in his answer,[5] traversed
all the material allegations in the petition, and these were re-
affirmed by the petitioner in his replication.[6]   Both parties
stated that they were ready to prove their statements as the
court should award.   Then follows a series of depositions :
the deposition of John Powele and John Glasse, ' made in the
presence of my lord Chaunceler at the More . . . by their
othes upon a boke';[7] 'the deposition of William Nynge'[8] ('The
seid William Nynge, sworn and dywely examyned before my
lord Chaunceler in the playn Court of Chauncery '); the deposition of William Aphowell, ' afore the Maister of the
rollez ';[9] the deposition of Stephen Stychemerssh the yonger,
' made before George, Archebisshopp of Yorke, primat and
Chaunceller of Englond ';[10] the deposition of William Elyot,
petitioner, in support of his own petition;[11] the deposition of
Robert Talbot;[12] the declaration of Stychemerssh the elder
(defendant), in support of his answer.[13]   The decree [14] runs :
' Memorandum quod pro eo quod, ista peticione ac responsione
ad eandem facta et replicatione in hac parte habita, necnon
desposicionibus et testimoniis tam ex parte . . . (of petitioner)
. . . quam ex parte . . . (of defendant) . . . in premissis coram
domino Rege in Cancellaria sua factis et habitis, lectis et
auditis, ac materia in eisdem plenius intellectis (*sic*), visum

---

[1] X. 76.
[2] LXVIII. 49.
[3] LIX. 285, *Cases*, p. 232.
[4] *Supra*, p. 132.
[5] XXIX. 12, *Cases*, p. 216.
[6] XXIX. 10, *Cases*, p. 217.
[7] XXIX. 11, *Cases*, p. 218.
[8] XXIX. 9, *Cases*, p. 218.
[9] XXIX. 8, *Cases*, p. 218.
[10] XXIX. 7, *Cases*, p. 218.
[11] XXIX. 6, *Cases*, p. 219.
[12] XXIX. 5, *Cases*, p. 219.
[13] XXIX. 4, *Cases*, p. 219.
[14] XXIX. 13, *Cases*, p. 214.

est Curie Cancellarie predicte . . .' that the petitioner had proved the allegations in his petition, &c.; an order was made accordingly.

From this case and others[1] we gain some insight into the method of examination in chancery. The party or witness appeared 'in his proper person' in the chancery, and was examined before the chancellor or the Master of the Rolls, or some person properly qualified. The examination was under oath; it is sometimes said to be on the sacrament,[2] sometimes 'on a boke'.[3] If the defendants lived at some distance from London, or were ill and unable to appear, a commission by a writ of Dedimus potestatem[4] would be granted to take the defendant's answer and also to examine witnesses. A certificate of the answer and testimony would then be taken into chancery.

The care which the chancellor exercised in ascertaining the true state of a case is evident from such documents as these. Evidence verbal or written was placed on the same footing, but the chancellor compelled a petitioner to prove his case. If he deemed the evidence insufficient or conflicting, he would call for more,[5] and no decree could be had until it was produced. There do not appear to have been any rules of evidence nor presumptions as to the burden of proof. The whole proceeding was thoroughly informal.[6]

---

[1] e.g. XIX. 354 d–354 e, *Cases*, pp. 206–207.
[2] XIX. 345, *Cases*, p. 204.
[3] XIX. 354 d, *Cases*, p. 206 (Examination of David Gogh).
[4] 10 S. S. xxvii–xxviii; and see XXV. 111. 110 (10 S. S. 141–2).
[5] Y. B. 16 Ed. IV. 9. 10.
[6] I have omitted consideration of those cases in which an issue of fact was tried in the common law courts.

CHAPTER IV

THE THEORY OF CONTRACT IN CHANCERY

IN the fragmentary view of the jurisdiction of equity which is presented in the preceding chapters we have noticed very summarily some of the principles which underlay the intervention of the chancellor. It now becomes necessary to gather these together and present them as a whole. Such a task one must approach with great diffidence, and with the consciousness that the danger of error is very great. In the first place, the extent of the equitable jurisdiction in contract is a matter of considerable uncertainty. Few of the petitions are endorsed with judgement. In the majority of cases, it has been necessary to fall back on inference and to sketch probabilities. But secondly, even if one knew precisely what the chancellor did, it would still be difficult to determine the principles on which he acted. Herein the student of the common law has a conspicuous advantage. The Year Books give not alone the decision of a case, but the discussion and arguments which preceded it. The contentions of counsel, the pointed interjections of the judges and the comments of the reporters are excellent material out of which to frame a theory.

In equity, unhappily, it is otherwise. Beyond an occasional case involving a subpoena which has crept into the Year Books, we have no reports; there are only the bare pleadings which came before the chancellor. These are drawn often by petitioners unskilled in legal technicalities and forms; for in many cases the litigant drafted his own petition. Equity gave judgement ' secundum conscientiam et non secundum allegata ',[1] a fact which doubtless accounts for the looseness of phrasing and ungainly diffuseness of many complaints. The facts are often presented carelessly, the demand for relief is

---

[1] Remark of the chancellor in Y. B. 9 Ed. IV. 14. 9.

vague, and even where a petition is endorsed there is slight indication of the process of reasoning which leads to the decision. Confessedly, any theory which can be put forward must be built up of fragments ; it cannot go beyond the inherent limitations of the material.

Absence of Remedy at Law.

The primary limitation imposed on the use of the subpoena lay in the fact that it could be brought only in case the petitioner could show an absence of remedy at law.[1] The burden of establishing this fact lay upon the petitioner ; if he failed to make out such a case the bill must be dismissed. Such, at all events, was the theory. However, the chancellor did not interpret this limitation strictly ; he recognized a variety of circumstances which might produce a failure of legal remedy, and if the constant complaint of serjeants and judges is any criterion, we may assume that in spite of this limitation he found means of invading what was regarded as the peculiar domain of the common law. It becomes important, therefore, to observe in what, as a matter of practice, absence of remedy at law consisted.

1. First and foremost are the cases which did not fall within the class of any contracts recognized by the common law. Such, for example, were parol agreements which lay outside the scope of Debt ; in fact, these include all the informal agreements which were later protected by Assumpsit, and some others besides.

2. Cases in which the technicalities of procedure or proof prevented a remedy being given in a particular case. Of these we may instance as examples, suits by one partner or executor[2] against another ; suits to recover debts proven

---

[1] Y. B. 39 H. VI. 26. 38 (per Jenney) : 'cest action de Subpaena ciens ne gist mes ou il n'y ad ascun remedy a le Comone Ley : donque il suera en cest Court de conscience'. This does not apply to petitions brought by the king, or by officers of the chancery.

[2] Cf. X. 151 (Petitioner and defendant were both appointed executors by the will of the testator. The defendant was in possession of an obligation which belonged to the testator, and though he refused to take part in the administration of the estate he would not give up the obligation. In consequence, the petitioner could not recover the debt due to the estate, nor

by sealed instruments which have been lost or destroyed ; suits by the assignee of a chose in action.

3. Cases in which the inequality of the parties, or the failure of common law process, resulted in the practical denial of a remedy.

4. Cases in which a remedy was given at law, but it was insufficient.

This is exemplified by the suits to recover specific chattels, and for the specific performance of contract.[1]

This classification is intended to be suggestive rather than exhaustive. Absence of remedy at law formed the condition precedent to the use of a subpoena; but it does not follow that the chancellor granted relief in every case in which a petitioner would have been helpless at law. True, Archbishop Morton in the heat of argument declared emphatically that no one who came to chancery should leave the court without a remedy,[2] but this rough-hewn clerical maxim was never intended to be interpreted literally. Rather does it suggest the motive which prompted the chancellor's intervention, and of this we must say a few words.

The Motive of the Chancellor.

In an interesting case, of which there is fortunately a comparatively full report, the chancellor set out certain specific cases in which relief would be granted by subpoena. Mordant, counsel for the defendant, immediately generalized these instances, and affirmed that the jurisdiction of the court of chancery was dependent upon breach of confidence.[3] The chancellor, however, refused to accept 'breach of confidence' as the sole ground of appeal to equity; instantly he cited an

could he secure the obligation by bringing Detinue against the defendant ; for he could not bring suit against the defendant at law).

[1] Of course it is to be noted that the chancellor enforced specific performance of contracts before the common law had developed an action applicable to parol contract.

[2] Y. B. 4 H. VII. 4. 8.

[3] '*Mordant*: In touts les cases per Monseignur le Chancellor ils sont mesles oves confidence, et pur ceo qu'il n'ad ascun remedy per le Comon Ley, uncore sur le confidence que les parties mettrent in les autres a avoir les choses accordant a le covenant entre eux . . . est bon conscience qu'il sera aide per cest Court . . .' Y. B. 7 H. VII. 10. 2.

example which suggested a wider principle : ' If one has no writing (i. e. deed) and his debtor dies, there is no remedy by the common law ; nevertheless here by this court of[1] conscience he will have a remedy.'[2]   Huse and Bryan JJ. accepted the implication ; for the reporter is particular to note that they affirmed *clearly* that a remedy existed in conscience where there was none at common law.[3]

This remark of the chancellor becomes significant when we remember the social conditions of the fifteenth century.[4] Feudalism was beginning to give way, but one of its greatest monuments, the common law, had yet to shake off the shackles of its origin.   Not only was there a revival of culture, but a tremendous impetus was given to commercial enterprise. One has only to read the calendars of chancery to discover the introduction of a strong foreign element in English trade and commerce.   Agreements and arrangements of daily occurrence demanded recognition ; but a system of law inextricably interwoven with tenure in land could not easily adapt itself to a changing environment.   The deficiencies of the common law became the more apparent as trade increased ; merchants were not prepared to embody their contracts in a highly technical form.   The very essence of business development lies in the possibility of fluid and formless agreements which may be easily made and easily changed.

Nor was it only the commercial class which felt the restraint of a rigid and unyielding system of law.   There were hosts of ' accords ' and ' bargains ' among people of humble life, who from ignorance or lack of means did not observe the technicalities of legal forms.   The parties agree to sell land, or to make a marriage settlement ; there is no clerk or ' learned man ' present, and the agreement remains formless because there is no one of sufficient skill to incorporate it in a deed. The reality of agreement is present, but it lacks the sacra-

---

[1] The Year Book reads ' in '.   I have translated otherwise because of the common reference to chancery as the ' court of conscience '.   Perhaps a better rendering would be : ' . . . by this court (i. e. chancery) he will have a remedy in conscience '.   The meaning is the same in either case.
[2] Y. B. 7 H. VII. 10. 2.   [3] *Idem.*
[4] See Vinogradoff, L. Q. R., xxiv. 373.

mental mantle of form.   And so the bargain is no bargain at
law.   It needed the touch of humanism to render the law
sensitive to the practical needs of the fifteenth century.

It was this breach which the chancery undertook to fill.
Behind the scattered remarks of the chancellors, behind the
petitions themselves, we see the motive which prompted the
relief: the desire, namely, in the interests of commerce, and,
if you will, of the community at large, to supply the defects,
the 'gaps' of the common law.   Let us look at them again
by way of *résumé*.

Money is lent abroad.   The common law cannot take
jurisdiction, but equity intervenes.   Services are rendered
or goods are sold, but no definite recompense is agreed upon
by the parties; services are rendered to a third party at the
request of the defendant; a debt is assigned by parol; an
obligation which proves a debt is lost or mislaid.   In all such
cases the creditor will fail if he brings Debt ; in chancery
he finds a remedy.   Again, a foreign merchant [1] is temporarily
in London ; his ship is unfreighted in the dock, and he cannot
wait to bring suit at law.   The chancellor takes cognizance of
his claim and provides a speedy remedy.   A debtor acknow-
ledges a debt by signing a bill 'testifyinge the same after
the course of Marchaundice ' ; subsequently he refuses to pay
' contrary to the Cours of trewe Marchaundice '.[2]   The proof
is insufficient at law ; it is accepted in chancery.   Constantly
in the chancery petitions we find references to the customs
of merchants, the ordinary course of commercial dealings,
which, while sufficient as business transactions, failed to meet
the requirements of the common law.   In a well-known
passage [3] the chancellor treated the law merchant as synony-
mous with the law of nature which it was his peculiar duty to
observe, and one cannot read the petitions without feeling

---

[1] Cf. the remark of the chancellor in Y. B. 13 Ed. IV. 9. 5 : ' Cest suit
est pris par un marchant alien que est venue par safe conduct icy, et il
n'est tenuz de suer solonque le ley de le terre a tarier le trial de xij homes,
et autres solempnities de le ley de terre, mes doit sues'icy, et serroit determine solonque le ley de nature en le chancery et il doit suer la de heur en
heur et de jour pur le sped des Marchants . . .'

[2] XXVIII. 210.   [3] Y. B. 13 Ed. IV. 9. 5 (*ad fin.*).

convinced that merchants appealed to him with the conviction that they would secure a ready hearing.[1]

Again, a vendor agrees to convey land on the payment of the purchase price. The money is paid over, but the vendor breaks the agreement. Land is promised by way of a marriage settlement, the marriage is performed, but the promise remains unfulfilled. In neither case will the common law aid the disappointed promisee. In both cases he finds relief in equity. We might continue to note particular examples, but those which have been given must suffice. The point we wish to stress is this: as one traces the chancellor's jurisdiction step by step, one finds that equity is continually providing, or endeavouring to provide, for such cases as were neglected by common law, wherever some general interest would derive benefit from their recognition. This is the motive which stirred the chancellor to action.

The mere fact, however, that the common law provided no remedy for a particular case was not in itself enough to induce the chancellor to intervene. Something else must exist. And so we find that a petitioner always bases his claim for relief on a principle, ordinarily expressed by two words, 'reason and conscience'. The ordinary phrasing of the petitions is easily seen from one or two examples. The defendant has promised to convey land on marriage, but he has broken his promise; the petitioner asks that he be made to 'appere afore you (i. e. the chancellor) in þe Chancellerie of our lord þe kyng atte a certain day and upon a certeyne peyne by you to be lymyted, there to aunswere unto þe seid premisses and þere mak hym do þat *good feith, right and conscience* aske and require, for þe love of god and by way of charite. . . .'[2] Another asks that the defendant be brought into chancery by subpoena and there examined 'issint que

---

[1] The desire to protect merchants, especially foreign merchants, was responsible for many interventions of the chancellor. It even had an effect upon the common law of the fifteenth century. For example, the doctrine that 'a bailee might be guilty of theft if he "determined the bailment" before he misappropriated the goods . . . seems to have been forced upon the judges by the chancellor for the satisfaction of foreign merchants'. P. & M., ii. 179, note 2.

[2] XVI. 386, *Cases*, p. 197.

remedie ent soit fait a dit suppliant solonc ceo que reson et concience demaundent. . . .'[1] The statements above given are fairly typical of the whole of the chancery material.[2] The particular form of expression may vary, but the principle alluded to is the same. Wherever a matter of conscience arises, remedy is to be found in chancery, though there be none at law.[3]

Reason and Conscience.

The use of these words was no peculiarity of the chancery. We find common law judges referring to matter of conscience and right,[4] but conscience as a principle is found in chancery alone. To the lawyer schooled in the traditions of the common law, the operation of this principle seemed too much a matter of whim and caprice. The chancellor's disregard of precedent, his tendency to isolate a particular case and decide it upon principles of natural justice, appeared to open the door to wanton interference with the law of the land. In one of the sixteenth-century tracts a 'Serjaunte at the lawes of England' complains bitterly of what appears to him the haphazard action of chancery. And what is this 'conscience' which avails the chancellor? he asks. It is 'a thinge of great uncertaintie; for some men thinke that if they treade upon two strawes that lye acrosse, that they ofende in conscience, and some man thinketh that if he lake money and another hath too moche that he may take part of his with conscience; and so divers men divers conscience; ... so me seemeth, that

---

[1] VII. 250, *Cases*, p. 179.

[2] e. g. IV. 100, *Cases*, p. 173 ('que le dit suppliant purra aver ceo qe reson et bon conscience demaundent'); X. 39 ('de faire droit a dit suppliant solonc ceo que droit, bon foy et conscience demaundent'); XV. 140 *a*, *Cases*, p. 192 ('to do and receyve þat gude fath and consiens requireth'); XIX. 404 *a*, *Cases*, p. 207 ('contrary to all good feith and conscience'); LIX. 114, *Cases*, p. 225 (The defendant' refuses to build a mill, 'contrarie to his seid promyse, good feithe and conciens'; petitioner asks that he be 'rewled and juged as good conciens requyreth'); LIX. 117, *Cases*, p. 226 ('contrarie to his seid promyse and good conciens').

[3] Cf. Brooke, Abr., *Parlement et Statutes*, 33 : ' ... ou matter est enconter reason et le party n'ad remedy a le common ley il suera pur remedy in parliment, et nota que a ceo iour plures de ceux suitz sont en le court de Chauncerie'. The reference is to 37 Ass. pl. 7, but it appears to be incorrect.

[4] e. g. Newton C.J. in Y. B. 20 H. VI. 34. 4.

if the kinges subjects be constrayned to be ordered by the discretion and conscience of one man, they should be put to a greate uncertaintie. . . .' [1]

Some utterances of the chancellor, as reported in the Year Books, seem to give pertinence to this criticism, if they are read as unrelated statements. The principle enunciated is often vague and indefinite ; it seems to shift and vary according to the idiosyncrasies of the particular chancellor. One of two executors releases a debt due to the estate of the testator without the consent of his co-executor. Both the executor and the debtor are brought into chancery by subpoena. Counsel for the defendant contends that as each executor has full power, his act cannot be attacked. But the chancellor brushes aside this technicality. Each rule of law, he says, is, or ought to be, conformable to the law of God (le Ley de Dieu). Then with an eye to the particular facts of the case at issue, he reduces the law of God to one specific statement : ' le ley de Dieu est q'un executor qui est de male disposition ne expenderoit touts les biens, etc.' If the executor who has expended the assets of the estate does not make amends according to his ability, ' il sera damne in Hell ' ; but the chancellor is not content to stop short with forecasting the melancholy consequences of such recalcitrance. He immediately asserts that to provide a remedy for such a case is ' bien fait accord al' conscience '. [2] Again, an obligee brings suit upon an obligation in a different county from that in which it was made. The obligor appeals to chancery, and the chancellor holds that the action is brought against conscience, ' car le verity de nul chose poit estre conus cibien en nul lieu q'en le com' l'ou le chose fuit fait.' [3] Obviously the chancellor is acting upon some principle of general jurisprudence, but we see the principle, not in its large outlines, but as it is specifically applied to a particular case. The only way in which we can hope to solve the riddle is by bringing analogous cases together.

In so doing, *Doctor and Student*, that amazing treatise

---

[1] Hargrave's Law Tracts, 326.   [2] Y. B. 4 H. VII. 4. 8.
[3] Y. B. 9 Ed. IV. 2. 5.

in which St. Germain embodied his wide knowledge of both canon and common law, is of great assistance.[1]   We observe that the canon law did find a guiding rule in conscience, and this peculiar coincidence points, it seems irresistibly, to a 'process of indirect reception of canon law' in chancery.[2] This 'conscience', however, is not the conscience of some particular individual at which the serjeant of law levelled his criticism.   It is rather a broad and flexible principle.   To trace it even in outline would lead us into the network of canon law ; and so far as St. Germain is concerned, the question has been carefully analysed elsewhere.[3]   Suffice it to say that St. Germain states distinctly that equity makes exception from the law on the ground of reason and conscience.   In chancery we find the general principle applied to concrete legal problems, and our interest here lies not so much in the source of the doctrine as in the way in which it worked out in practice.   Now the application of the principle of conscience in chancery resulted in the formulation of three distinct classes of cases which found protection in the subpoena : (1) cases in which parties had failed through ignorance or carelessness to avail themselves of their rights; (2) cases of transactions based on confidence ; (3) cases of parol contract.   The second class involves matters which are essentially equitable in the modern sense of the word.   This we may ignore and give our attention to the other two.

I. *Cases in which a party has failed to avail himself of his rights.*

We find the most pertinent illustration of this class of cases in the chancery doctrines with regard to obligations under seal.   A debtor has paid a debt proved by an obligation, but he has neglected to have the obligation cancelled or to secure an acquittance.   In consequence he has no proof of payment which will be accepted by the common law.   Again, an obligation

---

[1] In this brief consideration of Doctor and Student I have followed the analysis of Professor Vinogradoff in L. Q. R., xxiv. 373 ff.
[2] Vinogradoff, L. Q. R., xxiv. 378.   [3] Vinogradoff, *loc. cit.*

is made to secure the performance of a certain act, or it is conditioned by parol. The obligor might have protected himself had he taken the pains to have the condition (or intent of the obligation) inserted in the deed itself. The law treats this mistake on the part of the obligor as his folly; it refuses to modify a general principle to do justice in a particular case. An obligation is made in payment for the conveyance of land; the vendor keeps the bond, but refuses to make conveyance. In such instances the chancellor intervened to protect the obligor. But the rights of the obligee were also regarded. If he had lost his obligation, or mislaid it, but is able by extraneous evidence to establish a just debt, equity will assist him in obtaining it.

It was not alone in the domain of obligations that the chancellor found application for this principle. A does work for B, but there is no agreement as to the definite sum he is to receive for his labour. Goods are sold, but the price is not fixed. A benefit is conferred upon a third party at the request of the defendant. Goods are bailed to A, but they come into the possession of C, and the bailor cannot connect the possession so as to bring an action against C. There is no question in any of these examples of the right to recover, but the case cannot be brought within the scope of a common law action.

In brief, all these transactions are from the point of view of common law irregular. The law does not order a man to pay a debt twice or to perform services gratuitously. It offers him certain means of protecting himself, but if he fails to avail himself of these, he places himself beyond its protection. The chancellor, on the other hand, who was not bound by precedent, nor under the necessity of maintaining the supremacy of inflexible legal rules, was able to decide each particular case on a principle of general jurisprudence. If we apply the text of 'reason and conscience' to the situation, the answer is plain. And so upon this principle chancery 'excepted' from the common law.

II. *Enforcement of Parol Contract.*

In the *Diversity of Courts* it is written that ' a man shall have remedy in Chancery for covenants made without specialty if the party have sufficient witness to prove the covenants '.[1] I do not propose to introduce any further evidence in proof of this statement. I believe it has been shown that the chancellor did enforce certain parol promises, and that he did so upon the principle of reason and conscience. It is granted even by Professor Ames that the chancellor did enforce certain parol agreements, but this admission is qualified by the assertion that he did so ' only upon the ground of compelling reparation for what was regarded as a tort to the plaintiff or upon the principle of preventing the unjust enrichment of the defendant '.[2]

If then it be said that the promisor is under an obligation to perform his promise, upon what principle did the chancellor enforce this obligation ? Now every breach of contract which is accompanied by damage bears a strong analogy to a tort, if in fact it does not amount to one. But an obligation arising from a tort is plainly distinguishable from one arising from contract. In the one case it proceeds contrary to the will of the person bound ; in the other it is in accordance with, and in fulfilment of, his will. Does the chancellor then enforce the obligation, because the breach of promise amounts to a tort to the plaintiff, or because he holds that one who has for legitimate cause made a promise ought to carry it out ? In other words, in his analysis of agreements, did the chancellor proceed upon a principle of tort or of contract ? This is the question which I shall endeavour to answer. But first I shall examine some illustrative cases.

1456. A was to marry B, daughter of C. It was agreed that A should make an estate of lands to himself and B, &c., and that C ' for the . . . mariage and ioynture ' should make an estate of lands to A and B and their heirs. The marriage took place ; A made the estate to himself and B, but C refused to carry out his part. A accordingly brought a subpoena against C. The chancellor, after examining the evidence,

---

[1] Holmes, Early English Equity, L. Q. R., i. 172.
[2] Ames, H. L. R., viii. 257.

decided that the matter set up in the petition was true and just, and decreed that, as B was dead leaving issue, C should make an estate of the land to A and his heirs.[1]

1464-5. A made B 'le proctour de son benefice et luy promise per fidem que il luy garderait indempne'. A resigned the benefice to B's damage and B brought a subpoena for the breach of promise. The chancellor remarked : 'Pur ceo que il est en damages par le non perfourmans de le promise, il avera remedye icy.'[2]

1467-1468. A was bound to B in an obligation of £100. B told A that if he would furnish C (B's son) with goods and money on request, he would make payment therefor. A furnished C with goods and money to the value of £94, receiving from C, in the name of his father, bills witnessing the delivery of the goods, &c.; at the same time C promised on behalf of B that A should have deduction of £94 on the obligation of £100. Afterwards A tendered B the bills for £94 and £6 in money, and desired him to receive them on satisfaction of the obligation. B refused, and A brought a subpoena. Much evidence was introduced by both parties. The chancellor decided that A had proved his case, and that the obligation of £100 should be considered 'vacuum et nullius valoris'. Accordingly he ordered it to be cancelled.[3]

1470-1471. A at the request of B, and on his promise to save him harmless, became surety to C for the debt of D. D did not pay the debt, and in consequence A was threatened with suit by C. As B had died, A called upon B's executors to carry out the promise ; but they refused. He accordingly brought a subpoena. The chancellor decreed that the executors should discharge A against suit from C.[4]

What situation do these cases disclose ? There has been a breach of promise by non-feasance which is succeeded by damage, immediate or prospective, to the promisee. This element of damage is frankly suggestive of tort. It would be possible, if we did not scruple to strain our reasoning, to resolve the gist of the cause of action into a tort to the plaintiff, even a deceit. Such would be the line of reasoning followed by the common law. But I do not think one could

---

[1] XXV. 111 (10 S. S. 141).　　　[2] Y. B. P. 4 Ed. IV. 4.

[3] XXIX. 13, *Cases*, p. 214. I have simplified the facts, and omitted consideration of the defendant's answer (XXIX. 12, *Cases*, p. 216).

[4] XLIV. 142, *Cases*, p. 222. For the defendant's answer, see XLIV. 143, *Cases*, p. 224.

make a greater mistake than to impose upon the cases in equity
the peculiar theory of the common law.

In the first place, why did the common law treat a breach
of promise as a deceit to the promisee? I believe a ready
and conclusive answer is found in the history of Assumpsit.
Here we find another example of the manipulation of the
substantive law through the exigencies of procedure. From
the standpoint of contract, a breach of contract was a breach of
covenant, but I scarcely need remark that a breach of covenant
was actionable only in case the covenant was under seal. It
was never suggested by any common law judge that a breach
of covenant was a tort, a deceit to the plaintiff. Such
reasoning was unnecessary. But the promise may be the same
in essence whether it be under seal or no. A for £50 in hand
paid promises to convey Blackacre to B. A breaks his
promise. If the promise is under seal, Covenant lies, *because
the promise is broken*. The law says in effect that one who
makes a promise in a deliberate and formal way is bound to
fulfil it, irrespective of the situation of the promisee. If, on
the other hand, the promise is verbal, Assumpsit lies.[1] But
herein the law adopts a different line. Assumpsit lies because
by the breach of promise *A has deceived B*. It does this in
order to bring a breach of contract within the scope of an
action which sounds in tort. Thus on substantially the same
state of facts the law adopts a contractual theory for breach
of promises under seal, a theory fundamentally tortious for
breach of verbal promises. There is no logical basis for this
distinction; counsel and judges were aware of this, as the
constant argument in the early cases in ssumpsit, 'this is
a breach of covenant', bears witness. The distinction finds
its justification in the history of the forms of action and there
alone. Had the ingenious suggestion of Blackstone,[2] that
Assumpsit is an action on the case analogous to Covenant,
been literally true, the law might have adopted a different
theory for parol contract.

In equity the situation is different. There was no pro-

---

[1] I refer, of course, to the action in the sixteenth century.
[2] Blackstone, iii. 158.

cedural necessity for treating a breach of contract as a tort. There was no division into forms of action; there were no technicalities of pleading to obscure the real issue. We stand, so to speak, before breach of contract as a question of first impression. Analysis may lead us in the direction of tort or contract; but both ways are open, and there is nothing to compel us to take the one in preference to the other. I wish, therefore, to submit such evidence as I have been able to find which indicates the attitude of the chancellor in questions of contract.

1. The chancellor was an ecclesiastic, and probably carried with him into the chancery the principles and theories of the ecclesiastical court. It is notorious that the ecclesiastical court did assume jurisdiction over *laesio fidei*. What more natural than that the chancellor should have proceeded upon the ground of breach of faith? There is at least a suggestion of this in the petitions. In *Wheler* v. *Huchynden*[1] a pledge of faith is alleged, and it is quite common to find a petitioner saying that the defendant, 'promitted by hie feith'[2] or 'promytted by his feith'[3] or promised 'on his faith and troueth'.[4] In one of the cases[5] stated at length above, a promise 'per fidem' is set forth. It would be venturesome, however, to assert that breach of faith was the sole ground upon which chancery took jurisdiction. It has been argued that if the chancellor proceeded upon this ground, 'equity would give relief upon any and all agreements, even upon gratuitous parol promises'.[6] I do not think it necessary to base the chancellor's jurisdiction on breach of faith alone; but that he did enforce gratuitous promises cannot be doubted.[7] In this

---

[1] 2 Cal. Ch. ii. [2] XIX. 345, *Cases*, p. 204. [3] XVI. 277.
[4] XIX. 91. [5] Y. B. P. 4 Ed. IV. 4, *supra*, p. 161.
[6] Ames, H. L. R., viii. 255.
[7] In XLIV. 142, *Cases*, p. 222, there is a clear case of a gratuitous promise which was enforced against the promisor's executors. See also XIV. 5, *Cases*, p. 188 (Promise made by a surety); XV. 248 (Money advanced to A upon the promise of B, assuring payment); XV. 52, *Cases*, p. 191 (Promise to carry a letter); XXXI. 82, *Cases*, p. 219 (Promise to respite an action); XXXI. 118 (Promise by arbitrators to deliver an award *in writing*). The following promises connected with marriage appear to have been gratuitous : VII. 250, *Cases*, p. 179; XVI. 386, *Cases*, p. 197; XXVIII. 299, *Cases*, p. 213.

connexion, however, I do not wish to consider breach of faith except in so far as it tends to point to the promise as the essential factor in the chancellor's consideration of parol contract. The fact that some petitioners take occasion to mention a pledge of faith, coupled with our knowledge that gratuitous promises were enforced, seems to me a very strong indication that chancery was employing a purely contractual principle.

2. If we turn to the petitions and notice the way in which complainants state their case, we find that it is the promise of the defendant upon which stress is laid. If in fact the chancellor did consider breach of promise a deceit to the plaintiff, it is very curious that pleaders who were constantly appearing before him do not make use of so convenient an allegation. But they do not do so. Rather do they say that the defendant has made a promise which reason and conscience require him to perform. The defendants refuse to make a conveyance 'solonque lour covenantz',[1] or 'accordantz as covenantz et bargoyne suisditz';[2] another defendant is asked 'to shewe whi your seid besecher shuld not be content *after promys made* betwix them'.[3] Emphasis is laid upon the promise as the indispensable part of the case.

3. In certain cases the beneficiary brings the subpoena. These cases have been considered at length already[4]; at this point I wish merely to refer to the significance of the right of action in the beneficiary. It seems to mean this. If there is sufficient cause for a promise which is deliberately made, the chancellor holds the promisor to his obligation at the behest of one who has a right to obtain some advantage from the fulfilment of the promise, although he is not the promisee. The principle upon which the subpoena is allowed cannot be 'detriment to the promisee', for the complainant is not the promisee; it cannot be a 'tort to the plaintiff', for there is nothing but a breach of promise. But there is a reason why the promise should be fulfilled, and this reason lies in the circumstances under which the promise was made; it is

---

[1] IV. 96, *Cases*, p. 173.   [2] IV. 100, *Cases*, p. 173.
[3] LXXI. 7, *Cases*, p. 233.   [4] *Supra*, p. 126.

suggestive of the fundamental canonistical doctrine of 'cause'. Marriage seems to have been an adequate 'cause' for a promise, and it is for the enforcement of promises given for marriage that we most frequently find beneficiaries appealing to equity.

4. Again, if we look at the conditions under which an implied contract arises, some light may be thrown upon the whole question. The petitioner at the request of X became 'plegge' to the king for a farm which X held of the king, and through X's default has had to pay.[1] Again, petitioner 'atte request and praier' of B became bound to C as surety for B's debt, and as B has failed to meet his obligation C called upon the petitioner.[2] A at B's request 'undertook' for B in Ireland for certain customs; B inconsiderately sailed away and left A to meet his obligation.[3] In none of these cases is there an express promise, but a promise is raised by the relation in which the parties stand to each other. As the petitions phrase it, inasmuch as the petitioner has been *put 'in charge'* for the duty of the defendant and at his request, reason and conscience require that the defendant should *discharge* him. Even where, under similar circumstances, there is an express promise, the same process of reasoning is adduced to support its enforcement. Reasoning, therefore, from the implied to the express contract, we may conclude that the promise is enforced because there is some imperative reason why the promisor should fulfil his obligation, and this reason is found in the circumstances under which the promise was made.

5. Finally, the suits brought for specific performance of contracts to convey land lend support to the view here advanced. While there are many cases in which the promisee has paid the whole purchase price, there are many others in which he has paid nothing, but alleges that he is ready to pay. The only damage sustained is the 'loss of the bargain', that is, the loss of the advantage which would accrue to the promisee, if the promisor carried out his promise. The obligation is purely contractual; there is not the faintest suggestion of a tort.

[1] X. 186.   [2] XVI. 440.   [3] XV. 237.

For these reasons I believe that the attitude of the chancery towards contract was radically different from that of the common law before consideration became the recognized test of the enforceability of promises. The common law looked primarily at the promisee ; it compelled him to show that he had sustained damage other than that which resulted directly from the breach of contract. He must convert the breach of promise into a tort, a deceit, to himself. Chancery, on the other hand, scrutinized the position of the promisor. It asked whether he had made such a promise as in reason and conscience he ought to perform. In such an inquiry the benefit to the promisor or the immediate detriment to the promisee was a matter of secondary importance. It was forced into the background, while the promise and the circumstances under which it was made held the centre of the stage.

It is with considerable hesitancy that I venture to make any generalizations, but an examination of the chancery proceedings has led me to the following conclusion. I believe that the chancellor held that one might make a valid promise to do anything which was reasonable and possible, and that the obligation resulting from such a promise ought to be performed because the promisor had deliberately and intentionally assumed the obligation.[1] By this I do not mean that the chancellor enforced any and all promises. But in his analysis of parol contract he did not require as an essential condition to a right of action that the promisee should have been deceived or that the promisor should have been benefited. Rather did he inquire whether the enforcement of a particular promise would further some general interest. If the promisor has led the promisee to alter his position on the strength of the promise, there lies upon him a moral duty to fulfil that promise. It is desirable, in the interests of the community at large, that such promises should be enforced. A pays B £50 for a conveyance of land, or upon B's promise to deliver a letter A entrusts the letter to him. The cases are different from B's point of view. In the first case he has received a benefit ; in the second, there is no benefit. But in

[1] Cf. Spence, 852.

determining whether or no B shall be compelled to perform his promise, we look to some larger interest than that of the immediate parties to the contract. B induced A to give him the letter; he placed in A's mind a reasonable expectation that it should be delivered. Is it in the general interest that such an expectation should be fulfilled? The chancellor, I believe, determined that it was.

Closely connected with this factor is another. Some promises appear to have been enforced because of the object for which they were made. Thus money is promised for a marriage; the chancellor decrees that the promise must be performed. We might say that the promise is enforced because on the strength of it the promisee has entered upon marriage. But the fact that the beneficiary could bring the subpoena argues against this. I believe that such a promise was enforced because of the purpose for which it was given.

All this is admittedly speculative. One must be frank, and admit that it is impossible to determine absolutely the ground upon which chancery proceeded. But it seems to me that we are driven to seek the source of the chancellor's doctrines in the canon law. I have tried to state my reasons for thinking it impossible that the chancellor should have applied the theory of the common law. Hence we must look to the only other system from which he could possibly have borrowed his theory.

In the discussion of 'consideration' which St. Germain places in the mouth of the Doctor, we find it stated that a promise, to be enforceable, must have a *reasonable cause*. This cause may consist in a material advantage to the promisor, or in the object for which the promise was made. I do not think we can completely parallel the whole classification of promises, as set forth by the Doctor, in the cases in equity, but I do believe that all these cases can be explained from the principles of canon law. Therein seems to me to lie the only adequate and reasonable explanation. It is very probable that the chancellor as a judge in chancery did not proceed to the same lengths as he would have done in the ecclesiastical court. But when confronted with a new situation in chancery he did apply so far as possible the principles of that system in which as a churchman he was trained. This indirect reception of canon law is not demonstrable with mathematical precision; it seems to me, however, that the whole line of decision in equity points unequivocally towards the canon law.

I have attempted to set forth the main outlines of equitable jurisdiction in contract. Of the source of the chancellor's doctrines, the canon law, little has been said. But an investigation of the principles of the canon law with regard to contract is in itself a special study.

NOTE A

THE diversity of opinion in modern times with regard to the action of Detinue will appear from the following quotations:

'The action of detinue is an action of wrong . . .' Bayley B., in 1 C. & J. 570 (1831).

'Detinue falls within that class of actions called actions of contract, and the whole course of the proceedings shows that it is rather matter of contract than of tort . . .' Tindal C.J., in 3 M. & G. 557 (1841).

The County Courts Act, 1850 (13 & 14 Vict. c. 61), treats Detinue as founded on contract.

The Common Law Procedure Act, 1852 (15 & 16 Vict. c. 76), treats Detinue as a tort.

'Detinue is clearly in form an action *ex contractu* . . .' Erle C.J., in 11 C.B. [N.S.] 426 (1861).

'According to all authorities . . . detinue has always been considered to be an action *ex contractu* . . .' Byles J., *idem*, p. 427.

Tidd classes Detinue (with Case and Trespass) among 'actions for wrongs'. 1 Tidd's Pr. (8th ed.), pp. 4, 10–11.

Note also the interesting case of *Bryant* v. *Herbert* (1878) 3 C. P. Div. 389. The plaintiffs had delivered to the defendant a painting, in order that he might determine whether it was a genuine picture painted by himself or not. Having come to the conclusion that it was not genuine, the defendant refused to redeliver the painting, and the plaintiff accordingly brought Detinue against him. The question raised was whether the action was an action 'founded on tort' within the meaning of the County Courts Act (30 & 31 Vict. c. 142, s. 5). It was held that so far as this case was concerned, the action was founded on tort within the meaning of the Act, and though the judges did not profess to decide the historical question their comments are worth quoting.

Thus Bramwell L.J. said: 'But if the old learning, as it was called, is to be brought in to help us, I should come to the same conclusion (i. e. that the action is founded on tort). No doubt dicta and decisions are to be found that detinue is an action *ex contractu* or *ex quasi contractu*, &c., but there are dicta and decisions the other way. . . . The last case I know of is *Clemens* v. *Flight* (16 M. & W. 42). This clearly holds that the action is founded on a tortious detention.　I should therefore come to the same conclusion if these considerations governed the case.'

On the other hand, Brett L.J. (who concurred with Bramwell in the decision of the case) said : '. . . the action of detinue is technically an action founded on contract.　The action was invented to avoid the technicalities of the old law : the invention was to state a contract which could not be traversed.　Therefore I think the action of detinue, or the form of the action of detinue, so far as the remedy is concerned in its legal significance, was founded on contract.'

NOTE B

Trespass sur le Cas [1]

Un R. suist un bref de trespas sur le cas et counta coment le plaintif avoit bargaine certein terre pur certein some del defendant et monstre tout en certein, et que le covenaunt le defendant fut que il doit faire estraunge person avoir releas a luy deinz certein terme, le quell ne relessa poynt ; issint l'accion accrue a luy.

Elleker : cest accion sowne en nature d'un covenaunt, en quell cas il duist avoir ewe un bref de Covenaunt et non ce Accion : iugement de bref.

Newton : et en taunt que le trespas est conuz de vous et [vous] [2] ne monstrez autre matier, [nous] demandons iugement, etc.

Elleker : semble que le bref abatera ; qar divers cases devant cel iour ont estre tenuz pur ley en semble maniere, come en cas que ieo face covenaunt ove un Carpenter pur moy faire un meason deinz certein iour, il ne fait moy le meason, ieo n'avera null accion sinon bref de Covenaunt.　Et mesme le ley est s'un emprent sur luy de shoer mon chivall et ne face, Autre accion n'avera ieo sinon bref de covenaunt, s'il issint soit q'il ne face et faille l'especialte faille l'accion ; issint icy il ad empreint sur luy de faire estraunge per-

---

[1] This transcript is taken from MS. Harl. 4557, 112 verso ; the case is also reported in MS. Harl. 5159, 150 recto, but as there are only slight verbal variations they have not been noted.　For the Year Book report, see 14 H. VI. 18. 58.

[2] The words in square brackets are supplied.

sone relesser, le quell est un covenaunt, et est monstre que eux
n'ount relesse le quell n'est autre que covenaunt enfreint, pur que
semble [que] le bref abatera.

Newton : semble le contrarie et que le bref est bon ; qar en cas
de Carpenter que *Elleker* ad mys ieo voill bien q'il soit ley, mes s'un
Carpenter moy face covenaunt de moy faire meason bon et fort sur
un fourme en certein et il moy face meason que est deble et male et
sur autre fourme, i'avera bon accion de trespas sur le cas.   Auxi s'un
ferrour face un covenaunt ove moy pur shoer mon chivalle bien
et congeablement et il eux shoe et encludd i'avera bon Accion sur
mon cas.   Auxint si un leche emprent sur luy de moy sayner de mez
lessez, et il done A moy medicynez mes ne moy ensana, i'avera bon
accion sur mon cas ; auxint s'un home face covenaunt ove moy pur
arer mon terre en temps sesonable et il ce are en temps que ne
sesonable, i'Avera accion sur mon cas ; et le cause est en toutz lez
casez il ad enpris sur luy un matier en fait pluis que ceo que soune
en Covenaunt et issint est il en cas al barre, il ad emprise sur luy
q'un estraunger relesse al plaintif, le quel est un empris et en taunt
que ce ne fait le plaintif ad tort come en lez casez avaunt rehersez,
par que. . . .

Paston, J. : semble a mesme l'entent ; et A ceo que est dit que un
Carpenter face ove moy un covenaunt de faire a moy un meason, s'il
ne face ieo n'avera Accion sur mon cas, ieo die que si un oster
ou ferrour face covenaunt ove moy de shoer mon chivalle et il ne
face, pur que ieo passa Avaunt et mon chival n'ad solers et est perdu
pur defaut de solers, i'avera accion sur mon cas ; et si vous que estes
ad leges empristes sur vous par que i'ay perde i'avera accion sur mon
cas issint semble A moy en le cas Al barre que le bref est bon.

June, J. : semble a mesme l'entent, et come *Paston* ad dit, coment
que mon ferrour ne shoe mon chivalle i'avera accion sibien s'il
luy avoit shoe et cludd, quar tout ceo est dependaunt sur le covenaunt et en taunt que ne forsque accessorie et dependant sur ceo que
est le covenaunt sibien come i'avera accion de ceo que n'est forsque
accessorie, sibien avera ieo Accion de ceo que est principalle, par
que. . . .

Paston, J. : c'est tresbien dit.

APPENDIX OF CASES

Bundle IV, No. 69.

A tres reverent pier en dieu l'evesque de Duresme et Chanceller
D'engleterre.

Supplie tres humblement Reynold Barantyn que come nadgairs
estoit accorde perentre Robert Cluebrigg et le dit suppliant que
mesme le suppliant deinz certein temps ore passe ferroit enfeoffer
Katerine sa femme en certeins terres et tenements al value de quarant
marcz par an par terme de sa vie ; pur la greindre seurtee de quell
chose Drewe Barantyn, nadgairs citezein de Loundres, qi dieu assoill,
uncle de dit suppliant, estoit oblige a dit Robert en deux cents livres
et le dit suppliant adonques soy obligea a l'avauntdit Drewe en deux
centz livres par un estatut marchant al entent que le dit suppliant
garderoit le dit Drewe sanz damage et perde envers le dit Robert
touchant la seurtee par le dit Drewe a l'avauntdit Robert fait. Et
combien que mesme le suppliant ad complie et parforme les choses
desuisdit, issint que le dit Drewe ne nul autre pur luy n'est pas
unqore, ne iammes, sera endamage envers le dit Robert ne nul autre
pur le dite seurtee par le dit Drewe ensy fait ; nientmeins un William
Randolf et certeins autres persons, executours del testament de dit
Drewe, par force de dit estatut par le dit suppliant a dit Drewe ensy
fait, ont pursue mesme le suppliant et unqore pursuont a graunde
damage de luy et encountre l'entent suisdite : Qe pleise a vostre tres
gracious paternite de considerer les choses desuisditz et sur ceo
d'envoier pur le dit William d'estre devaunt vous a un certein iour
pur estre examine des ditz matiers, portant ovesque luy al dit iour le
dit estatut marchant et que vous pleise par vostre hault discrecon
d'ordeigner remedie en ceste partie come la bon foy et conscience
demandent, considerant que le dit suppliant autrement ne poet estre
aide, pour dieu et en oevere de charitee.

After
1417.

---

[1] The reader will observe many mistakes of grammar and orthography,
and some obvious *lapsus calami*, throughout the petitions. These are
intentionally reproduced from the documents, which are very erratic in
this respect.

Bundle IV, No. 96.

A tres noble et tres reverent piere en dieu L'evesque de Dusreme
(*sic*), chaunceler D'engleterre.

Suppliount humblement vos povres servantez, William Spenser et
Robert Clopton, qe come le xme iour de Jun darrein passe un John
Beverech del Counte de Cambrigge avoit venduz as ditz suppliantz
un mees ove les appurtenantz en Shymplyng en la counte de Suff'
pur xl livers, lez qeux sont paiez, par force de quell bargein ils ount
faitz grauntez costez entour le mees suisdit; et qe le xij^{me} iour de
Septembre adonqes proschein ensuant le dit John duist avoir delivere
seisin de mesme le mees as ditz suppliantz solonque lour covenantz,
le quel adonqes il refusa et unqore refuse a graunt perde dez ditz
suppliantz, considerantz, tres gracious Seignur, q'ils n'eient ent accion
par le comun ley, n'autre remedie sinon de vostre especial grace et
socour : qe please a vostre tres gracious Seignurie graunter ad ditz
suppliantz brief directe al dit John de estre devant vous en la chauncerie al certein iour sur certein peine par vous alimiter pur y estre
examinez et ent afaire come vous semble resoune, et ceò pur dieu et
en oevre de charite.

Date uncertain.

Bundle IV, No. 100.

A tres reverent pier en dieu et tres gracious Seignur l'evesque de
Duresme Chaunceller D'engleter.

Supplie humblement vostre humble servitour, John Burton de
Bristuyt, que come il le lundy proschien devant le fest de Seint Petre
l'advincle, l'an du regne nostre Seignur le Roy octisme, a Bristuyt
achata d'un Mark Wyllyam de mesme la ville certeins terres et tenementz c'estassavoir xij mees, v salers et iiij gardeins en Bristuyt
suisdit ove les appurtenantz, en noun de toutz les terres et tenementz
oretarde un Richard Neweton de mesme la ville ; sur quel bargayne
l'avantdit Mark ferroit astat sufficiant en ley et livroit seisin et
possession al dit John de les avantditz terres et tenementz ove les
appurtenantz quant il fuist par le dit John ou ascun autre en son
noun ent resonablement requis, pur un certein some d'argent, cestassavoir CCxl li, dount le dit John paia al dit Mark CC li, en partie du
paiement de lavantdit some de CCxl li. Et nient contresteant le
paiement devant mayns par le dit John fait et q'il ad souvent requis

After 1421.

le dit Mark de faire astat al dit John et luy lyvrer seisin et possession de les terres et tenementz suisditz en maner come avant est dit, le dit Mark ne voet faire astat ne lyvrer seisine et possession al dit John accordantz as covenantz et bargoyne suisditz de les terres et tenementz avantditz, a graunt anientisement et perpetuel destruccion de dit Suppliant s'il n'eit vostre gracious eide et socour en celle partie : Que please a vostre tres reverent paternite et gracious Seignurie, graunter brief direct al dit Mark pur apparere devant vous a certein iour sur peyn par vous alymyter d'estre examine de lez matiere suisditz et sur son examinacion luy ensy iustifier et govourner que le dit Suppliant purra aver ceo qe reson et bon concience demaundent en celle partie, Considerant, tres gracious Seignur, que le dit Suppliant ne poet mye aver remedie en ceo cas a la comune ley, et ceo pur dieu et en oevre de charite.

Plegii de prosequendo :

Willielmus Gastoigne de Brocley, Gentilman, in com' Som'.
Nichalaus Dany de Southpoderton, Gentilman, in com' Som'.

Bundle IV, No. 158.

8 Hen. V. Pleise a tres reverent piere en dieu et tres gracious Seignur l'evesque de Duresme Chaunceller D'engleterre considerer coment apres la mort Richard le Scrop, Chivaler Seignur de Bolton qui de nostre Seignur le Roy teigne en chief et qi heir est deinz age et en la garde nostre dit Seignur le Roy estoit a present, diverses patents, chartres, muniments et autres evidences touchantz le heritage mesme le heir a les mayns de William Mayhewe sont devenuz et unguor èn ses mayns estoient, de graunter un brief de peyne direct a dit William luy comandant d'estre devant nostre Seignur le Roy en sa Chauncellarie a certeigne iour par vous alimiter, ameignant ovesque luy les patentz, chartres, munimentz et autres evidences suisditz en salvacion del droit nostre Seignur le Roy et ceo pur dieu et en oevere de charite.

Endorsed : Decimo septimo die Octobris anno etc. octavo, concordatum est per consilium quod sub magno sigillo dirigatur Willielmo Meyhewe infrascripto essendi (*sic*) coram domino Rege in Cancellaria sua in crastino sancti Martini proximo futuro, deferendo secum litteras, patentes, cartas, munimenta et alia de quibus infra fit mencio.

Bundle VI, No. 20.

A tres gracious et tres reverent pier en dieu l'evesque de Wyncestre
chaunceller D'engletere.[1]

Suppliont humblement voz poverez Oratours William Overay de
Southampton et Agnes sa femme, que fut femme de Bartholomew
Marmoray, executors del testament du dit Bartholomewe, que come
un John Mascall, iadis Burgeis de Southampton suisdit, le trezime
iour D'apprill l'an du regne le Roy Henry quint, qe qieu assoill, sisme,
achata du dit Bartholomew a Southampton suisdit xl et vij bales de
waide pur iiij̄ˣˣ et xiij li. et ix d pur estre ent paier saunz delaie, dount
le dit John paia a dit Bartholomewe iesqes al sume de xxviij li., les
queux xxviij li. le dit Bartholomewe en sa vie sovent foith apres ad
demande de dit John Mascall et il les dits xxviij li. a dit Bartholomewe paier ne voleit ; le quel Bartholomewe fist la dite Agnes adonqes
sa femme et Tempane de Johane, son cosyn, ses executours, et devia,
les quex Agnes et Tempane come executours [du dit].[2] Bartholomewe
sovent foith apres la mort de dit testatour ount requie le dit John
Mascall a eux paier les ditz xxviij li. et il les paier ne voleit, et apres
le dit Tempane devia et la dite Agnes prist a Baron le dit William
Overay, les qeux William et Agnes sovent foith requis le dit John
Mascall a eux paier les ditz xxviij li. et il les paier ne voleit ; le quell
John Mascall fist ses executours, Margerie adonqes sa femme et
Henry Baron, et devia, apres qi mort les ditz suppliantz ount sovent
foitz requie les ditz Margorie et Henry Baron come executours a dit
John Mascall a eux paier les avantditz xxviij li. et ils les paier ne
volient, de qeux xxviij li. suisditz ne nul denier dicell le dit testatour
ne les ditz suppliauntz nient le pluis ne avoient ascun obligacion ou
autre suertee forsque le simple contracte suisdit, en quel cas les ditz
suppliantz sount saunz remedie a la comune ley, a graunde damage
de ditz suppliantz et en retardacion del execucion del testament suisdit,
s'ils ne aient vostre tres gracious Segnurie en icell partie : Please
a vostre tres gracious Segnurie de considerer les matiers suisditz et
sur ceo solonc vostre treshaut et tres sage discrecion d'ordener et

1424 to
1426.

---

[1] Bundle VI. No. 19 is a briefer statement of this case.
[2] Hole in document ; words in square brackets supplied throughout.

agarder que bone et due remidie soit fait en la mater suisdit as ditz suppliantz, come foy et bon concience le demaundent, pur dieu et en oevere de charitee.

Plegii de prosequendo :
Ricardus Thornes.
Johannes Sanky.

Bundle VI, No. 21.

A treshounree et tresgracious segnur et tresreverent piere en dieu l'evesque de Wyncestre et Chaunceller D'engletere.

Probably after 1413.

Supplient tres humblement les povres parochiens del esglyse de Kirkby en Kendale en la Countee de Westmerland que, come nadgairs lour esglise fuist abatuz par veillesse et autres feblesses, ils fisrent [agreement][1] ovesque un William Thornburgh Esquier, un des parochiens, q'il duist faire l'avauntdite esglise bien et covenablement estre fait, reedifie et relever honestment et [reparaille][1] pur sesze vyntz marcz, des queux l'avantdit William ad resceu quatorsze vyntz marcz et les ovesque luy retient ; et ensy est ore, tres gracious Segnur et pier en dieu, que l'avantdit William ne voet mye l'avantdit esglise faire estre fait ne reedifie issint que le Chauncell de mesme l'esglise est en point de chaier pur defaute de fesure et edificacon dicell a graunde tort, disease et pierd des toutz les parochiens avauntditz, et les queux parochiens, tres gracious Segnur, en cest matier par le comune ley ne poent mye estre eidez en ascune manere ne socourez : Si plese as voz tres hounree et tres gracious Seignurie et tres reverent paternite d'envoier par brief nostre Segnur le Roy pur l'avauntdit William de comparer devaunt vous en le Chauncellarie nostre Segnur le Roy sur un certein peine par vous alimiter et ensi ordeyner que cest matier par vous tres gracious Segnur poet solonc vostre tres sage et tres purveux[2] discrecon estre socouree et [remedie],[1] considerantz que les parochiens avauntditz ne purront mye avoir nul eide ne secoure a le comune ley, pur dieu et en overe de charitee.

Plegii de prosequendo :
Thomas de Tunstall, chivaler.
Robertus Belyngeham.

[1] Hole in document.   [2] Or ' purneux ' ?

Bundle VI, No. 299.

A tres reverent piere en dieux et son tres gracious Seignur, l'evesque de Wynchestre, Chaunceller D'engletere. Supplie tres humblement John Hogham[1], un des clerks del Chauncellarie nostre Seignur le Roy, qe come John Oklee, le lundi proschein devaunt le fest de Seint Michel l'archangele darrein passe, l'an du regne nostre dit Seignur le Roy q'orest quynt, tierce, a Loundres en la paroche de Seint Cristofore en la garde de Bradstrete, achata certeins draps, laynes et diverses colours pur xxvj li., queux luy doit et luy detient encountre droit ad damages de dit John Hogham de x li., dount il prie remedie, et ceo pur dieu et en oevere de charite.

After 1416.

Plegii de prosequendo:
> Ricardus Sturgeon.
> Willielmus Robroke.

Bundle VII, No. 104.

A tres reverent pier en dieux l'erchevesque D'everwyk Chaunceller D'engletere.[2]

Supplie humblement Roger Denys de Loundres, Fremason, que come bargaine ceo prist a Wyburton parentre le dit suppliant et Philip Proketour de Wyburton et Roger Robynson de mesme la ville en le fest de Seint Martyn, l'evesque, l'an de regne le Roy Henry quint, pier nostre Seignur le Roy q'orest, oeptisme, que le dit suppliant ferroit l'esglise et le steple de la dit ville de Wyburton[3] en manere et forme contenuz en un escript endente ent entre eux fait, preignant pur le dit bargayne C iiij$\overset{xx}{}$ x marcz, come en le dit escript plus pleinement est contenuz; et come en apres a la dit ville de Wyburton, c'estassavoir le lundy proschein apres le fest de Seynt Michell l'archangell adonqes proschein ensuant, bargaine ceo prist saunz especialtee parentre le dit suppliant et les ditz Philip Proketour et Roger Robynson, c'estassavoir que le dit suppliant ferroit xij corbellez en la dit esglise et q'il ferroit enbatailler le dit esteple ovesque legementz et tables accordantz ovesque franke pere, pur

1426 to 1432.

---

[1] Perhaps 'Hegham'.

[2] Bundle VII, No. 105, is another copy of the same petition; there are slight variations, which are noted.

[3] After 'Wyburton', VII. 105 adds: 'de pleyn overaigne et de pere appelle rough stones saunz table ou corbell', and omits from 'en manere' to 'preignant'.

quele ils luy paieront a taunt come il expenderoit entre la faisaunce
de le dit overaigne outre le primer covenaunt suisdit, que amount
a cent marcz, come il ad este aiugge par quatre maistres masons de
frank pere ; Et les dit Philip Proketour et Roger Robynson les ditz
cent marcz au dit suppliant paier ne voillent, et il est ensy, gracious
Seignur, que le dit suppliant ne poet avoir accion envers eux a le
comune ley par bref de covenaunt ne en autre manere, pur ceo q'il
n'ad mye especialte de le covenaunt, a graunde anientisement de dit
suppliant, s'il n'eit remedie par vostre Seignurie en ycell partie : Please
a vostre tres gracious Seignurie de considerer les premissez et de
grauntier severalx briefs directz envers les ditz Phylip Proketour et
Roger Robynson eux comaundantz de comparer devaunt vous a certein
iour et sur certein peine par vous alimitier de respondre a les premisses,
pur dieux et en oevere de charitee.

     Plegii de prosequendo :
        Ricardus Johnson de London.
        Willielmus Bridde de London.

Note on date of case.—The transaction is said to have taken place in
8 Hen. V ; as the petition is addressed to the Archbishop of York, it must
have come up later than this. John Kempe was made chancellor and Archbishop of York in 1426, and retained the office till 1432. The case therefore would seem to fall between those two dates. Kempe was again made
chancellor in 1450, and it is possible that this petition came up in his second
chancellorship. However, as that would imply a very great delay in
bringing the case up, the first date is taken as preferable.

Bundle VII, No. 112.

A mon Reverend piere en dieu l'ercevesque D'everwyk chaunceller
D'engletere.

Date
uncertain.
    Supplie tres humblement John Goldsmyth de Melton Moubray,
merchant, que come il eit vendu a un William Sakes, servant et
Chapman a John Trewe de Colchestre, marchant, troys quarts et
demy de woed al oeps et profyt de mesme le John Trewe pur un
certein some apaierz au certein iour, et fuist ensy, gracious Segnur,
que a les iours de paiement du dit some assignez le dit suppliant
venoit au dit John Trewe pur demander son paiement, le quel John
Trewe, ymaginant de defrauder le dit suppliant de son dit paiement,
disoit que son dit servant n'avoit acchatee de luy synon deux quarts
et demy de wood et le quell unquore fuist sy malveys et feble que ne
fuist de tiel value sicome le dit William l'avoit achate, la ou en fait
et loiaulte il avoit troys quarts et demy sicome il sera duement

par sufficiantz lettres testimoinalx provee, et ensy le dit suppliant est forbarre et delaie de sa monie et est verrayseble d'estre mys a graund damage et perde saunz vostre gracious eide et socour celle partie : Que please a vostre tres reverend paternite de considerer les premises et coment le dit suppliant a cause q'il n'ad ascun especialtee des premises est par le dit John Trewe celle partie estre decieu et sur ceo de vostre benigne grace grauntier deux briefs directz as ditz John Trewe et William d'estre devant vous au certein iour sur certein peyne d'estre examine sur la matiere avantdite et par leur examinacion de faire que droit et reason demaundent, en oevere de charitee.

Plegii de prosequendo :

Henr' Roos, clericus.

Reg' Sharp de Melton.

Bundle VII, No. 250.

A tres reverent piere en dieu et mon tres gracious Segnur L'erchevesqz d'everwyk et Chaunceller D'englitere.

Supplie humblement Robert Craunford, que come accorde soy prist parentre luy d'un part, et John Drayton et John son fitz d'autre part, cestassavoir a Aldurmeston en le counte de Worcestre le xxiiij e iour de septembr l'an du reigne nostre Segnur le Roy q'ore est quinte, que le dit John fitz John avoit et prendroit a femme Anne file a dit Robert et que deinz un moys apres les espousailles et mariage issint parentre eux faitz le dit John Drayton ferroit astat as ditz John fitz John et Anne des teres et tenementz a la value de xx marcz par an outre lez reprisez deinz le maner de Botilbrigge en le Counte de Huntyngden et Craunford en le Counte de Northanpton, a avoir et tenir lez dites teres et tenementz issint a la value de xx marcz par an as ditz John fitz John et Anne et a les heirs de lour deux corps engendrez ; pur cause de quel accorde la marriage soy prist parentre lez ditz John fitz John et Anne, et puis le dit John fitz John [avoit][1] issue parentre luy et mesme cesty Anne et morust, le dit estat nient fait, nient contristeant que le dit John Drayton a ceo faire sovent foitz ad este requis par les ditz Robert et Anne, a graunde damage du dit Robert et autres : Please a vostre gracious Segnurie deconsiderer (*sic*) lez premissez et que le dit suppliant n'ad mye remedie en celle partie par la comune ley et sur ceo de grauntier un brief sur certein notable peyne a dit John Drayton direct de comparier devaunt

After 1426.

[1] Hole in document.

vous a certein iour par vous alimiter en la chauncerie nostre Segnur le Roy al fyn pur illeoques estre examine de et sur les premissez, issint que remedie ent soit fait a dit suppliant solonc ceo que reson et concience demaundent, Et ceo pur dieu et en oevre de charite.[1]

Bundle IX, No. 132.

To the right worchipfull fader in god Bisshop of Bathe Chaunceller of Englond.

1439 to 1440.

Beseches mekely your pouer bedeman John Osgodby of London, Brewer, forasmoche as ther was a mater in debate by twyx John Kyffawe, Wodemonger, and Thomas Langley of London, Botelmaker, for the wheche mater were chosen arbitros ov bothe partyes and eyther party bounden to other in obligacions of xx li., the wheche obligacions were delivert to the arbitros ; and after thus come the said John Kyffawe, the too party, to your said besecher by asotelte and asked hym where was the obligacion, and your said besecher shewed yt to hym ; and whenne he hadde yt he held yt and wolnot gyffe yt agayne ; and your said besecher toke accions of detenue and detenue (*sic*) and canne have no recovere by lawe, and thus your said besecher ys lykly to pay this obligacion of xx li., w^t outen your gracious lordship or remedy to be putte on hys behalf : Wherefore lyke yt to your gracious lordship to consider this mater aforesaid and to graunte a wrytte under certeyn payn directe to the said Thomas[2] that he may apere afore yowe in the Chauncery atte certein day by yowe alymed and therto be examined afore yowe and thenne to reule the mater aforesaid as lawe and conciens wolle, for the love of god and yn the way of charite.

Endorsed: Memorandum quod quinto die Novembris anno regni Regis Henrici sexti decimo septimo, Willielmus Staynford de London, Gentilman, et Iohannes Alkyn de London, Gentilman, coram dicto domino Rege in Cancellaria sua, personaliter constituti manuceperunt pro Iohanne Osgodby, videlicet uterque eorum, quod in casu quo ipse materiam in hac supplicacione specificatam veram probare non poterit, tunc prefato Thome Langley omnia dampna et expensas que ipse ea occasione sustinebit eidem Thome satisfacient iuxta formam statuti in hac parte editi et promisi.

---

[1] There is a short endorsement, but it is too faint to be legible.
[2] At first sight this appears to be a mistake for ' John ' ; Thomas, however, is the party mentioned in the endorsement, so the presumption is that he got hold of the obligation.

Bundle IX, No. 206.

To þe ryght gracious Lord þe Chaunceller of England.

Besecheth ful humbly Richard ap Howell þat where as William, 1440 (?). Priour of þe cherche of Seint Cuthlace of Hereford, late be his Covent seall let to ferme to on Leonard Holand his manere of Prioures Frome wyth þappourtenances for a certein some yeerly to be paied to þe seyde Priour and his successours and under oþer certein condicions comprehended in an endenture betwen hem made as in þe seid endenture it is comprehended more pleinly þe whiche Leonard after þe same lees made unto hym, lete over þe same manior to þe seid suppliant be his lettre sealed under þe conditions aboveseid be vertue of which latter lees þe seid suppliant entred and occupied and whenne þe seid suppliant hadde sowen gret part of þe landes of þe seid manoir and done þere upon gret husbondrye þe seid priour and Leonard ymaginyng to putte þe seyd suppliant fro his ferme entretyd þe seid suppliant to leve þe terme þat he hadde in þe seid ferme and for þat so to be leved graunted be word þat þe seid suppliant shulde have all þe cornes growyng on þe same manoir frely to þe which þe seid suppliant agreed hym and upon þys dilivered to þe seid Priour by þadvys of þe seyd Leonard as well þe endenture made to þe seyd Leonard be þe seid Priour and convent as þendenture made be þe same Leonard un to þe seid suppliant, þe seid priour seyng boþe þendentures þus delivered un to hym wolde not suffre þe seid suppliant to have þe seid cornes aftyr þere seid covenant but hath takyn hem to hys owne oeps to þe grete hurt of þe seid suppliant in þis partie : That it plese un to youre gracious lordshippe to considere how þe seid suplliant hath no remedie at þe comon lawe an þere upon to graunte certein wryttes directid to þe seid priour and Leonard to be before you at a certein day to be examined of þe mater above seid and þere upon to do as consience and lawe wolle for þe love of god and in þe wey of charite.

Plegii de prosequendo :

Willielmus Watkyns de com' Buk', Gentilman.

Johannes Marchant de London, Gentilman.

Endorsed[1] : Memorandum Haec billa excerpta fuit ex bundello brevium in Cancellaria de Aᵒ 1ᵐᵒ H. 6ᵗⁱ.

---

[1] Written on the back of the petition in a large hand ; obviously a later addition.

Bundle IX, No. 335.

To hise fulgracius Lord the Chaunceller of England.

After
1432.

Rightmekely (*sic*) besechith Rauf Bellers that for as moche as William Harper of Mancestre and Richard Barbour weren endetted to the seyde Rauf in certain sumes of mone withoute specialte to be payed unto the seyde Rauf or to hise certain attorne at certain dayes past at the wheche dayes and longe aftir the seyde William and Richard weren required by the seyde Rauf to make hym payment of the seyde sumes, to the wheche request the seyde William and Richard wolde not obeye in any wyse soo that the seyde Rauf, consideryng that þe seyde William and Richard wolde make hor lawe in that partie agens faithe and good conscience, sued to the Archebisshop of Yorke, at that tyme chaunceller of England, for remedie in that caas, apon the wheche suggestion the seyde chaunceller graunted under certain payne writtes severally direct unto þe seyde William and Richard to apere afore hym in the chauncery there to be examyned apon the seyde matere ; by force of that oon of the seyde writtes the seyd Richard apered in the seyde chauncerie and there agreed with the seyd suppliant and the seyd William myght nat befande soo that the writ direct unto hym stode in none effect : wherefore liketh to youre gracius lordeship to graunte a writ under a certain payn direct to the seyd William to aper afore yowe in the chauncerie there to be examyned apon the matere aforeseyd for goddis luf and in werk of charite.

Bundle IX, No. 382.

To my full gracious Lord the Bysshop of Bath and Welles and Chaunceller of Inglond.

1442 to
1443.

Prayeth and mekely besecheth youre povere oratour William Parkoure, that whare the same suppliant and one Gilbert Bedenall of Benerley in the counte of York, Mercer, hadde theyr comon silver and golde in Mercerware to the price and value of xl S. and more pakked in fotepak and in hors pak to be demenet and reulet be adviss and labour of the sayd Suppliant unto theyr bother oeps sex yer to geder, that is to say fro the sevent yer of oure soveraigne Lord now beyng unto the xiiij yer of the same oure soveraigne Lord, with in whiche tyme of sex yer the same Gilbert had by thadvise (*sic*) and labour abovesaid all thencresse (*sic*) of the said silver and gode provenaunt, that is to say xxxiiij li., and the said Suppliant no part ne none cane gete by the comon lawe, whare by their covenaunt he shuld have the half: Wharefore lyke it unto youre graciouse lordship to graunte unto the said Suppliant a writte upon a certeyn peyn directe unto the same Gilbert to apper be fore yowe in the Chauncery of oure seid soveraigne lord at a certeyn day by yowe to be lymite to have and do in the maters abovesaid as gode treuth and conscience will, for goddes love and in way of charite.

Endorsed: Memorandum quod, sexto die Novembris Anno regni Regis Henrici sexti vicesimo, Henricus Thwaytes et Iohannes Muston coram prefato domino Rege in cancellaria sua personaliter constituti, manuceperunt, videlicet uterque eorum, pro Willielmo Parkour, quod, si ipse materiam in hac supplicacione specificatam veram probare non poterit, tunc predictus Willielmus (*sic*) prefato Gilberto pro omnibus dampnis et expensis que in hac parte sustentabit satisfaciet, iuxta formam statuti inde editi et promisi.

Bundle IX, No. 405.

Suppleaunt a vous umblement vostre povre oratour Richard Cordie, que come Thomas Rose vendit a luy un Mese, xl acres de terre, pur C marces de argent, des que C marces lxx marces furent paiez a luy et pur lez autres xx li. le dit Richard fuist tenuz al dit Thomas en un obligacion apaier a luy all iour comprise deinz mesme le obligacion; par force de quele le dit Thomas enfeffa le dit Richard par un fait de feffement de lez ditz mese et terre a avoir et tenir a luy et a ses heirz a toutz iours, et oblige luy et cez heirez a garrant all dit Richard et sez heires a toutz iourz; par lou graunde parcell de lez dit Mese et terre fuist tenuz en villenage par cause de quele Seignur de le dit terre ad ouste le dite Richard et le dit Thomas sue le dit Richard pur lez ditz xx li. comprise deinz le obligacion, sur quele grevaunce le dit Richard n'ad mie remidie al le comune ley: pur que plesit a vous de graunter un sub pena d'estre direct al dit Thomas d'aperer devaunt vous en le chauncerie all certein iour par vous limitez de estre examinez sur lez ditz maters, en honour de dieu et par voie de charite.

Endorsed: Memorandum quod vicesimo nono die Iunij Anno regni Regis Henrici sexti decimo octavo, Iohannes Dentard de villa Westm', yoman, et Willielmus Rous de Nenton in com' Surr', husbondman, coram dicto domino Rege in cancellaria sua personaliter constituti manuceperunt videlicet uterque eorum pro prefato Ricardo quod in casu quo ipse materiam in hac supplicacione specificatam veram

1440 to 1441.

probare non poterit, tunc prefato Thome omnia dampna et expensas qua ipsa occassione sustinebit satisfaciet (*sic*) iuxta formam statuti inde editi et promisi, &c.

Bundle X, No. 17.

A tresreverent pier en dieu l'evesque de Bathe son tresgracous Segnur.

After 1432.

Supplie humblement John Polyng, Qe come un Symon Blaundell apprompta de ly xx li. et ly bailla ij obligacons, un par le quell un Ric' Webber fuit oblige al dit Symon en ix li., l'autre par le quell un Thomas Trevily fuit oblige al dit Symon en vij li., de rescevoir lez sommes en iceux contenus en payement et satisfaccon pur l'afferant de lez ditz xx li.; a le quel payement lez ditz Ric' et Thomas al request du dit Symon agreerunt; puis le dit Symon morust intestat sauns ascuns biens aver, puis le dit Ric' fist un Isabell, sa femme, son exccecutrix et morust, quell Isabell puis prist a baron un Ric' Medros; Et sovent puis le dit suppliant ad requys lez ditz Thomas, Ric' Medros et Isabell de lez payer lez ditz dettes a eux proferant lez ditz obligacions et eux, veiantz que le dit suppliant ne puit ascun accon avoir vers eux a le comyn ley, ne voillent ly payer, a grant anyntysment du dit suppliant s'il n'eit vostre tresgracous eide: Pleise a vostre tresgracous Segnurie de considerer les premysses et de graunter al dit suppliant ij breves, un d'eux directe al dit Thomas, et l'auter as ditz Ric' Medros et Isabell sa femme, de comparer devant vous a un certeyn iour sur un certeyn peyne par vous a lymyter d'estre examines sur lez premyssez et d'ent faire droit solonc vostre tres gracious discrecon pur dieu et en oevre de charytee.

Bundle X, No. 207.

To my ful graciouse lord the bysshop of Bathe chaunceller of England.

After 1432.

Mekely besekes unto your graciouse lordship John Derehill of the shire of Cornwaill for as muche as the said beseker, atte the Instaunce and prayer of on William Bampton of the said Shire, yoman, And opon ful promisse to kepe hym harmelese, was bounden with the said William unto on Nicholas late Abbot of Newenham in the counte of Devonshire in an obligacon of a C mark to be paied atte a certain day conteyned in the said obligacon; Whereuppon on Tristram now abbot of the said abbaye be covyn and assent of the said William suyth and vexit your said beseker with divers writtes in the said counte and putte him to grete vexacion an coste for the said somme, to the undoyng of your said beseker in lasse than hit be remedyed by youre graciouse lordship : Please hit unto your good grace to graunt a writte sub pena direct to the said William atte acertain (*sic*) day and opon a certain somme by youe alimited to a piere a fore your graciouse presence, and after due examinacion had to fynde your said beseker sufficient suirte to kepe him harmlese agains the said abbot as he promised the said beseker, as reson and conscience woll after your highe and graciouse discrecon, For þe love of god and in Werk of Charite.

Bundle XI, No. 8 *a*.

To the full gracious fader in god Bisshop of Bath and Chaunceller of Inglond.[1]

Besechith mekely un to your gracious Lordship John Barnesby parson of the chirche of Slapton in the Counte of Norhampton, that where as the seide parson let his chirche to oon William Chacombe of Toucestre for the terme of thre yere of grete trist with oute any specialte and for as muche as the first two yeres were of grete derth and the thirde yere wexed grete chepe the seide William, seyng his avayle not so grete in the third yere os he had in the two yeres be fore, Also he seyng that your seide Besecher had no writyng to ground hym apon at the comyn lawe to conceyve any accion by and so with oute remedie, refusid to hold the third yere to the grete losse and harme of your seide Besecher the yerely value : Wherfor, please it to your full gracious Lordship to consider the mater above seide and there apon to graunte a writ sub pena directe un to the seide William to appere be fore you at a certeyn day under a certeyne peyne by you alymet and ther to be examyned of seide mater as concience will for the love of god and be way of charite.

After 1432.

    Plegii de prosequendo :

        Willielmus Asshely.

        Johannes Reynolds.

---

[1] Bundle XI, No. 8, is a copy of this petition, but it is not addressed to any particular Chancellor, and the 'pledges' are omitted.

Bundle XI, No. 47.

To my ful gracious Lorde bysshop of Bathe Chaunceller of
Engelond.

After
1432.

Besechith mekely un to youre gracious lordship youre pouer
servaunt John Leomyster, one of the Clerkes of the Chauncery, that
where one Thomas of Oclee of Erlygham in the Counte of Gloucestre,
Squyer, oweth to Robert Manfeld of Gynes x mark, the which x mark
was assyned be the seyde Robert Manfeld in recorde of the Mayre of
Caleys for to be payed to youre seyde suppliaunt for certeyn money
that the seyde Robert Maunfeld owed to hym; the seyde Thomas
of Oclee, late beyng at London, a fore worthy men knowleged the
dewete and payment ther of to be made to youre seyde suppliaunt,
the whiche he utterly seth hathe refused: Wherefore please hit un to
youre lordship to consider thys mater and ther upon of youre grace
to graunte the seyde suppliaunt a Sub pena direct un to the seyde
Thomas of Oclee, to appere a fore yow at a certeyn day and to be
examyned of this mater abovesayd and as ye may fynde be examinacion to remedy hit aftur youre discrecion, for the love of godde and
in wey of charitee.

Plegii de prosequendo:
 Thomas Asshecombe.
 Johannes Halle.

Bundle XI, No. 160.

To the right Reverent Fader in God the bisshop of Bathe
Chanceler of England.

After
1432.

Humely (*sic*) besechith youre poure Oratour John Pottok that
where he solde certeyns goodis and catalles to Harry Brome be the
handes of oone Margrete Wylton for x li. For the which the sayd
Harry was bound in an obligacion to your sayd besecher, the whiche
sayd Margrete lost the forsayd obligacion: That it please to your
gracious lordship consciensly to consider the premyse and [that][1] your
sayd besecher be cause that the sayd obligacion is loste hath noo
remedie atte the comune lawe to recover the sayd some and over that
of your good and gracious lordshyp to graunt your sayd besecher
a writte under a certeyne peyne agenst the sayd Harry to apeyr in

---

[1] Hole in document.

the Chauncerye at the xvme of Pasch' that next comyth, there to fore yow to be examyned upon the sayd mater as right and consciens requiren at the Reverence of godd and in weye of Charitee.

Plegii de prosequendo :
> Hugo atte Water.
> Johannes Corff.

Bundle XI, No. 427 a.

To the ryght reverent fadur in god Bysshop of Bathe Chaunceller of England.[1]

Mekely beseketh youre pore bedman Thomas Baby, Prest, that where as youre seid Suppliant delivered certein godes of grete trust to on John Bramfeld of London, Prest, and therupon borowed XX. S. to be paid agen atte certeine day be twene hem acorded, atte whiche day youre seid Suppliant come and paid to the seid John the seid XX. S. and required the seid John to deliver hym the seid godes ; and the seid John aftur the seid payment ensured youre seid suppliant on faith and on his pristhode [to] delyver the seid godes on the morow, and in the mene tyme the seid John solde awey the seid godes to a straunge man in grete disseit to youre seid Suppliant and to that entent that yef he toke an accon of detenu agene the seid John that he myght have come in and waged his lawe ; and so your sayd Suppliant shuld be withoute remedie in grete hyndryng to hym withoute your speciall grace in this mater had : Wherfor, plese hit un to youre high grace to consydre these premysses and in relevyng of youre seid Suppliant to graunt a wryt directe to the seid John to aper a for you atte a certein day in the chauncerie under a certein peyne by you lymyted, there to be examyned of this mater as trouth and cociens (*sic*) woll, for the love of God and in the wey of charite.

Endorsed : Memorandum quod tam infrascriptus Thomas quam infrascriptus Iohannes pretextu cuiusdam brevis domini Regis eidem Iohanni directi et in Cancellaria eiusdem domini Regis ad diem in eodem breve contentum ad respondendum super hiis que sibi per peticionem istam ad persecutionem predicto Thome obicerent, ibidem personaliter comparuerunt. Qua quidem peticione in Cancellaria predicta in presentia parcium predictarum lecta, ac materia in eadem nec non responsionibus et replicacionibus utriusque parcium illarum

After 1432.

---

[1] Bundle XI, Nos. 427 *b*, 427 *c*, 427 *d*, are copies of this pleading, and are substantially the same except that they are not endorsed with judgement.

pro iure suo in hac parte probando plenius auditis et intellectis, consideratum fuit per curiam Cancellarie predicte quod predictus Thomas recuperet bona infrascripta, videlicet unam murram et quatuordecim solidos et octo denarios pro sex coclearibus parcell bonorum predictorum.

Bundle XII, No. 201.

A tres reverent Segnur l'evesque de Bathe et de Welles
Chaunceller D'engletere.

After 1432.

Supplie humblement vostre povre oratour Richard Pers, que come John Alewent et Thomas Fylder, servantz le dit Richard en son service esteantz en alant en sez bosoignez hors de la meere, par dyvers enemyez nostre Segnur le Roy furent sur la meere prisez ensemblement ove autres bienz le dit suppliant et cariez en la Mounte de Seynt Michell et illoqs raunsome a xl marcz; a cause de quele le dit suppliant vient a un William Becche et ovesque luy accorda qu'il duist delyveres lez ditz prisons hors del dit prison, A cause de quele le dit William preist del dit Suppliant xl marcz, et nient [obsteant][1] le dit William riens a ceo fist, par qi lez ditz prisons, pur ceo que lour raunsom ne vient a iour a eux limite, furent graundement distressez, stokkes et malement tretes, issint q'ils furent en despeire de lour viez, a final destruccon des ditz prisons et a graund anientissement le dit suppliant, saunz vostre tres gracious eide et socour: Que please a vostre tres gracious Segnurie de considerer lez premissez et coment le dit Suppliant n'ad mye remedie solonque la cours del Comune ley et sur ceo de grauntier al dit Suppliant bref de sub pena direct al dit William d'estre examine devaunt vous de lez premissez a certein iour par vous limitez et sur ceo faire solonque ceo que bon foy et concience demaunde, Et ceo pur dieu et en overe du charite.

Plegii de prosequendo:
Edwardus Mills.
Johannes Boteler.

Bundle XIV, No. 5.

To the most reverent Fader in God John Erchbysshop of
Caunterbury Chauncellere of Englond.

1443 to 1450.

Besechuth humbully youre pore and contynuell oratoure, Conrade Goldsmyth, that where oon Laurence Walkere the Saturday next byfore the Fest of the Purification of oure lady, the yere of the regne

---

[1] Hole in document.

of the Kyng oure sovereyne lord, that is to say Kyng Harry the Sixte, aftur the conquest xxj⁰, att Teukesbury bought of youre seide besechere ij clothes and half of blankett for vij li. to be payode to the same besechere in the Fest of the Anunciacon of oure lady thenne next sewyng, for whiche payement as woll and trewely to be made oon Symkyn Bakere of Teukesbury undurtoke and bykome borowe for the seide Laurence, in as muche as the seide supliant wold nothur have solde nor delyverode the seide clothe un to the seide Laurence butt only uppon trust of the seide Symkyn and that he wolde undur-take for . . .[1] payement of the seide sume which he feythfully pro-myttode un to the seide supliant that he schulde be satisfiode and payode ther of atte his day, of which sume remayneth yett iij li. un payode which nothur the seide Laurence nor the seide Symkyn yett hathe satisfiode nor payode un to youre seide besecher ; and the seide Laurence is wythdrawen and dyssnode[2] to strange places unknowen so that youre seide besechere may noo remedye have agenst hym thaughe he sewe hym by wrytte nor agenst the seide Symkyn by the cours of the comyn lawe : Pleasith youre gracious Lordship to consyder these premissez and ther uppon to do the seide Conrade to have dewe remedy agenest the seide Symkyn, for the love of God and in Wey of Charyte.

Plegii de prosequendo :

Ricardus Bury de Solbe in Com' Glouc'.

Henricus Wakfeld de Camden in eadem Com'.

Bundle XV, No. 20 a.

To the ryght worchipfull fader in god the Erchebysshop of Canterbury and Chaunceller of Inglond.

Besechith mekely youre servauntz and continuell oratours, Sir William Drury, Knight, and Johane his doughter, lathe the wyfe of Robert Aysshefeld the yonger, that, where as accorde was hadde be twen the seid William and Robert Aysshefelde, Squyer, the older, that the seid Robert Aysshefeld the yonger, sone to the seid Robert Aysshefeld the elder, shulde wedde the seid Johane, doughter of youre seid suppliaunt, and the seid Robert Aysshefeld the fader shulde do lawful estat to be made of alle his meses, londes and tenementz in the townes of Michel Yernemouthe and Southton to

After 1432.

---

[1] Hole in document. [2] The word is uncertain.

the seid Robert the sone and Johane and to the heirs of the seid
Robert the sone of the body of the seid Johane be gotyn, and that
the seid Robert the sone and Johane his wyfe shulde be made suer
in lawe of a yerely rente of x marcs to take in the maner of Lytylhawe
duryng the lyve of the seid Robert the fader, and also that the seid
Robert the sone and Johane shulde be made suer be the seid Robert
the fader and his feffes of the seid maner in Lytylhawe to have it after
the decesse of the seid Robert the fader to the seid Robert the sone
and Johane and to heyrs of Robert the sone of the body of the seid
Johane be gotyn ; wheche Robert the fader be cause the same maner
is helde of the kyng in chief, sued a licence that he myghte of the
same maner enfeffe Hug' Bekenham and Water Gerard en fee, and
that thei ther of myghte make estat a geyn to the seid Robert the
fader terme of his lyve, the remaindre ther of to the seid Robert
the sone and Johane in the some a bove seid, as in the seid license
more pleynly apereth, and ther of made estate to the same Hug'
and Water to the same entent ; for the whech mariage and estates to
be made your seid suppliaunt, William Drury shulde paie to the seid

Robert the fader viij $\overset{xx}{}$ x marcs, wher of the seid William hath paied
a gret parte and the residue he muste content at the dayes assignad ;
and nout wythstandyng that the seid mariage was finished and day
a poynted at twene theme of the seid estates to be made, for as
muche as it happed the seid Robert the sone to dye in the mene
tyme, the seid Robert the fader wulde nout suffre the seid estates to
be made accordyng to the acordes a bove seid : Please hit youre
gracious Lordshippe to consedre these premisses and howe of this
mater youre seid suppliauntes have no remedye atte Comone lawe,
and theruppon to graunt to youre seid suppliauntes Writtes sub pena
directe to the seid Robert Aysshefeld, Hug' and Water to appere
a fore you atte a certeyn day under a certeyn peyne by you to be
lymyted, to be examened of these premisses and theruppon to rewle
hem to make the seid estates acordynge to the seid accorde, as good
feith and conscience requiren, atte the reverence of god and for
charite.

Plegii de prosequendo :

Johannes Hervy de Lavenham, Gentilman.
Rogerus Brook de Bernaham, Gentilman.

Note.—For the defendant's answer see Bundle XV, No. 20 *b.*

Bundle XV, No. 20 *b*.

The answer of Hug' Bokenham and Water Bayard, Clerk, to the
   bille goven agens hem be Sir William, Knyght, and Jane his
   doughter, in þe Chauncerye.

The seid Hug' and Water for answer seyn that they were enfeffyd
in yᵉ seid Maner of Lytelhaghe for discharge of suyrte of an obligacion
in which þe seid Hug' and Water were boundyn to the seid Sir William
in xl marcs atte request of þe seid Robert Asshfeld; And also to
make estate of þe seid Maner to þe seid Robert Asshfeld terme of
his lyfe withoutyn enpechement of wast, the remayndre thereof to
Robert Asshfeld, his sone, and to Jane, doughter of the seid
Sir William, accordyng to þe licence, upon certeyn condicions, which
were rehersyd attwyn them, of certeyn payments and suyrtees to be
payed and made be þe seid Sir William to þe seid Robert Asshfeld,
the fadir, be the fest of of (*sic*) lammesse last past; For þe which þe
seid Sir William and Robert ben in controversie be bille here in
this place, wherfore so that bothe parties can agree them that the
condicions be parformyd, orell yf it can be provyd they be parformyd
on the þe (*sic*) said Sir William's part, that we may be saved harmless
agens þe said Robert Asshfeld and have lyvere of þe seid obligacion,
we be redy and at alle tymes shall be to make estate accordyng to
the seid licence; wherfore we praye to be dismyssed oute of court
with oure resonable costes.

Note.—Bundle XV, No. 21, is a petition addressed to the chancellor by
the same complainants, but they pray for a 'sub pena Against Robert
Asshfeld' alone. The petition sets up substantially the same facts, and
concludes with the prayer that the chancellor '. . . rewle the saide
Robert Asshefeld to do in seid mater as moche as he may do accordyng
to the seid accord, as good feith and conscience requiren, atte the reverence
of god and for charite'.

Bundle XV, No. 52.

Unto the ful reverent fader in God the Archbisship of Caunterbury
Chaunceller of Ingelond.

Besechen to your high lordship Thomas Acton, William de Lones,   **After**
William Abraham, John Aleyn and Richard Hervy herby to consider   **1444.**
that where thei hade C tonne Wyn wᵗ other godes to the value of
v C (i. e. 500) li. laded in a ship called the Mighell of Dertmouth
comyng fro Burdeux toward London, the which wyn and godes were
taken uppon the See by one Thomas de la Tere of Bretayne sithen

trewes hade bitwene our soverain lord þe king of Ingelond and the Duke of Bretayne, for the which wyn and godes your seid besechers sued a lettre undre the prive seall of our seid soverain lord directe to the same Duke to have her seid wyn and godes agein or elles an answer wherfore thei shuld nat be restored to hem; And therupp on your seid besechers comoved w^t an herande of armes to have delivered þe same lettre to þe seid Duke and from him to have brought to hem an answer; ther come the fifte day of May in the yere of our soverain lord aforseid xxij in the parisshe of Seint Martin in the vynetrie of London one Robert Wenyngton by covyn of þe seid Thomas de la Tere and covenaunted and undretoke to your seid besechers to deliver þe seid lettre and bryng in to þe seid parisshe a redy answer of þe same lettre fro the Duke aforseid atte fest of lamasse then next suyng, at which v day þe same Robert reseyved the seid lettre and yet brought none answer to hem there of; So that your seid besechers are nat restored to her wyn and godes bicause none answer is hade, to her harmes of M^l li.; and the seid Robert hath housed and herberwed þe same Thomas de la Tere takyng godes out of Bretayne for þe seid wyn and godes sithen the resceyt of the lettre aforseid: Wherfore please it to your gracious lordship, consideryng þe premisses aforseid, to graunte a writte upon a certein peyne directe to the seid Robert him comaundyng to appere afore you in the Chauncerie at a certein day by you limyt for to be examined and answer to þe mater afore rehersed and whether he hath delivered þe seid lettre or none and upon þe seid examinacon hade to content your seid besechers for her costes and damages and that for the love of god and in wey of charite.

Note.—The right-hand edge of this document is much worn; in fact the whole petition was difficult to decipher.

Bundle XV, No. 140 *a*.

To the moste reverent fader in god Archbysshop of Cantuar' Chaunceller of Englond.

After
1443.
Humble besechith Hammond Sutton that where late hit was accorded and agreed by twix John Bussy, knyght, and your saide besecher, þat John, sone and heire apperaunte of the saide John Bussy, shuld wedde and take to wyff Agnes, doghter of your saide besecher; For which maryagge so to be hadde and (*sic*) a sure estate of landez and tenementz of the yerely value of xx li. a boffe all charges

and reprys to be made by the saide John Bussy or other persones for hym to the saide John the sone and Agnes and heire heires of ther bodys comynge with in a moneth after the mariage made. Not with stondyng the saide John Bussy Knyght yite hath not made no suche astate of dyvers landez and tenementz to the saide John sone and Agnes after the Fourme of the saide accorde, bot yt to doo he utterly refuseth agenste all gude faith and consciens : Please hit to your right gracious lordeship to considre thez premissez and þat your saide besecher in this partye hath no remedy by the comune lawe, and ther uppon to graunte to hym a wryte directed to the saide John Bussy, Knyght, hym comaundyng to appere by fore yowe at a certayn day uppon a certayn payn by yowe to be lymeted, to be examined of this aforsaide and ther uppan to do and receyve þat gude fath and consiens requireth in this party, and he shall pray to gode for yowe.

Plegii de prosequendo :
Johannes Burton.
Ricardus Leek.

Bundle XV, No. 140 *b*.

This is the answer of Sir John Bussy, Knyght, unto þe bill ageynes him in the chauncery be Hamond Sutton.

First the saide Sir John saith that the mater contened in the saide bill is not mater sufficiant to pute hym to answer to, and if it be sufficiant he says hit is mater determinable at the comen lawe ; Neverþeless for the declaracon of the trouth of the mater he saith þat upon the trety of the mariage betwix the saide John the son and Agnes, hit was agreede þat a ioyntoure of xx li. of lyflode shulde be made to þe same John the son and Agnes and to þe heires male of their ij bodyes begoton, for defaute of suche issue the remeigner to the Right heires of the saide Sir John Bussy : bot for asmyche as hit was doubted whether the saide lifelode were tailled to the saide Sir John Bussy and to the heires of his body comyng or no, hit was appoynted be the counsell of bothe parties, for perill of a remitter be cause the saide John the son was at that tyme far with in age, þat astate of the saide lifelode shulde be made to vj persons, iij at the denomination of the saide Sir John and iij at the denomination of the saide Hamonde, in fee simple and þat the same vj persons at þe full age of the saide John the son shulde make astate of the saide lifelode to the same John the son and Agnes and to the heires male of their ij bodyes comynge, the remeigner over in the forme as it is above saide: beforce (*sic*) of which accorde and appoyntement and accordyng to the same the saide Sir John Bussy made astate of xx li. of lyfelode to Thomas Savage, Clerk, John Langholme and William Percy, chosen be the same Hamond and to John Boure, Clerk, John Denton and Richard Byngham, chosen be the saide Sir John, in fee simple to performe the saide entent, be virtue of whiche astate the saide vj persons are seised at this day of the same lyflode in fee simple, with oute þat the saide Sir John and Hamond were acorded þat the same Sir John or other persons for hym shulde make any astate to the saide John the son and Agnes and to the heires of their ij bodyes comyng with in a moneth aftur the saide mariage made in the maner as it is supposed be the saide Hamond be his bill; and praith þat he may be dimissed and þat he may have his damage for his wronge vexacon.

Bundle XV, No. 141.

To the moste reverent Fader in gode Archbysshop of Canterbury Chaunceller of Englond.

After 1443. Humble besechith Hamond Sutton, that wher late accorde of mariage toke be twix John Bussy, Knyght, and your saide besecher, that John, sone and heire of the saide John Bussy, shulde wedde and take to wyf Agnez, doughter of your saide besecher; For which mariage so to be hade and asure astate of landez and tenementz of the yerely value of xx li. aboff all chargez and reprysse to be made to the saide John Bussy to Thomas Savage, Clerk, John Langholm, William Percy, John Boure, Clerk, John Denton and Richard Byngham, to that intente that whan John the son of the saide John Bussy come to the agge of xxj yere þat þai shuld make astate of the saide landez and tenementz to the saide John son of the saide John Bussy and Agnez his wyf and to the heirez malles of ther bodez comyng, your saide besecher shuld pay to the saide John Bussy ij C and lx marces, of the which some the saide John Bussy is contented be youre saide besecher with owte any state maide to the saide per-sonez so named Feffes of the saide landez and tenementz; Wheruppon your saide besecher suede agens the saide John Bussy afore the Kyng in his chauncerie to have hade remedy in theiz premissez, uppon the which a trete was takyn be twix the saide partez be mediacion of William Stanlowe and other of theire Frendez to abyde the rewelle and ordinaunce of John Tailboys, Esquyer, Robert Sheffeld, Thomas Fitz William and William Stanlowe of the mater a boffe specified, so that awarde made be hem in that partye shulde be wretyn and inseelled under theire seelez of the saide arbitrures a fore the Quindecim of Seint Michell last passed, which arbitred and awarde be dede indented maide and enselled under all their sellez excepte the seele of the saide William Stanlowe, the which be the excitacion procuryng and styrryng of the saide John Bussy and Kateryn his wyff hath refused to putte to his seelle to the indenture of the saide awarde to the intent þat the saide award shulde not be effectuell nor avaylleable in lawe, notwithstondyng both the saide Hamond and John Bussy to the award and ordinaunce aforesaide hath pytte to þeir seellez, as it apperith of recorde and so remaneth the saide Feffement not execute, nor the saide award effectuell nor avaylleable in gret hurte to your saide besecher agens all gud fath, reson, and consiens : Please hit to your gracious Lordeschip to considre theiz premissez and theruppon to have the saide John Bussy to for yowe and to be examined þerof and of all the circumstance of the same and so to do dewe remedy and redresse theiz premissez to your saide besecher, as gud fath and consiens requireth.   For the loffe of gode and in Wey of Charite.

[Plegii de prosequendo :]
    Robertus Hawton.
    Thomas Baylton.

Bundle XV, No. 181 a.

To the right holy fader in god Archebysshop of Caunterbury
Chaunceller of Englond.

Besechith mekely youre humble servaunt, John Serle, that where as debate was betwene Richard Fortescu, John Silverlok of that part, Thomas Wollywrought and the saide besecher of the other part, of the right and title of the mesis, landes and tenementz that nywly were the right and possession of on John Braklee in Plympton erlys, Plymphome and Loghetorre, in the Countee of Devon, and after that by mediacon of frundis to bothe parties aforsaid the said Richard, John Silverlok, Thomas Wollywrought and the said besecher com-

After 1438,

promitte ham to stande to the awarde, arbitrement and iugement of Sir John Fortescu, Knyght, and Water Burell by the said parties indifferently chosyn, of the title, right and possession of the said mesis, landes and tenementz; wherof the said arbitrours takyng on ham the charge of the said arbitrement, awarde and iugement, awardede and demyd the thursday next after the fest of seint Peder de Advincla, the yere of kyng Harry the sixt the xvj^te yere at Plympton erlis in the said Countee, that the said Richard Fortescu and John Silverlok afore the fest of Seint Michell thenne next suyng after the said day of awarde, arbitrement and iugement sholde enfeffe the said Thomas and the said besecher to the use of the said besecher in a miese with apurtenaunce in the said Towne of Plympton erlis in the west part of the geldhalle of the said Towne to have and to hold to hem and to theire heirs in fee to the use of the said besecher; whiche awarde, arbitrement and iugement the said John Silverlok for his part hath parformid and the said Richard hath not parformyd ne fulfilled the saide awarde, arbitrement and iugment, and utterly hath refusid and in to this tyme haldith the possession of the said mese with apurtenaunce to the dishereteson of the said besecher, withoute your gracious help and socour in this partie: Plese to your gracious Lordship to considere the premissis, that the said besecher hath no remedie by the comyn lawe, to graunte a wryt sub pena directid to the said Richard Fortescu to apere afore yowe in the Chauncerie of oure soverain lord at a certein day by yowe lymet and on a certeyne payne ther to be examynyd on the mater aforesaid and ther on to do as reson and consciens askith, at honour of god and foe (*sic*) charitee.

    Plegii de prosequendo:
        Johannes Heryng.
        Willielmus Mychell.

Bundle XV, No. 181 *b*.

This is the answere of Richard Fortescu Esquyer to the bille of John Serle.

The said Richard seyth that the mater specefyed in the said bille ys noo mater sufficiant in lawe to putte hym to answere too; where fore he askeyth Juggement and prayith to be Dymyssid oute of this Court Wyth hys resonable costes and damages, &c.

Bundle XV, No. 181 *c*.

This ys the replicacon of John Serle to the answere of
Richard Fortescu.

The said John seyth the mater specified in his bill in (*sic*) mater
sufficiant in lawe and mater determinable by this Court, to the whiche
mater the seid Richard answereth nat, Wherefor he askyth iugement
and prayth that he may have the effect of the seid bille.

Bundle XVI, No. 386.

To the right reverent fader in god and our right gracious lord the
Archiebisshop of Cauntbury Chaunceller of Englond.

Mekely besechen your pore and continuell servantz Robert Harry
of Bradstede and Isabelle his Wyfe, that where on William Shoeswell
þe yonger, fader unto þe seide Isabelle, desired þe seid Robert to
wedde and take to wyfe þe seide Isabelle and yf the seid Robert wolde
so doo þe forseid William promysed and graunted unto þe seid Robert
and Isabelle yn mariage xl marces yn money to be paide at Ester
laste passid and on þat to deliver to þe seid Robert and Isabelle
goodes and catelles to þe value of xl marces whiche þat on William
Shoeswell þe elther, fader unto þe seid William Shoeswell þe yonger,
in his laste dayes delivered unto hym saufly to kepe to þe use of þe
seide Isabelle and to be delivered unto here assone as she were
maried ; And now hit is so þat þe seid Robert hath wedded þe same
Isabelle and þereuppon he hath come to þe seid William Shoeswell
þe yonger and requyred hym diverse tymes setthe þe seid feste of
Ester to fulfill his graunte and promysse and þe seid William Shoeswell
þe yonger yn no wise will paye þe seid xl marces neyther deliver þe
seid goodes and catelles after his promysse and þe byqueste of þe seid
William Shoeswell his fader but atte þe oeptas of seint hillary laste
passid afore þe Justicee of þe Comone place hath done his lawe yn
a writte of dette by your seid besechers in þis partie sewed þat he
owed your seid besechers no peny ne no suche goodes ne catelles
þann withholdith where of your seid besechers have notable witnes
and profes of þe contrarie to þair grete hurte and losse for ever of þe
seid dette, goodes and catelles, wiþoute your gracious socour and
helpe yn þis partie to þaim shewed : Plese hit unto your gracious
lordship to consider þe seid premysses and þereuppon to graunte
unto your seid suppliantz a writte directed unto þe seid William
Shoeswell to appere afore you in þe Chauncellarie of our lord þe kyng

Date uncertain.

atte a certein day and uppon a certeyne peyne by you to be lymyted there to answere unto þe seid premisses and þere mak hym do þat good feith, right and consience aske and require for þe love of god and by way of charite, Consideryng þat your seid suppliantz ben wiþoute remedie after þe cours of þe comone lawe, yn so moche as þei have no specialte to shewe for þaim yn þis partie.

Plegii de prosequendo:

Thomas Hever de com' Kent.

Robertus Parler de Brastede.

Bundle XVI, No. 412.

To the ryght holy fadre in god and my goode lorde Archiebisshop of Canterbury and Chanceller of England.

Date uncertain. Besechith mekely your poure bedeman John Palgrave, That where the sayde John boght of on Cristain Gymbald certain londes and tenementes in the towne of Pesynhale in the shire of Suff' for sufficiant record and for certaine sommes of money to be paiede to the saide Cristian att certain daies betwixte the saide parties lymyted; And for be cause ther was no clerk nor lerned man there to make upp their dedes accordyng to the sayde covenauntes, It was appointed and accordid betwixte the saide parties that att a certaine day by thaime assigned they shuld have mette and paied the furst paiement and made upp here dedes; And noghtwithstondyng that this sayde bargan was sufficiently made [and of goode][1] record and the sayde john was redy with the saide furst paiement att þe saide day, the sayde Cristian by styrryng of oother evill willid poeple (*sic*) refusith utterly the [saide][1] bargain unto grete hynderyng of your saide besechiere without youre gracious lordship in this party: Wherfor please hit unto youre gracious lordship, consideryng that youre saide suppliaunt may have no remedy att the comune lawe, to graunte a write under a certaine paine directe unto the saide Cristian to appere afor you in the Chauncerye atte certaine day by you to be lymyted, there to be examyned uppon the mater aforsaid, he there to have and receyve that by youre gracious lordship shall be awarded in that partie, For the love of god and in Wey of charite.

Plegii de prosequendo:

. . .[2] Stapilton de villa Westm', yoman.

Johannes Ceyfi de villa Westm', Cordwaner.

---

[1] Hole in document.   [2] Illegible.

Bundle XIX, No. 26.

To the most reverent fader in god and right gode and gracious lord the Archebisshop of York Cardynall and Chaunceller of Inglond.

Besechith mekely your poore Oratour John Carter of Beverley that where [he][1] and Roger Kidall were possessed ioyntly of ix Stockfisshes and an C iiij Saltfisshes þe which [were][1] putte in to a hous to have ben uttered and sold to their bother use and profite Wheruppon the forseid Roger all the forsaid Stockfissh and Saltfisshe hath manured, occupied and putte unto sale and noon accompte nor profite therof, ner of any parcell therof, will yelde to your said Oratour, to his perpetuell undoyng withoute your full gracious lordship be to hym shewed in this behalf, for he may have no remedie by the Course of the comone lawe in this partee : Wherfor, those premisses tenderly considred, please it your gode gracious lordship to graunt a writte sub pena to be direct to the forseid Roger to appere afore the Kyng our soverayne lord in his Chauncerye at a certayn day by you to be lymitted there to be examyned of the premisses and theruppon to do as faith and conscience requireth, for the love of god and in the waye of charite.

Plegii de prosequendo :
    Johannes Killyngholme.
    Nichelaus Elys.

1450 to 1454.

Bundle XIX, No. 59.

To the most wurshippful and reverent fadir in god the Cardinall and Archebisshop of York Chaunceller of Jnglond.

Besechith mekely your pour and continuell oratour John Mercer, that where as oon John Halsnoth was seysyd of a Meese and xvj acres of lond wythynne the Parysh of Cranebroke in his demesne as in fee and there of soo seysyd of gret fayth and trust enfeffid oon Simon Doreham and other to have and do (*sic*) hoold to theym and theyre heyres for evermòre to the use and behoft of the seyd John Halsnoth and hys heyres, aftyr whych feffement, accord and aggrement was had betwene your sayd Suppliaunt and the seyd John Halsnoth that your seyd suppliant shold have the sayd Mies and

After 1450.

[1] Hole in document.

xvj acres of lond to hym and to hys heyres for evermore, And that the seyd Halsnoth shold require hys seyd feffez to make an astat to your seyd Suppliaunt and to such as he wold name wythynne a moneth next aftir the seyd accord ; for the which Mies and xvj acres your seyd Suppliaunt shold paye to the seyd John Halsnoth atte tyme of the makyng of the seyd astate xliiij mark, wherof part is payd. And now gracious lord the seyd moneth and more is passyd and your seyd suppliaunt hath required the seyd feffes to make astat to hym accordyng to the seyd aggrement, the whych they all been redy for to doo except oonly the seyd Simon Doreham, With that the seyd John Halsnoth woold there to require hem ; and the seyd Simon Doreham seyeth that he hath bought the seyd Mies and xvj acres of lond of the seyd John Halsnoth to thentent (*sic*) to put your seyd Suppliaunt from his seyd bargayne, where of trowith the seyd Simon had never noo maner of covenant of the seyd londys and tenementes afore the seyd aggrement had bytwne your seid Suppliaunt and the seyd Halsnoth, but oonly syn, how be it þat the seyd Simon had very knowyng of the seyd bargayn had betwene your seyd besecher and the seyd John Halsnoth long tyme byfor the seyd bargayn had bytwene the seyd Simon and John Halsnoth, the whych is agenst all reson, feyth and good concience : Wherefore please it youre good and gracious lordship tenderly to concider thyse premisses and that your seyd suppliaunt hath noo remedy atte the comyn lawe, to graunte to hym severall wryttes sub pena direct to the seyd John Halsnoth and Simon to appere atte a certeyn day be yow to be lymyted and that the seyd John Halsnoth may be compellid to require his seyd feffez to make astat to your seyd Suppliaunt, and also that the seyd Simon may be compellid to make astat forth wyth his cofeffees to your seyd suppliaunt as good feyth and concience will for the love of god and in wey of charite.

Plegii de prosequendo :

Thomas Reynold de London, Gentilman.

Ricardus Richard de London, Grocer.

Bundle XIX, No. 58.

This is the answere of John Halsnoth and Simon Durham agenst the bill of John Mercer in the kynges Chauncerye.

John Halsnoth and Simon Durham by protestacion seith that the mater in the seid bille comprehended is not sufficient in lawe for hem

to answere to whiche [they] praye that theire avantage there of alwey
to be saved. Furþermore, where as the said John Mercer hath surmytted and aleyde by his seid bill that the said John Halsnothe
shulde have be seised of a mees and xvj acres of lond within the
paryssh of Cranebroke in his demene in fee and so seised of greet
trust shuld have inffeffed the said Simon Durham and other to the
use of the said John Halsnoth and of his heires, after whiche feffement accorde and agrement shuld have be bytwene the said John
Mercer and the said John Halsnothe þat youre seid suppliant shulde
have the seid mees and xvj acres of lond to him and to his heires
and that the said John Halsnothe shuld require his seid feffees to
make estate to your seid suppliaunt at whiche tyme as he wold name
within a moneth next after the said accord as in the said bill is
conteyned ;

Therto the said John Halsnothe and Simon answere and seye for
declaration of trouth that longe tyme afore that ever the said John
had eny possession in the said mees and xvj acres of lond on
John Robert of Cranebroke þe elder was seised þerof in his demenes
in fee whiche said John Robert in and of the said mees and xvj acres
enfeffed the said John Halsnoth, Simon Durham and oþer to have to
hem and to her heires forever, by vertue of whiche þey were þerof
seised ; whiche said Simon and oþer so beyng ioyntly seised with the
saide John Halsnoth afterward into the possession of the said John
Halsnothe by her dede relessed all her right title and clayme þat þey
had þerin in any wyse by vertue of the said feffement ; whiche seid
John Halsnoth þerof so beyng soll seised sold the said mees and xvj
acres to the said Simon Durham, by cause of which sale he infeffed
þerin the said Simon Durham and oþer to þe use and behoove of the
said Simon and of his heires forever by vertue of whiche þey were
þerof so seised, withoute þat ever eny accord and agrement were
made or had bitwene þe seid John Mercer and John Halsnoth for þe
seid mees and land, and withoute þat the said Simon were ever
enfeffed by the said John Halsnoth to his use in þe seid mees and
land in maner and fourme as it is surmytted by þe seid bill ; which
mater þey be redy to averr as þis Court will award, and prayen to
be dismyssed oute of Court and her damages for their wrongefull
vexacion.

Bundle XIX, No. 57.

Thys ys the replication of John Mercer to the Answere of Simon
Doreham and John Halsnoth.

Ther to the seid John Mercer seyth that, where as the seid Simon
and John Halsnoth seyen that ther was never non accord and aggrement hadde betwene the seid John Mercer, Suppliant, and the seid
John Halsnoth for the seid Mees and lond and that the seid Simon
was never enfeffed by the seid John Halsnoth to his use in the seid
Mies and lande in maner and fourme as it is surmittid, Therto the
seid suppliaunt seith that ther was accord and aggrement hadde
betwene the seid suppliant and the seid John Halsnoth for the seid
Mies and land in maner and fourme as the seid suppliaunt hath sur-
mitted by his bill, and that the seid suppliaunt gaf notys to the seid
Simon Doreham of the said bargayn long tyme afore the seid John
Halsnoth solde the seid Mies and land to the seid Dorham; the
whiche matiers the seid suppliaunt ys redy for to prove as this Court
will awarde; and in as moche as the seid Simon and John Halsnoth
with seyen not that the seid Simon was enfeffed to the use of the seid
John Halsnoth atte tyme of the Bargayn of the seid suppliant made
and longtyme syn and that the seid Halsnoth hath reseyvid parte of
the seid money by force of the seid Bargayn, the seid Suppliant
prayeth that the seid John Halsnoth may be compellyd to make his
feffeez to make estate to the seid besecher of the seid Mees and lond
and that the seid Simon may be compellyd to make an astat in like
wyse therof to the seid suppliant in maner and fourme, as the seid
suppliant hath disyryd be his bill as good feith and concience
requireth.

Bundle XIX, No. 56.

Thys ys the reioinder of Symon Dyrham and John Halsnoth to the
replicacon of John Mercer.

Where the seid John Mercer seith that ther was accord and agrement hadde bytwene the seid John Mercer and the seid John
Halsnoth for the seid meas and land as he hath surmetted by hys
byll, Therto seith the seid Simon and John Halsnoth that ther was
non accord ne agrement had by twene the seid John Mercer and the
seid John Halsnoth for the seid meas and land in maner and fourme
as he hath allegged by hys bille, the whiche he ys a redy to averr as
the Court will award. And also where as the seid John Mercer

surmetteth in hys replicacon that the seid Symon and John Halsnoth wythseyeth not that the seid Symon was enfeffed in the seid meas and lande to the use of the seid John Halsnoth, to the whiche the seyd Symon hath sufficiantly answered ageinste the seid bill, And to the whiche the seid John Mercer hath not sufficiantly replyed, wherfor he prayeth that he may be dismyssed.

Bundle XIX, No. 347.

To the right reverent fadur in god Cardinall of Yorke Chaunceler of Englond.

Besechith lowly Richard Onehand of London, Draper, that where Johane, late the wyff of yon Etton, Squyer, owed un to your seid besecher ix li., on Phelypp Lewston labored to the frendes of the seid Johane to have her to wyff; which Johane agreed to have the seid Phelypp to housbond so that he wold pay your seid besecher the seid ix li. and also to pay the residue of her dettys of the seid Johane. And afterward the seid Phelypp came to your seid besecher and lett hym to have knowlege that he shuld be payed of the seid ix li., and promytted hym that he shuld be payed ther of with yn short tyme. Which Phelypp afterwarde wedded the seid Johane and after that tyme your seid besecher hath often tymes required the seid Phelypp to make hym payment of the seid ix li., which to do utterly he refuseth a genst alle good feith and Concyens : Wherfore pleaseth your gracious lordeshipp tenderly to consyder thes seid premysses and ther uppon to geve in comaundement to the seid Phelypp to a pere a fore [you] atte a certen day by you to be lymeted to aunswer to thes seid premysses and that he may be compelled to pay your seid besecher the seid ix li. as good feith and concyens requireth, for the love of god and in wey of charite.

Plegii de prosequendo :
    Robertus Blewet.
    Thomas Staff.

After 1450.

Bundle XIX, No. 346.

This [is the] aunswer of Philip Leweston a genst the bille of Richard Onehand.

Where the seid Richard by his bille surmytteth that Johan, late the wyf of yon Etton, owed un to hym ix li., sche owed hym no peny, ne never was cause ne contracte by twyx them wher of eny dette

shuld growe [out]¹; wher he aldith² that sche schold agre to take
the seid Philip Leweston to husbond so that he wolde pay the seid
Richard ix li., ther was never soche langage by twyx [the]m³ ne
y promytted hym never payment of thes ix li. as he surmyttith by his
bille; and pray that y may be demyssed owte of court and to have
my damages amged⁴ to me for his wrongfull vexacion, a cordyng to
the statutes ther uppon ordened.

Bundle XIX, No. 345.

Memorandum, that Phelipp Lewston come to Ric' Onehandes
Shopp in the parissh of Seynt Marie Lothawe in Walbroke Warde in
London in the Monthe of Jule the date of our lorde M¹CCCCxxxviij,
the reign of kyng Henry the vj^te xx^te,⁵ he promytted Ric' Onehand
in presence of Alyson, his wife, ix li. for the deute of Johane, late the
wife of Jon of Etton, to pay well and truly atte Ester twolf monthes
after that promyse, by hie feith; and heruppon my wife and I will
swere uppon the sacrement that this is true that we swere, and her-
upon will bryng Ric' Hyfeld, Thomas Herford, Harry Mesant,
William Dodde, Thomas Godyng and Thomas Steven and xx^ti goode
men mo to conferme this true that my wife and I will swere.

Also oon John Scot, apperyng in hys propre person in the kynges
Chauncerie, seys upon hys sacrement that he ij yere nowe agone
herd Phelip Leweston in Westmynster Hall sey to the seid Richard
Onehand that the seid Richard Onehand was a foole on a day; for
if ye hadde made obligacion as I bad you, y wolde have sealid it at
that day and then ye shuld have be sekyr of your money.

Bundle XIX, No. 354 a.

Addressed to the Cardinal and Archbishop of York.

After   The complainant, Robert Ellesmere of London, makes out the
1450.   following case in his petition :

One William Serle of London came to him (i. e. the complainant),
and said he had certain 'terms' (i. e. leases) of certain lands to sell
of the value of £6 yearly. There was much discussion about this,
and finally it was 'accorded' that complainant should come with

---

¹ Hole in document.
² i. e. 'ald', to hold; query perhaps 'aloith'.
³ Hole in document.
⁴ This word is uncertain.
⁵ Evidently one of these dates is wrong; for 20 Hen. VI would be 1442.

counsel to Serle's house at a certain day to examine the evidence of title. Complainant went, examined the said evidence 'and liked þeym wele, . . . wherupon it was ful accorded and covenanted between þeim þat þe said Robert shulde have þe said termes for the summe of xl li. betwene þeim accorded, And þat at a certaine day þey shulde mete at a place lymited to ensele and delyver þe writing of þe said covenaunt' at the payment of the said sum. The parties came to the place assigned and complainant offered payment and ¦demanded the sealing of the said writing and livery of the evidences. The defendant (William Serle) 'utterly' refused to seal the writing or to deliver the evidences, and still refuses, so that complainant has lost his bargain and is without remedy at law. He prays for a subpoena directed to the defendant, and general relief.

Bundle XIX, No. 354 *b*.

The defendant's answer.

The defendant says first that this case is not properly brought in chancery; for the complainant has a remedy at law, namely by an action of Covenant, which, says the defendant, is maintainable by custom of London without specialty.

Secondly, the defendant denies that there was ever such bargain or 'accorde' as the complainant has alleged in his petition.[1]

Bundle XIX, No. 354 *c*.

The complainant's replication.

In reply to the defendant's first contention, he says:

' Furst, where as the seid William seith that the custome of the Cite of London is and tyme with oute mynde hath ben, that accions of covenaunt are and have been of the seid tyme maintenable with Inne the said Cite as well withoute specialte as with specialte, and seith that all bargaynyng as touchyng the seid termes of the same mees was hadde betwene him and the seid Robert with Inne the seid Cite, the which is mater determinable by an accion of covenaunt with Inne the same Cite,

' Therto the seid Robert seith by protestacon that he knoweth noon suche custome with Inne the Cite of London, ne that the seid bargayne and covenaunt was made with Inne the seid Cite, but he seith that, for asmoche as the seid William Serle hath confessed

---

[1] This document is in a very bad condition.

the same covenaunt and bargayne as it appereth by his answere, he asketh iuggement and prayeth that the same William may be compelled to make him astate.'

Complainant then replies to the rest of the defendant's answer.

Bundle XIX, No. 354 *d*.

This is the examinacion of John Cresswell, Squyer, upon the mater in the Chauncerie of oure soverayne lords the kynge betwyne Robert Ellesmere, Goldsmyth, and William Serle, Carpenter.

Firste, the saide John saith that he was presente whenne the saide Robert Ellesmere and the saide William Serle, as touchynge the termes comprehended withynne the bill of the saide Robert, were fully accorded, the whiche bargayne the saide William Serle rehersed to the said John Creswell, the wyfe of the saide William beynge presente, and by thassente (*sic*) of here they were fully appoynted and accorded that at oure lady day the Annunciacion, that last was, the saide Robert shulde come and have his bargayne and paye his money; at whiche tyme of the saide accorde, if the saide William and his wife wolde have saide nay, the saide Robert wolde have hold him plesed and not desired it. All whiche comunicacion the saide John Creswell herde and was presente; And þereupon they wente to the Swan beside Seynt Antonyes and there they dronke to gederes upon the saide bargayn atte the coste of the saide Robert Ellesmere; alle whiche mater be trewe and that he woll swere upon a boke.

This is the examynacion of David Gogh upon the saide mater.

David Gogh, examined upon a boke, saith that he was presente whenne the evydences touchynge þe saide termes was redde, and the saide Roger[1] asked on George Houton, a man of Counsell, reder of the saide evydences, wheder they were gode for hym other no, And the saide George avised the saide Robert to take the bargayn, saynge that the evidence was gode, and this the saide David herde, the saide John Creswell saynge, thanne ye be accorded, and the saide William Serle sayde, yea.

Bundle XIX, No. 354 *e*.

The trouth is this, that I, George Houton, was desired by Robert Ellesmere to goo and to have sight of the evidences of William Serle concernyng the bargeyn of certeyn termez of a mees of the same

---

[1] Query: for 'Robert'?

William that the seide Robert shulde bye and bargeyn of hym ; the whiche George hadd sight of the seid Evidences, understandyng theym gode and sufficiant, counseld the seid Robert the (*sic*) bargeyn the seide termez with the seide William, with that he myght conclude for a competent some of money ; the same Robert then desired to wete of me, the seid George, what some I wolde thynk were competent to be goven therfor ; I seide xxx li. were y nough and þen the seid Robert answered me and seide that he wolde geve xl li. rather than leve the bargeyn, wheruppon the seid Robert comyned w^t þe seid William and his wiff, þe seide George and oon John Creswell, stondyng by the same Creswell herkenyng better and more takhede as at that tyme to the comynycacion betwen them then I, the seid George, did spake and seid un to them, then ye be accorded ; then I, the same George, geveng better Erys to their speche, desired to knowe howe they were accorded ; then seide the seid Robert, I shall geve a grete some of money ; what some I, the seid George, desired to wete and he answered me and seid, xl li. and it most be purveyd agenst our lady day Annunciacion at whiche tyme it is accorded that the seid William shall delyver unto me, seide the same Robert, all the seid Evydences to geder w^t other Evydences to be engrosed of the seid bargeyn ; and yet, seide the same Robert, I thank the godeman here, he puttyth me at my choyse whethir I woll have it or leve it at þe seid day ; then, seide I, the seide William be ye accordeth in the maner as Robert here hath rehersed and he seid, ye, Then goo We drynke ; and so We did unto the Swan, a brewehaus fast by Seynt Antoines and then departed, &c.

Note.—A further deposition (Bundle XIX, No. 354*f*) is omitted, as it does not contribute any additional information.

Bundle XIX, No. 404 *a*.

To the most reverent fader in god my good and gracious lord my lord the Cardynall of york Chaunceller of England.

Besecheth mekely your contynuell bedman John Isaak of Bourne in the Counte of Kent, that where as John Isaak, fader unto your said besecher nowe ded, by his lyve bought of oon Robert Bisshoppesdane and Johane his Wief ij acres of lond lyeng in the said toun of Bourne for a certeyn some of money which he payd weel and truly unto the said Robert and Johane, and whan he had payd þe money the said Robert and Johane agreed and made faithfull promyse unto hym to make a sufficient estate unto hym and to his

After 1450.

heirs when he or his heirs wold theym þerto requyre, and thenne sone after dide aswell (*sic*) þe fader unto your said besecher as the said Robert, after whoos deeth your said besecher, sone and heir unto the said John, hathe dyverse tymes required the said Johane to make estate unto hym accordyng unto hir said promyse ; the which to doo she utterly refuseth contrarie to all good feith and conscience : Wherfore plese hit your goode lordshipp tenderly to considre the premysses and hou your said besecher may have noo remedy as by the comon lawe to graunt a writ of sub pena direct unto the said Johane to apere be fore the kyng in his Chauncerye at a certeyn day by you to be lymyted, there to be examyned uppon the premysses and to doo and resceyve as the Court wyll award, atte reverence of god and in wey of Charytee.

[Plegii de prosequendo :]

Johannes Doyle de Cantaur', Armig'.

Ricardus Pargate de eadem, Gent'.

Bundle XIX, No. 404 *b*.

This is the answere of Johanne Byschopysdane to the bille of John Isaake.

ffyrst she seith that she ouwyth not to answere to noo mater that is comprehendith in the bille of the seid John, but she seith for here answere that she never solde, concentyd, nothir agreed to no sale of the seid land whiche is conteyned in the bille of the seid John ; Wherefore she prayeth to be dismyssed oute of court as faith and consciens requireth and that the seid John may satysfye here here costys for that he hath wrongfully vexithe here accordyng to the statut in suche case provydyd.

Bundle XIX, No. 492.

To the most reverend Fader in god the Archibisshop of York Cardynall and Chaunceller of England.

1450 to 1454.

Sheweth mekely to your gracious lordship Thomas Bodyn of London, that where accord and covenant was made betwene hym and one Robert Chirche, Citezin and Haberdassher of London, the xv^th day of Feverere the yere of the reigne of King Henry the vj^the after the conquest the xx^th, be the medeacion of the frendez, beyng thenne your said suppliant with in age of xiiij yere, that he shuld be prentice to the said Robert in and of the crafte of haburdassher fro the Feste of Alhalowen then last passed unto the yend of xij yere thenne next comyng, So alwey that the said Robert shuld fynd to scole at hys awen costes and charge the said Thomas duryng two the furst yeres of the said terme, that is to say a yere and half therof to lerne grammar and the resydue of the said two yeres, which amounteth to half a yere, to scole for to lerne to write, and theruppon the said Thomas by the advise of his frendez, trustyng to have be founde to schole in fourme aforsaid, graunted the same xv^th day by dede indented thenne made betwene hym and the said Robert to be true Apprentice to the same Robert duryng the said terme of xij yere, of which terme of xij yere he hath contynued in the Service of the said Robert as his prentice in the said crafte from the said Feste of Alhalowen unto the yende of viij yere and more and often tymes in the bigynnyng of the same terme and mony tymes sithon the said Thomas with his frendes hath prayed and required the said Robert to putt and fynd hym to scole in fourme aforsaid after the effecte of the said covenaunt and accorde, the which to doo the said Robert wolnot (*sic*), but that to doo at all tymes utturly hath refused, to the grete hurte, harme and losse of the said Thomas : Please hit your good and graciouce lordship to consider the premisses and that the seid Thomas therof may have no remedy by the course of the comone lawe of this land, And theruppon to graunt a writte to be direct to the said Robert to appere by fore the kyng in his Chauncerie at a certeyn day and uppon anotable (*sic*) payne, by your gracious lordship to be lymyted, there to answere and to doo and resceyve of and in thise premisses as by the Courte of the same Chauncerye thenne shall be ordeigned, and he shall pray to god for you.

Bundle XIX, No. 493.

This is the Answer of Robert Chirch agenst the bill of Thomas Bodyn.

Frist (*sic*) the seid Robert, by protestacion y^t the mater in ye seid bill conteyned is not sufficient to put hym to answer in y^is courte, saith y^t ye seid Endenture of Apprentice by ye which the seid Thomas was bounde to ye seid Robert with all ye circumstaunce y^eof was made and had with in the Cite of London where by ye custom of the same Cite ane accon of covenaunt ys mayntenable as well withoute Especialte as with Especialte, so y^t yf eny sich covenaunt of fyndyng at scole of the seid Thomas had be made and broken like as the seid

Thomas hath surmittyd, he myght yerof have had and yit may have covenable remydy by pleynt within ye seid Cite after the fourme and cours of the Comone law yere ; and foryermore, for ye more declaracon in yis mater, ye seid Robert seith yt nygh aboute the fest of all halowen the yer of the reign of our soveign lord yt [now is]¹ xixth, ye seid Thomas and Robert by ye mene of one Henry Wakefeld were agrede and Endentures yeruppon made, yt the same Thomas shuld be apprentice with ye seid Robert for ye terme of xiij yere yen next folowyng so yt sufficient suerte were founde for the seid Thomas to be trewe apprentice with ye seid Robert duryng ye terme aforsayd ; Wherupon ye seid Thomas abode with ye seid Robert fro yt tyme unto ye terme of hillary ye xxth yer of ye seid kyng yen next cumyng and no suerte for the parte of ye seid Thomas by all yt tyme was founde, wherfor ye seid Robert at yt tyme was in full·purpose no more to have had to do with ye seid Thomas in so myche ye ye (*sic*) seid Endentures en every parte afore yt tyme made werbroken (*sic*) and noght enrolled and so both parties at yere large, so yt ye seid Thomas myght their have departyd if hym had list but yit ye seid Henry eftsones entretyd ye seid Robert to take ye seid Thomas apprentice for ye terme of xij yere next folowyng ye fest of halowen yen last passyd, promittyng to gete suerte for ye seid Thomas to be true apprentice duryng ye same terme, so yt ye seid Thomas in ye seid terme shuld have covenable lernyng and doctrine as resonably for ye profite of sich apprentice shuld belong, the which he had withoute yt all ye seid Robert at yt tyme or eny tyme seth made covenaunt with the seid Thomas to fynd hym att scole in sich maner and fourme as ye seid Thomas hath surmittyd ; Wherupon ye seid Endentures of Apprenteshode were made like as ye seid Thomas hath declaryd, the seid Thomas beyng at yt tyme in ye xiiij yer of his age or nygh upon, by virtue of which Endentures ye seid Thomas and by the enrolment yerof was admitte as alaufull (*sic*) apprentice after ye custom of the seid Cite ye xxx day of Octobr ye yer of the reign of ye Kyng aforsaid xxj, the which terme ye seid Thomas on his parte hath not truly kept but by hys owne knowlage in hys seid bill nygh ye iij parte yerof, yt is to witte all most iiij yer, wrongfully of hys obstinate willfulnes hath broken and disobeyed, which not withstondyng, ye seid Robert seith yt ye seid Thomas is and afore his departure was sufficiently lernyd and instruct both in redyng and also in wrytyng as unto sich apprentice resonably may suffice, and over all yis ye seid Robert seith yt he

¹ Hole in document.

and ye seide Thomas ye vij day of Fevr' nowe last passyd at ye grete instaunce of ye seid Thomas were put in award of iiij notable and thrifty persones, then Wardenz of ye Craft of haberdassher of ye seid Cite, Arbitrours bytwix hem both indeferently chosen of all maner causes, accons, querelez, debates and demaundes betwix hem afore y^t tyme in eny maner of wise had, movyd, or hangyng, The which arbitrourz with in ye day to hem yerof limite demyd, awarded and finally determynyd betwix ye seid Robert and Thomas, The which award, deme and determinacon ye seid Robert is and at at (*sic*) all tymes hath bene redy onhys (*sic*) parte to kepe and performe, notwithstondyng y^t ye seid Thomas y^t at to hym yerof fulfill will in no wise nor obey; The which maters and ich of hem ye seid Robert is redy to prove like as this Courte will award, Wherfor he prayth to be dismist oute of thys Courte and to be restoryd to hys Costes and Damage for hys gret and wrongfull vexacon after the fourme of the Statute, &c.

Bundle XX, No. 39.

To þe most reverent Fader in god the Archebisshop of Yorke Chaunceler of Inglond.

Besechith mekely Bartholomew Couper, Citezin and Draper of London, that where he now late, that ys to wete the xx day of Decembr the yere of oure sovereigne lorde the kyng that nowe ys the xxix, bargayned with one John Broke of Stoke Neyland in the shire of Suff' for to have of him an C clothes called Suff' streytes for a certeyn some of money betwene hem accorded; And moreover that thei weren accorded that the seyd clothes shuld be of certein divers colours convenient for such parties beyonde þe see as the seyd Bartholomew at þat tyme notified unto the seid John that he wolde sende hem unto; Wherupon then iiij^{xx} clothes, parcell of the seid C clothes, at that tyme weren delyvered, And the residue, that ys to say xl clothes, bi the same accorde should have ben delivered unto youre seid besecher at the feste of Estre then next folowyng, at whech feste the seyd John of the seid clothes made no deliverance nor yet hidder to have none made ne none woll make, notwithstondyng that often tymes he hath ben requyred, to grete hurt and hinderance of youre seyd besecher, for as much as the seid iiij^{xx} clothes that he hath resceyved may not be uttered nor solde to his profite nor availe till he be content and perfourmed of the hole nombre accordyng to þe seid bargeyn: Please youre graciouse lordeshippe considred for as

1452 to 1454.

much as youre seyd besecher hath no writing to prove the seid covenaunt that remedie faileth him at the comone lawe, to graunte a writte sub pena direct unto þe seid John comaundyng him upon a certein peyne to appere before oure lorde þe king in his Chauncerie at a certein day bi you to be lymyted, there to be examened in þe premisses, And therupon such rule and ordinance bi you to be made as gode feyth and conscience requyren.

      Plegii de prosequendo:

          Johannes Rede.

          Ricardus Lawe.

Bundle XXVII, No. 467.

To the right reverent fader in god and good and gracious lord
the Bisshopp of Excestre and Chaunceller of England.

After
1460.

      Besechith mekely youre good lordshipp Andrewe Wolson, Brick-maker, to consider howe oon Herry Johnson, Berebruer, hath attained an Accion of dette of x li. agenst hym in London for a bargayn that was made betwene them in Lambith where they bothe dwell like as all ther neghbours, and reporte that yf the seid Andrewe wolde be served of Bere of the seid Herry youre seid besecher shuld paye noe redy money therfore but Brike and so everich [1] of hem shuld have of other ware for ware ; which bargayn youre said besecher is redie to parfourme and at all tymes hath ben and nowe the seid Herry wold have redie money of youre seid Suppliaunte, the bargayn notwith-standyng, albe hit youre seid besecher myght have ben served of an other Berebruer, like as he was before of hym ware for ware, had nought the said Herry have ben, and so entendith to recover the seid money of youre said besecher agenst all feith and good conscience, to his utter undoyng, withoute youre gracious lordschipp to hym beshewyd (*sic*) in this behalf: Wherfore please it youre good and gracious lordschipp tenderly to consider the premisses and heruppon to graunte a Corpus cum causa for youre besecher And he shall con-tynually pray to god for youre mooste noble estate.

Bundle XXVIII, No. 210.

To the Bischop of Excestre Chaunceler of Englond.

After
1460.

      Mekely besechith your gracious lordschip your pore Oratour William Grene, Marcheaunt of the Staple of Caleys, that where he Delivered C li. sterling at Brugges the secund Day of April last

---

[1] 'everich,' each one (Halliwell).

passid to Thomas Mollesley, factour and attorny veryly knowyn un to John Warde of Loundon Grocer, and to the use of his seid Master to be repaied agen to your said oratour at Loundon the secunde Day of May thanne next folowyng, as more plenely apperith by a bill Directid by the same Thomas un to the said John Ward, his maister, of the hand of the said Thomas Wretyn and signid with his said Masteres Mark, testifying the same after the cours of Marchaundice, at which Day nor no tyme sythen the said John paiyd not your said suppliaunt the said C li. nor noo peany therof, notwithstondyng the seid bill testifying the premissis hath ben shewyd unto hym the said sume accordyng to the same Demaund and that he to pay utterly hath refusyd and yit refusyth contrarie to the Cours of trewe Marchaundice to the utter Destruccon and undoyng of your said Besecher : Wherfor please it your gracioux lordschip the premiss tenderly to considere and to graunte a Writte of subpena directe to the said John Warde to appier afore the Kyng in his Chauncerie at a certeyn day there to Answere to the premiss and your said suppliaunt shall pray to god for you.

    Plegii de prosequendo :

        Rogerus Chesshure, clericus.

        Johannes Aleyn de London, Gentilman.

Bundle XXVIII, No. 299.

To the Reverent Fader in god Bysshoppe of Exceter and
Chaunceler of Engelond.

Mekely besechith youre poore Oratrice Elizabeth, late the Wyff of John Gambon the yonger, that where, upon the Marriage made and hadde betwene the saide John and Elizabeth, it was appoynted and concluded betwene Jamys Derneford, Fader of the said Elizabeth, and John Gambon the elder, Fader to the saide John Gambon the yonger, that the same John the Fader or his feffees shoulde by thair dede graunte an Annuyte of x li. or ellis make a sure and sufficient astate of londes and tenementes to the yerly value of x li. over all charges and reprises to the said Elizabeth for terme of hir lyfe within iij Mouneththes (*sic*) after the said mariage, And that the said Annuyte or londis should be made as sure to the said Elizabeth as it coude be made by advyse of the Councell of the said Jamys her Fader for terme of hir lyfe ; Natheles after that mariage made and solempnyzed betwene the said John Gambon the yonger and Eliza-

After
1460.

beth the said John Gambon the yonger died afore any graunte or
astate to the said Elizabeth of such Annuyte or londes to be made,
how be it that the same Elizabeth ofte tymes sithe the Dethe of the
said John Gambon the yonger hathe required the said John Gambon
the fader to graunte or make to hir astate of the said Annuyte or
londes accordyng to the appoyntements and conclusions abovesaid,
And that to do the said John the Fader agenste goode faithe and concience hathe utterly Refused and yeit refusith, to the importable
hurte and grete impoverysshment of your said Oratrice which hathe
neyther londes nor goodes for hir sustinaunce nor can ne may
Recovre or have other then by the mene of concience : Wherfor
please it your gracious lordshippe the premisses tenderly to concidre
and ther upon to graunte a Writte of Sub pena to be directe to the
said John Gambon the elder to appere afore the Kyng in his Chauncery atte a certeyn day by your lordshipp to be limited and under
a certeyn payne there to Aunswere unto the premisses And to abyde
there such Rule as your lordshipp and the said Courte ther upon
shall concidre and determine, And this for the love of god and in
Way of charyte.

Plegii de prosequendo :

Ricardus Pree de London, Gentilman.

Thomas Harryes de Lanevet in Com' Cornub', marchant.

Bundle XXIX, No. 13.

To the reverende Fader in god and full gode and graciuos lorde
the Bisshop of Excerter, Chaunceller of Englonde.

1467 to
1468.

Humbly besecheth youre gode and gracious lordship your contynuell Oratour, William Elyot of Brystowe, Mercer, graciously to
conceyve that where the seid William and oon John Elyot, Fader
unto the same William, stondeth bounden bi theire obligacions [in
the somme of a C li. to oon Stephen][1] Stychemerssh for certeyn marchandize of him bought ; wheruppon, and also upon the Frendelynesse
bitwene theym, the seid Stephen specially instanced and desired
youre seid bisecher, forasmoche as he in the fourme aforseid was to
him so endetted, to deliver [to Stephyn Stychemerssh, sone of the][1]
seid Stephyn, his Fader, all [such][1] marchandize and money as his
seid sonne at eny tyme wolde of him desire to have, promysyng and

---

[1] Illegible ; supplied from the defendant's answer (Bundle XXIX,
No. 12), which repeats verbatim the substance of the petition.

grauntyng your bisecher to make him payment therfore ; wherupon
the sonne of the seid Stephyn, bi the auctorite and name of [his
fadre come to your seid Besecher at] [1] Bristowe and there [desyred
of] [1] him certeyne marchandize and money to the sume of iiij xiiij li.,
Offeryng him oon obligacion and billes remembryng the same and
promised him in the bihalf of the seid Fader that at what tyme after
he brought the same [obligacion and billes to his fadre] [1] that then he
shuld have deduccion of the same somme of iiij xiiij li. uppon the
obligacion of C li. ; wherupon youre seid bisecher, trustyng specially
to the promise and graunte made afore tyme bi his seid Fader,
delyvered to the sonne the seid marchandize [and money to the] [1]
some of iiij xiiij li., takyng of the same sonne for his remembraunce
an obligacion and divers billes provyng the same delyveraunce, to the
whiche receyte, aftir that the seid Fader had notice therof, the same
Fader bifore worshipfull and full credible persones specially thanked
your seid bisecher for the good will that he at his seid instaunce had
shewed his seid sonne in that bihalf, and eftsonys accordyng to his
seid instance aggreed to the same receyt and bifore the seid persones
made feithe and promise that your bisecher shulde lose no peny therby ;
And howe be it that your seid bisecher oftymes sithen hath [tended]
the seid Fader vj li. in money and the obligacion and billes of the
seid somme of iiij xiiij li., desiryng him to take the same vj li. with
the obligacion and billes aforseid in full contentacion and payment of
the seid obligacion of C li., The seid Fader, for asmoche as of late
[he] hath notice that his seid sonne hath indaungerd himself in the
parties of portynggale to his displeasure, Therupon refuseth to be
charged with the contentacion and payment of the seid somme of
iiij xiiij bi his seid sonne at his instance and in his name in fourme
aforseid receyved or to make deduction perof upon the seid obligacion of a C li. ; And so demaundeth and entendeth to levye of your
bisecher the hole sume of the seid obligacion of a C li., to his utter-
most undoyng, without your gracious helpe in this bihalf to hym bi
you be shewed : Please it your gode and gracious [lordship, consider-
ing] [2] the premisses, to directe a writte Sub Pena unto the seid Fader
comaundyng him bi the same upon certeyne payne bi you to be limited
to appere afore the kyng, oure soverain lorde, in his Chauncery at a

---

[1] Illegible ; supplied from the defendant's answer.
[2] Illegible.

certeyn day bi you to be assigned, there to be ruled in the premisses as [reason][1] and good conscience requiren, and your seid bisecher shall pray to god for you.

Plegii de prosequendo :

Johannes White de Redyng in Com' Berk', Gardener.
Edward . . . [1] de Mussenden in Com' Buk'.

Endorsed : Memorandum quod pro eo quod, ista peticione ac responsione ad eandem facta et replicacione in hac parte habita necnon desposicionibus et testimoniis tam ex parte infrascripti Willielmi Elyot quam ex parte infrascripti Stephani Stychemerssh patris in premissis coram domino Rege in Cancellaria sua factis et habitis, lectis et auditis, ac materia in eisdem plenius intellectis (*sic*), visum est Curie Cancellarie predicte quod materia in eadem peticione contenta pro parte dicti Willielmi vera et veraciter probata existit, ac pro eo quod infrascrepte sex libre, residue Centum librarum, in dicta peticione specificate in plenam satisfaccionem eorundem Centum librarum in Curia Cancellarie predicte per predictum Willielmum oblata sunt, infrascripto Stephano Stychemerssh, patri, solvende et in eadem Curia in manibus Ricardi Fryston, clerici, restant eidem Stephano libande ; Ideo, vicesimo die Iunij, Anno regni Regis Edwardi quarti sexto, consideratum est per dominum Cancellarie Anglie quod infrascriptum scriptum obligatorium Centum librarum eidem Stephano per predictum Willielmum ac Iohannem Elyot, patrem eiusdem Willielmi, factum, vacuum et nullius valoris penitus existat et quod idem Stephanus idem scriptum obligatorium in Cancellariam predictam deferat ibidem cancellandum et dampnandum aut sufficientes litteras acquietancie pro scripto illo et pecunia in eadem contenta prefatis Willielmo et Iohanni sine dilatione fieri et deliberari et in Cancellaria predicta de recordo irrotulari faciat.

Bundle XXIX, No. 12.

This is the Answere of Stephen Stichemersh to the bill put Ageynst hym by William Eliot of Bristowe, merchaunt.

Fyrst, he seith by protestacion that the mater conteyned in þe seid bille is not sufficiaunt in lawe ne in Consciens, wherby he aught by this Court to be put unto answere ; bot for more pleyn declaracion

---

[1] Illegible.

of trowth the seid Stephen seith, where it is surmysed by the seid bill that the seid William . . .

(Here follows a copy verbatim of the chief allegations of the petition ; this is omitted.)

. . . herto the seid Stephen seyth that well and trew it is that the seid William and John were boundyn to hym in þe seid obligacion in a C li., of which somme thei feithfully promitted hym paiement at the daie conteyned in the same obligacion ; and the seid Stephen seith þat he never instanced ne desyred your seid besechers to deliver to his sone marchauntdyse and money, grauntyng to mak paiement þerof as is surmised by thair seid bill. And also the seid Stephen seith that is (*sic*) seid sone toke marchauntdise of your seid besechers to his owne use and noght to þe use of the seid Stephen in maner and fourme as is conteyned in þe seid bill; Wheruppon his seid sone become bounde to your seid besechers by his obligacion for the same marchauntdise which was bowght of your seid besechers be his seid sone unknowyng to the seid Stephen and withoute assent or Agreament or eny comaundment goven by the seid Stephen to his sone to doo, insomuch as when the seid Bargeyn was in making, thar was certayn merchauntz of Byrstowe (*sic*) at (*sic*) counseled your seid besechers to be wele avysed, for thei underestode veraly þt þe seid Stephen wold never answer of on peny for his seid sone. And also the seid Stephen seith þat your seid besechers never tendyd þe seid vj li. and a obligacion to the seid Stephen as is surmysed bi thair bill ; all which materez þe seid Stephen is redy to prove as this Courte of reason and Consciens wyll rewle hym, and prayeth þat he may be dismissyd with his Costes and his damages for his wrongfull vexacion, accordyng to the statutz in such case ordenyd.

Bundle **XXIX**, No. 10.

The replication of William Elyot.

William Elyot in his replication reaffirms all the matter set up in his petition and concludes :

'. . . All which maters your seid Suppliant is redy to prove as this Courts will A warde ; wherefor he prayeth that the seid Stephen Stychemerssh myght be comytted to warde therefor to A byde un to the tyme he have brought the seid obligacion of C li. into this seid courte to be cancelled and made voide, as good feith and conshens (*sic*) requyreth.'

Bundle XXIX, No. 11.

The deposition of John Powele of Bristol and John Glasse '. . . made in the presence of my lord Chaunceler at the More the xxix day of Novembre by their othes upon a boke', &c.

They swear that, the 13th day of November, 3 Ed. IV, William Elyot came to Stephen Stychemerssh and desired to have the obligation by which he and his father were bound to the said Stephen, and that he (William Elyot) then offered to deliver an obligation and certain bills containing £94, which Stephen, the son, had left with William Elyot for the discharge of £94 against the obligation held by Stephen the elder (i. e. the defendant) '. . . which Stephen thelder (*sic*) seid to the seid William: I thank you of that ye have do, but what nede ye to doubte of your obligacion ; ye shall never lose peny therby and all thinges that ye have delivered to my son afore this I have content and paide you, and also ye nede not to be so hasty, for your day is not yet come'.

Bundle XXIX, No. 9.

The deposition of William Nynge.

The seid William Nynge, sworn and dywely examyned before my lord Chaunceller in the playn Court of Chauncery, the xxvj day of January, the iiij^{the} yere of kyng Edward the iiij^{the}, seith and deposith . . .

(This deposition confirms the allegations in the complainant's petition.)

Bundle XXIX, No. 8.

The deposition of William Aphowell '. . . afore the Maister of the rollez '.

(This deposition is in further confirmation of the complainant's allegations.)

Bundle XXIX, No. 7.

This is the deposicion of Stephen Stychemerssh of London the yonger, Squyer, made before George, Archebisshopp of Yorke, primat and Chaunceller of Englond, the viij day of July, the vth yere of Kyng Edward the iiij^{the}.

First, the seid Stephen, sworn upon a boke and duly examyned before the said primat and Chaunceller of Englond, saith and deposith, by the othe þat he hath made, that all such marchaundise and money that he hath resceyved of oon William Elyot of Bristowe, which amountyth to the some of iiij^{xx} and xiiij li. howe he resceyved hit by the comaundement of Stephen Stychemerssh of London, theldyr (*sic*), fader unto the seid Stephen the younger, and in his seid Faderz name as his Factour and never otherwise.

Item : The seid Stephen the yonger by his seid othe seith that his seid Fader also comaunded hym that, as sone as he had receyved the seid marchaundise of the seid William Elyot, that then the seid Stephen the yonger shuld send to his seid Fader for an obligacion by the which the seid William Elyot and oon John Elyot were bounde to the Fader of the seid Stephen, the yonger, in C li. and that he shulde scrybe the hole some of the receyt of the seid marchaundise upon the bak of the seid obligacion.

Item : The seid Stephen the yonger by the othe that he hath made saith that he myght not send for the obligacion ; Wheruppon he made an obligacon in his owne name to the seid William Elyot, the which obligacon the same William in no wyse wold receyve of the seid Stephen þe yonger as his dede but at the Speciall request of the seid Stephen, the yonger, he receyved hit for a remembraunce unto the seid Stephen, the Fader, and noon other maner.

Bundle XXIX, No. 6.
The deposition of William Elyot.

(A long deposition by William Elyot in support of his own petition.)

Bundle XXIX, No. 5.
The deposition of Robert Talbot.

(A deposition by one Robert Talbot which seems to be in support of the allegations in the defendant's answer.)

Bundle XXIX, No. 4.
The declaration of Stephen Stychemerssh the elder.

(A long declaration by the defendant in support of the statements in his answer.)

Bundle XXXI, No. 82.
To the most reverent fader in god George Archebisshop of
York primat and Chaunceller of Englonde.

Mekely [besecheth your pouer][1] and contynuell Oratour John of Kent, of London Skynner, that where as oon Gararde Morys of London, Barbour, hath [commenced an accion][1] of trespas agenst

1470 to 1471.

[1] Hole in document.

oon Gyles Thornton, Gentylman, for whom your said besecher became suerte, and it was so, gracious lord, [that the said][1] Gararde promytted unto the said Gyles for to take respyte and sparynge of the callyng uppon the said accion unto the tyme [that the said][1] Gyles had ben beonde the see and comen ayen with oure Soveraygne Lady the quene, in trust wheroff the said Gyles departed ovre see [in the][1] ship of Thomas Danyell, Esquyer, the whyche the said Gyles wold nat have doon, had nat the said promyse have been made by the saide Garard unto hym ; And contrary therto now the said Gararde calleth uppon the said accion and so intendyth to condempne the said Gyles for defaute of answere, agenst all feyth and goode conscience : Wherfore please it your goode and gracious lordship tenderly to consydre the premisses and hereuppon to graunte a certiorari directed to the Shirffes of London for the said Gyles and your said pouer suppliant shall specially pray to gode for yowe.

Endorsed: Coram domino Rege in Cancelleria die Mercury, videlicet xxij die Novembris.

Bundle XXXI, No. 374.

To the right reverent fader in god and gode and gracious lord
the Archbisshop of York and Chaunceller of Englond.

Probably 1470 to 1471.

Mekely besechith youre gode and gracious lordship Thomas Cranwys, Clerk, that wher as oon John Benet and other his cofeffees late beyng seased of a tenement in their demesne as yn fee and the seid John Benet so beyng seased therof enfeffed your seid besecher and oon Thomas Benet, Chapeleyn, to thuse (*sic*) and behofe of your seid besecher and albe it that all the cofeffees of the seid John Benet have relesed unto your seid suppliaunt except on Robert Benet, Clerk, which atte tyme of the feffement so made was at Rome, and in the meane tyme the seid John Benet dyed and anoon after his disceas the seid John Benet, Clerk, came fro Rome and your seid besecher came unto hym and requyred hym to relees unto hym as his cofeffours had doon, which to doo he refused, seyng that that (*sic*) the seid John Benet shuld have be indettyd unto hym in the some of v marcs of the which he seid he wold be content or that he releced, and herapon the seid Thomas Benet, cofeffour[2] with your seid besecher, came to hym and seid that yf he wold take to hym xxvjv S. . . . d.[3] he wolde brynge to hym a relees to the seid

---

[1] Hole in document.
[2] Query : a mistake for ' cofeoffee ' ?   [3] Illegible.

John Benet Clerk and your besecher, puttyng full Truste in the seid Thomas Benet, yn asmoche as he was his Cofeffour[1], toke to hym the seid xxvj s. v ... d.[2] for the getyng of the seid relees and it is so, gracious lord, that your seid besecher hath often tymes requyred the seid Thomas Benet to delyver hym the seid relees of the seid John Benet Clerk and also to relees unto hym the right that he hath forthwith your seid besecher in the seid tenement and gardyn, which so to do he utterly hath refusid and yet doth agenst all right and conscience : wherfor please it your gode and gracious lordship, the premissez tenderly to consider and that your seid besecher can have no remedy at the comyn lawe, to graunte a writte sub pena to be direct to the seid Thomas Benet streigtly comaundyng hym by the same to appere afore the kyng in his Chauncery at a certayn day and under a certayn payne by your lordship to be lymyt ther to be examined of the premyssez and to do and receyve as right and conscience shall requyre, for the love of god and yn the wey of charyte.

Plegii de prosequendo :

Simon Reynold de London, Gentilman.

Johannes Payn de eadem, Gentilman.

Bundle XXXIX, No. 55.

To the full reverent Fader in god the bisshop of Bathe Chaunceller of Englond.

Besechet lowely your pore oratour John Langton, Chaunceller of the universite of Cantebrigge, that where the seyd Chaunceller and universite by the assent and graunt of our soverain lord the Kyng have late ordeyned to founde and stablisse a college in the same toun it to be called the universite college and to endowe it with diverses possessions in relevyng of the sayd universite and encresing of clergie therof, And how late acorde took bytwix oon Sir William Byngham that the seyd Chaunceller and scolers shuld have a place of the seyd Sir William adioynyng on every side to the ground of the seyd Chaunceller and universite that they have ordeyned to bild her seyd college upon for the augmencacon and enlargeyng of her seyd college and to edifie upon certein scoles of Civill and other faculteez, and for to gif the sayd Sir William a noder place therfor lyeng in the sayd toun bitwix the whit Freres and seint Johns Chirch and do it to be amorteysed suerly after the intent of the seyd Sir William of the cost of the seyd Chaunceller and universite, os the ful reverent fader

After 1433.

---

[1] See n. 2, p. 220.   [2] Illegible.

in god, the bisshop of Lincoln, in whos presence this covenaunt and acorde was made, wole recorde; And it is so, reverent lord, that the seyd Chaunceller and universite acordyng to this covenaunt have ordeyned the sayd Sir William a sufficeaunt place lyeing in the seyd toun of Canterbrigge bytwix the said Whit Freres and seint Johns Chirch and extendyng doun to the Ryver of the same toun wyth a gardeyn therto, which place is of better value then this other place is, and profred to amorteyse it at her own cost acordyng to the covenaunt forseyd, and therupon diverse costes and grete labores have made and doon late therfor; And also required diverses tymes the seyd Sir William to lepe[1] and performe on his party these seyd covenauntz, the seid Sir William now of self wille and wythoute any cause refusith it and will not doo it in noo wise: Plese it to your gracious lordship to consider thes premisses and therupon to graunt to your seyd besechers a writ sub pena direct to the seyd Sir William to appere afore yow in the Chauncery of our lord kyng at a certein day upon a certein peyne be yow to be limited, to be examened of these materes forseid and therupon to ordeyne by your gracious lordship that the said Sir William may be compelled to do that trowth, good feith and consciens requiren in this caas, considering that in alsomich as there is no writing bitwix your seyd besechers and the seyd Sir William thei may have noon accon at the comyn lawe, and that for god and in wey of charite.

Bundle XLIV, No. 142.

To the Right Reverent Fader in god the Bisshop of Bathe Chaunceller of England.

1470 to 1471.

Mekely besechen youre humble suppliauntes, Mathew Phylipp, Citezin and Alderman of London, and Thomas Coke, knyght, that where Johanne Reynolde, William Reynolde and Thomas Baldewyn, executours of the testament of Richard Reynolde, afore this tyme bargayned and solde unto oon Richard Wright certayne wollen Clothes, Corses,[2] lases and Rybons and divers dettis belonging unto the said Johanne, William Reynolde and Thomas Baldewyn as executours of the testament aforesaid, for the some of xij l., paiable at certayne daies bitwex thaim accorded; for the which some youre

---

[1] Query: a mistake for 'kepe'?
[2] 'Corse,' a silk riband, woven or braided (Halliwell).

said besechers oonly at the speciall instance and praier of Piers Ardeyn, knyght, late Chief Baron of the Kynges Eschequer, be came suertees unto the said Executours and were bounde ioyntly and severally to thaim in the said some by divers obligacions for the said Richard Wright, which Richard thanne hadde wedded the Nece of the said Piers Ardeyn. Which Piers promised faithfully and wolde that thei therof shulde bee saved harmles, and after the said Piers made his executrix Kateryn, thanne his wiff and now the wiff of Sir John Cheyne, Knyght, which hath taken uppon here the administracon of the goodes of the said Piers as his Executrix ; and moreover it is soo that sith the decesse of the said Piers, the said William Reynolde, oon of the Executours of the said Richard Reynolde which survived his coexecutours, hath taken an accon of dett in London of Clxx li., parcelle of the said some of xij li.^{xx}, which accon was nowe of late removed afore the Kyng in his Chauncery by a Certiorary, and afterward, for certayne consideracons movyng youre good lordship, Remitted agen, soo that youre said suppliauntes stande yet bounde in the said somme of Clxx li., parcell of the said xij li.^{xx}, and in greet iupardie therof, and have no suerte for thair indempnite in that behalve nor remedy by the comon lawe but stande destitute of remedye w^{t}out your gracious lordship to thaim be shewed in this partie : Please it the same youre good and gracious lordship the premisses tenderly to consider and theruppon to graunte a writte sub pena to bee directed to the said John Chayne, Knyght, and Kateryn, his wiff, which have goodes sufficient in thair handes that were the said Piers Ardeyn's, lawfully to content the said Clxx li. if it bee due, comaundyng thaim by the same to appere afore the Kyng in his Chauncery at a certayn day and under a certayne payne by youre good lordship to be limited, there to answere to the premisses and theruppon that it may please your good lordship to sette such direccon and rule therin for the indempnite of your said suppliauntes as shalbe (*sic*) thought to your good lordship to be accordyng to faith, reason and good conscience, and this at the reverence of god and in wey of Charite.

Plegii de prosequendo :

Ricardus Whyte de London, Gentilman.

Ricardus Lowe de London, Gentilman.

Endorsed :

Coram domino Rege in Cancellaria sua in quindena Sancti Martini proxima futura.

Memorandum, that the xj day of Febr', xlix yere of the reigne of Kyng Henry the vj^te, &c., This bill withynwriten atte the suyte of Thomas Cook, Knyght, and Mathewe Philipp agenst the withynwriten John Cheyne, Knyght, and Kateryn, his wyfe, executrix of the testament of Piers Ardeyn, Knyght, the aunswer, replication,[1] and reioynyng[1] to the same, alle proves also and examinacions and othir circumstancez dependyng uppon the same of both partiez pleynly herd and understoud, with gode and ripe deliberacion theruppon had, it is considerid and iuged by the reverend fader in god, George, Archebisshop of York,[2] Chaunceler of England, and by consideracion of the Courte, that the seid John Cheyne and Kateryne shal acquyte and discharge the seid Thomas and Mathewe agenst the withynwriten William Reynold of and for the withynspecified obligacions and every some therof, accordyng to the seid peticion of the seid Thomas and Mathewe, &c.

Bundle XLIV, No. 143.

This is the answer of John Cheyne, Knyght, and Kateryne, his wiff, to a bill of Subpena brought agaynst theim by Mathew Phillypp and Thomas Cooke, Knyght.

By protestacion that the mater conteyned in the bill is nat sufficiaunt in lawe netheir in conscience to putt theim to answer ; Nevertheles, for trouth of the mater, the seid John and Kateryne saith that wher In the forseid bill is conteyned . . .

(Here follows a brief summary of the complainant's bill.)

Theirto the seid John and Katerine seith that the seid Mathew Philypp and Thomas Cooke wher never bounden unto the seid Johane Raynold, William Raynold and Thomas Baldwyn at the instaunce and praer of the seid Sir Piers Ardeyn in maner and fourme as they have supposed by their bill ; and forthermore they say that the seid Sir Piers Ardeyn never made suche promyse unto the seid Mathewe Philypp and Thomas Cooke to save theim harmles in maner and fourme as they have surmytted ; and more over the seid Sir John Cheyne and Katerine, his wiff, sey that sith the deth of the

---

[1] Only the answer is preserved.
[2] Chancellor Oct.–April, 1470-1 (restoration of Henry VI).

seid Sir Piers Ardeyn and byfore this bill of Subpena sued they have paid for the dettes of the seid Sir Pyers Ardeyn dyvers grette and notable somez of money and have parfourmed and don otheir dedez of charite accordyng to the will of the seid Sir Piers Ardeyn and emoung otheir in Bylddyng of his Chaunterye and the Chyrche Stapill in the Town of Latton, in the Counte of Essex, to the grete charge and costes of the seid Sir John Cheyne and Katerine, his wiff, ov which charges and costes the seid Sir John Cheyne and Katerine, his Wiff, have nat nor hade nat in their handes at the tyme of this bill brought nor no tyme sith netheir goodes ne catalles of the seid Sir Piers Ardeyn to the value of the seid somez conteyned in the seid obligacions; all which maters they ar redy to prove as this Court will award Jugement and praith that they may be dismyssed.

Bundle LIX, No. 114.

To the right reverent Fader in god the Bisshop of Lincoln
Chaunceller of England.

Mekely besecheth youre good and gracious lordship John Whithed, Esquier, that wher as oon Robert Orchard late in an accon of waste suyd by the seid John Whithed ageyn the seid Robert before the kinges Justices of his comone benche for brennyng[1] of a water Mill, whiche the seid John Whithed had before leten to ferme to the seid Robert for terme of certeyn yeres, was condempnyd to the seid John Whithed in xxx li., and the seid Robert Orchard also at the suyte of the seid John Whithed by processe thereuppon had was for the same xxx li. in prison and execucon unto the tyme that John Spryng of Suthampton, Peautrer, grauntyd and feithefully promysyd to the seid John Whithed that, yf he wold relesse and discharge the seid Robert Orchard of his seid imprisonment and execucon and suffere hym to go at his liberte, that then the seid John Spryng at his owne propre cost and charge wold sufficiently and substancially edifie and bilde the seid mill ageyne bothe in tymber werk and stonys to the same expedient by a certeyn day nowe long tyme past; Wheruppon the seid John Whithed, trystyng the promysse of the seid John Spryng, at his desyre immediatly relessyd and discharged the seid Robert Orchard of his seid execucon and lete hym go at large at his liberte, and howe be hit that the seid John Spryng before the seid day reedified not the seid Mill in fourme aforseid nor no

After
1475.

---

[1] 'Brenne,' to burn (Halliwell).

part thereof and that the seid John Whithed often tymes sythe the seid day hathe requyred the seid John Spryng to reedifie and bilde the seid Mill as ys aforeseid acordyng to his seid promyse, that to do at all tymes as yet he hath refusyd, contrarie to his seid promysse, good feithe and conciens, of whiche your seid besecher hathe no remedie by the comone law of this land : Wherefor pleaseth hit youre good and gracious lordship, the premissis tenderly considered, to graunt a writ Suppena to be directed to the seid John Spryng comandyng hym by the same to appere before the kyng in his Chauncery at a certayne day and undur a certeyne payne by youre lordship to be lymitted and ther to be rewled and Juged as good conciens requyreth, for the love of god and in wey of cheryte.

[Plegii de prosequendo:]

Johannes Purvyer de London, Iremonger.
Thomas Clyfton de eadem, Draper.

Endorsed: Coram domino Rege in Cancellaria sua in quindena sancti Iohannis Baptiste.

Bundle LIX, No. 117.

To the right reverent Fadere in god the Bisshop of Lincoln Chaunceller of England.

After 1475. Mekely besecheth youre good lordship Richard Colnet that where as oon John Hill of the Cite of Wynchestre in a pleynt of Detenue of a Cloth of the value of x mark by the seid Richard Colnet late ageyn the same John Hill before the Mayre and Baylyes of the same Cite affermed, was condempnyd to the seid Richard Colnet in vij li., and thereuppon in prison in kepyng of the seid Baylyes and execucon for the same and so restyd in execucon till the seid John Hill desyred the seid Richard Colnet to relesse and discharge hym of his seid execucon and to geve hym dayes of payment of the seid vij li., promyttyng feithefully to the seid Richard Colnet that Immediatly after that he were at large and so discharged of his seid execucon that he wold do make an obligacon of the seid vij li. to be payd to the seid Richard at certayn dayes betwene them then acordyd ; whereuppon the seid Richard, trystyng to the promyse of the seid John, relessyd his seid execucon and caused the same John Hill to be at his liberte, Sithe whiche Relesse and discharge the seid Richard hathe often tymes requyred the seid John Hill to do make to hym the seid obligacon of vij li. acordyng to his seid promyse and that to do the seid John Hille at all tymes hathe refusyd and yet refuseth, contrarie to his seid promyse and good conciens, of whiche youre seid besecher hathe no Remedye by the comone lawe of this land : wherfor pleaseth hit youre good and gracious lordship, the premisses tenderly considered, to graunt a writ Subpena to be directed to the seid John Hill comaundyng hym by the same to appere before the Kyng in his Chauncery at a certeyn day and under a certeyn payne by youre lordship to be lymytted and there to be rewled and Juged as consciens requyreth, for the love of god and in wey of cheryte.

Plegii de prosequendo :

Willielmus Lyngard de London, Grocer.

Ricardus Farlyng de London, Yoman.

Endorsed: Coram Rege in Cancellare (*sic*) sua in xvie sancti Iohannis Baptiste.

Bundle LIX, No. 132.

To the Right reverent Lorde and Fader in god the Bisshop of Lincoln and Chaunceller of Englond.[1]

Mekely besechith youre goode and gracious lordship Richard Massy of London Goldsmyth that where Edmunde Chertesey late of Rouchester in the Countie of Kent, Gentilman, promysed to youre saide besecher if he wold marye Maryon, doughter of the saide Edmunde, I marcs of lawfull money, in trust of which promysse youre saide besecher toke the saide Maryon to wif, at which tyme of mariage the saide Edmunde paied to youre saide besecher xx li. parcell of the saide I marcs and as for xx marcs residue of the said some youre said besecher is not as yit contented [nor][2] paied and afterward the saide Edmunde made John Bamme his executour and dissesed, the which John Bamme hath godes the which were the saide Edmunde at the tyme of his deth sufficient to content the saide xx marcs and more and the saide John Bamme hath often tymes ben required by youre saide besecher to content and paye hym the same xx marcs and he that to doo hath at all tymes refused contrary to goode consciens, wherof youre saide besecher hath no remedy by the Cours of the Comon lawe. Please it therfore your goode lordship the premisses tenderly considered to graunte a Writte Subpena tobe (*sic*) directed

After 1475.

---

[1] See Bundle LIX, Nos. 137-9, for amended bill, answer, and replication.

[2] Hole in document.

to the saide John Bamme comaundyng hym by the same to appere be fore the kyng in his Chauncerie at certeyn day and uppon certeyn payne by youre goode lordship to be lymitted to answere the premisses and to doo as goode consciens requireth and your saide besecher shall praye to god for your goode lordship.

Plegii de prosequendo :

Jacobus Galon de London, Gent'.

Edwardus Bowdon de eadem, Yoman.

Endorsed: Coram domino in Cancellaria sua in quindena Pasche proxima futura.

Bundle LIX, No. 133.

The Answer of John Bamme to the byll of Ric' Massy.

The seid John Bamme, by protestacon that the mater conteyned in the bill of the seid Richard Massy is nat sufficient in lawe nor Conscience wherto the same John owe to answer, seith that Edmund Chertesey namyd in the bill of the seid Richard made his executours Alianor Chertesey, late the wife of the seid Edmund, Wyllyam Chertesey, Squyer, sone and heir to the same Edmund, and the forseid John Bamme, which Alianor and Wyllyam as well admynystred the godes of the seid Edmund as the forseid John Bamme, and for asmoche as the same Alianor and Wyllyam be yit in playn life and nat namyd in the bill of the seid Richard, the same John Bamme praieth that the byll of the forseid Richard therfor be abated and that the seid John Bamme be dysmyssed owte of this Courte.

Bundle LIX, No. 137.

To the right reverend fader in god and right gode and gracious lord my Lord of Lincoln Chaunceller of Englond.

After 1475. Mekely besecheth your gode and gracious Lordship, your humble Oratour, Richard Massy of London, Goldsmyth, That where Edmond Chertesey, late of Rouchestre in the Countie of Kent, Gentilman, promysed unto youre seid besecher if he wold marye and wedde Maryone, doughter of the seid Edmond, 1 marc of lawfull money of Englond. In trust of whiche promisse, youre seid besecher toke the seid Marione to wife ; at the tyme of which mariage the seid Edmond payed to the your seid besecher xx li. parcell of the seid 1 marcs, and as for xx marc, residue of þe seid 1 marc, your seid besecher is not

yet payed nor contented; and afterward the seid Edmond made
Alianore, his wif, Willyam Chertesey and John Bamme his executoures
and dyed.   The which executoures have goodes which were þe godes
of þe [seid] [1] Edmond the tyme of his deth sufficient to contente your
seid Oratoure of þe seid xx marc and more.   And how be it that your
seid besecher hath often tymes required the seid executoures to pay
unto hym the seid xx marcs, yet that to do they at all tymes have refused and yet doth, ageyn all right and conscience, wherof your seid
Orator hath no remedy by the comyn lawe of the land: Please
it þerefore your gode lordship, the premisses considered, to graunte
severall writtes of sub pena to be directe to the seid executoures
Comaundyng them to appiere afore the kyng in his Chauncerye
at a certayn day and under a certayn payn there to answere unto the
premisses, and furthermore to do therin as by the seid Courte shal be
demed and awarded, and that for the love of god and in wey of
charite.

    Plegii de prosequendo:

        Jacobus Galon de London, Gent'.

        Edwardus Bowdon de eadem, yoman.

Endorsed: Coram domino Rege in Cancellaria sua in quindena
Pasche proxima futura, breve directa Iohanni Bamme.   Et memorandum quod xviij die Aprilis emanarunt duo alia brevia directa
infrascripto Willielmo Chertesey et Alianore Chertesey respondendum
Crastino Sancti Iohannis Baptiste futuro.

Memorandum quod xiij die Octobris anno presenti dies data
est partibus infrascriptis ad producendum testes ad probandum
materiam infrascentum (*sic*) hincunde usque Crastino Sancti Martini
proximo futuro ex assensu utriusque partis.

Bundle LIX, No. 138.

The defendants' answer.

Defendants in their answer say by protestation that the matter
contained in the bill is not sufficient to put them to answer.   They
then set up other facts, denying that Edmund Chertesey ever promised
more than £20, which, they say, is paid; they also allege against the
complainant a promise of his own which, they say, remains un-
performed.   Also they say that they have administered fully, &c.

        [1] Hole in document.

Bundle LIX, No. 139.

The complainant's replication.

Complainant in his replication reaffirms the facts set up in his petition, and denies those alleged by the defendants in their answer, and concludes with the prayer that . . . 'the same executours may be rueled to pay to hym the same xx marcs accordyng to conscience'.

Bundle LIX, No. 185.

To the right reverent Fader in god the Bisshop of Lincoln
and Chauncellar of England.

After
1475.

Mekely besechith your gracious lordship Adam Knyght of Shrowesbury where on John Adams of Acton Burnell sold to your said suppliant certeyn wolles beyng in an house at Acton Burnell in grete at aventure for vij marcs to be paied at such tyme as your said suppliant shuld fette the said wolles, before which tyme your Oratour paied to the said John Adams for the [saide][1] wolles v marcs, parcell of the said vij marcs; And afterward he send his servant dyverse tymes for the said wolles to have lyvere therof accordyng to his bargayn and therof he was denyed, for the said wolles were not the said John Adams at the tyme of the said bargayn; by which bargayn soo untruely made the proprete of the said wolles vested not in youre said suppliant, and so [he] is withoute accion by the Cours of the comen lawe to his grete hurte in lesse your gracious lordship be shewed to hym in this behalfe: Please it therfore the same your lordship, the premisses considered, to graunte a writte of sub pena to be directe to the said John Adams comaundyng hym by the same to appere before the kyng in his Chauncerye at a certen day and upon a certen payn by your lordship to be lymet to answere to the premysses and thanne and there such direccion to be had heryn by your said lordship as shalbe thought to the same accordyng to reason and conscience, and this for the love of god and in wey of charite.

Plegii de prosequendo:

Johannes Baker de London.
Willielmus Hauke de eadem, yoman.

[1] Hole in document.

Bundle LIX, No. 227.

To the right reverend Fader in god and my gode lorde the
Bisshope of Lyncoln Chauncellar of Englonde.

Mekely besecheth your gode and gracious lordshipp your Poure 1480 to
Oratour Roger Godemond, that where he afore this tyme uppon a x 1481.
yere past and more was bounde to one Alice Reme, Wedowe, be his
syngle Obligacion in x marke sterlyng paiable at a certeyn day in the
seid Obligacion specified, and afterward the same Alice made her
executours John Hale and one Thomas Plane and died, after whos
dethe your seid Oratour truly paied and full contented the seid
executours of the dewete of the seid obligacion, trustyng be that payment to have be discharged of the seid Obligacion lefte the same
Obligacion in the handys of the seid executours and trustyng that
the seid executours wolde have delyvered the seid Obligacion to
your seid besecher at all tymes when they hadde ben therto requyred ;
and afterward the seid John Hale died after whos dethe the seid
Thomas Plane as executour of the seid Alice, not withstandyng the
seid payment hadde and contentacion of the Obligacion made,
suethe an accion of dette nowe late afore the kyngis Justice of the
Comen place upon the seid Obligacion agenst your seid besecher,
not dredyng god ne th'offens of his owne consciens, intendyng be the
same accion shortly to condempne your seid besecher in the seid
x marke, be cause the seid payment can make no barr at the comen
lawe and so to be twys satisfied upon the same Obligacion for one
dewte, contrary to all reason and gode conscience, wherof your seid
besecher is withoute remedy be the Comen lawe withoute your gode
and gracious lordshipp to hym be shewed in this behalve : Please it
therfor your gode and gracious lordshipp the premysses tenderly to
consyder and to graunte a writte Suppena to be directe to the seid
Thomas Plane comaundyng hym be the same to appere afore the
kyng in his Court of Chauncerie at a certeyn day and upon a certeyn
peyn be your lordshipp to be lemette, there to answere to the premysses and to bryng afore your seid lordshipp the seid Obligacion to
be cancelled, and ferthermore that he may have ynyongcion no
further to procede in the seid accion at Comen lawe till your seid
lordshipp have examyned the premysses and sett such rewle and

direction in the same as shall accorde with reason and gode consciens, and this for the love of god and in the Wey of Charite.

Plegii de prosequendo :

Ricardus Somer de London, Gentilman.

Thomas Mey de London, Gent'.

Endorsed : Coram domino Rege in Cancellaria in Crastino Ani marum futuro.

Memorandum quod termino Sancti Michaelis, videlicet sexto die Novembris Anno etc. xix°, iniunctum fuit Thome Sharp, attorn' infranominati Thome Plane, quod ipse sub pena Centum marcarum minime prosequatur versus infranominatum Rogerum Godemond in quodam placito debiti super demandum decem marcarum coram Iusticiis Regis de Banco suo, quousque materia infraspecificata plene determinata fuerit et discussa.

Bundle LIX, No. 228.

This is the answere of Thomas Plane on of the executours of Alice Reme, Wedowe, to the bill of complaynt of Roger Godmond.

The seid Thomas Plane by protestacon sayeth that the mater conteigned in the bill of compleynt of the seid Roger is not sufficient in lawe to put hym to answere to the same ; for plee he sayeth that the seid Roger paid not the seid x marcs nor non parcell there of to the seid Thomas plane ne to John Hale his coexecutour in maner and forme as the seid Roger be his seid bille of complaynt hath surmyttyd ; all whiche maters the seid Thomas plane is redy to averre as this court will award, and askith iuggement and prayeth to be dysmyssed out of this court wyth his resonable costys and expenses for his wrongfull hurte and vexacon in that behalf don, had or susteyned.

Bundle LIX, No. 285.[1]

Addressed to the ·Bishop of Lincoln.

1479 to 1480. The complainant is one Cecil Merfyn, executrix of the testament of John Merfyn.   The substance of her petition is as follows :

John Merfyn and William Clyfford bound themselves jointly and severally in an obligation of £140 ... to the use of Agnes, wife of William Halowe, late the wife of Henry Cheveley ... to the intent that an estate of lands and tenements of the annual value

[1] The substance of the petition is given ; the endorsement is transcribed in full.

of 12 marks should be made to the said Agnes within two years following.   After the decease of John Merfyn and William Clyfford, complainant caused a sufficient estate to be made to Agnes within the time limited . . . 'accordyng to the trewe intent of the makyng of the seid obligacon,' . . . yet Geoffrey and William Hamond (the defendants) will not give up the obligation, nor make acquitance thereof, but are now suing an action against the complainant in the king's court, 'callid the Comone place,' upon the said obligation, which is against all reason and conscience.   Complainant says she has no remedy at law.   She prays for a subpoena to be directed to the defendants, Geoffrey Blodwell and William Hamond, and asks general relief.

The petition is endorsed as follows :

Coram domino Rege in Cancellaria sua in xv Sancti Iohannis proximo futuro.

Memorandum quod termino sancte Trinitatis, videlicet nono die July anno regni Regis Edwardi quarti decimo octavo, Ista peticione per infrascriptam Ceciliam Merfyn coram dicto domino Rege in Cancellaria sua versus infrascriptum Galfridum Blodwell et Willielmum Hamond exhibita, ac responsione[1] prefati Galfridi eidem peticioni facta, lectis, visis et auditis et ad plenum intellectis, advocatis que (*sic*) tam infrascripto Willielmo Halowe et Agnete uxore sua quam prefata Cecilia Merfyn et super materia (*sic*) huius peticionis diligenter examinatis, iidemque Galfridus, Willielmus, Agnes et Cecilia fatebantur et recognoverunt infranotatam obligacionem factam et delibatam fuisse prefatis Galfrido et Willielmo ad intencionem infraspecificatam, ipsi Willielmus Halowe et Agnes tunc ibidem presentes recognoverunt de fore satisfacta et contenta iuxta allegacionem peticionis predicte et secundum causam ob quam ipsa obligacio facta fuerat, unde dicta Cecilia peciit quod dicti Galfridus et Willielmus Agnes, uxor eius, per auctoritatem huis Curie ad dictam obligacionem sibi delibandam et cancellandam compellantur, quamobrem dicta obligacio per prefatos Willielmum et Agnecem prefato (*sic*) Cecilie per auctoritatem Curie Cancellarie predicte et per consensium parcium delibata fuit cancellandum.

Bundle LXXI, No. 7.

Right mekely besechith youre continuell oratoure, Richard Dryf-   Date feld of London, Clerke, that, ther as William Brampton, Citeceyn uncertain. and Scryvener of the said Citee, made contracte of Mariage by

_____
[1] No answer is preserved.

his owne pursuyng by twene the seid Richard and Denys, the Doughter of Thomas Sele, the said William Brampton promysyd to the said Richard x marcs of sterlinges and other x marcs in howsold to be paied by the handes of the said William Brampton, of the whiche the said Richard hath reseyved vj marcs in mony and in howshold the value of viij marcs, whiche the said Richard hath divers tymys asked in presence of worthy men ; but for as muche as the same Richard hath noght to shewe for hym in wrytyng the said William Brampton wolnot (*sic*) do hym ryght, sayng that he can never recover any thyng of hym be the comyn lawe, and thus with owt youre gracious lordschip youre said besecher ys with owte remedy : where fore plese hit your god and gracious lordschip to make the said William to appere afore yowe in the Kynges Chauncellarie and to shewe whi youre said besecher shuld not be content after promys made be twix them, and also to abyde and resayve that schall [be] ordeynyd at that tyme by youre full and gracious lordship, and this for the love of god and in Way of Charite.

Bundle LXXI, No. 8.[1]

The answer of William Brampton.

William Brampton says in substance :

That the said Richard by mediation of friends ' laboured to þe seid Thomas, fader of þe seid Denys, . . . of his owen desire willing to have . . .' the said Denys as his wife.   And as William Brampton is a cousin of Denys, complainant asked him to come and ' to here the comunicacon bitwene þe seid Richard and Denys, upon which comunicacon the seid Richard desired xx marcs w^t the seid **Denys** ; To which matier it was answerd by þe seid William in name of þe seid Thomas and his frendes, þat, yf þe seid Richard wold have þe seid Denys to wyf, that he and all the frendes of þe seid Denys wold make hir worth x marcs in money and in godes ; To which the seid Richard agreed and þerupon wedded þe seid Denys and of þe seid x mark in money and godes the seid William and frendes of the seid Denys hath content þe seid Richard and more ' . . . , &c.

---

[1] As this document is very long the substance of it only is given.

INDEX